D1087505

MISSION TO IRAN

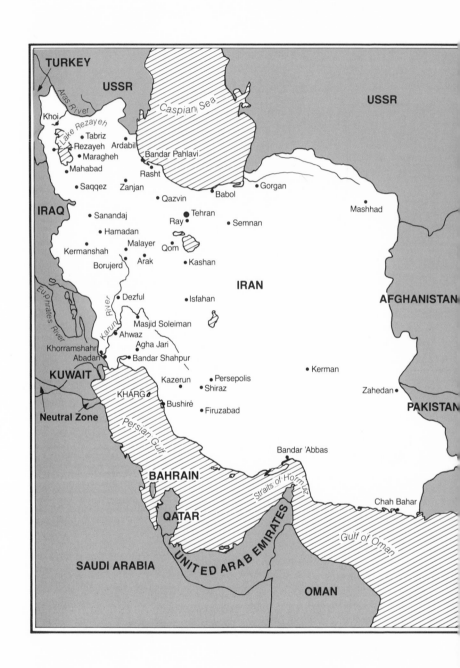

MISSION
TO
IRAN

William H. Sullivan

W · W · NORTON & COMPANY

NEW YORK   LONDON

Published simultaneously in Canada by George J. McLeod Limited, Toronto.

Printed in the United States of America

First Edition

Library of Congress Cataloging in Publication Data
Sullivan, William H. (William Healy), 1922–
  Mission to Iran
  Includes index.
  1. Iran—Politics and government—1941–1979.
2. Sullivan, William H. (William Healy),
1922–   . 3. Diplomats—United States—
Biography. 4. United States—Foreign relations—
Iran. 5. Iran—Foreign relations—United States.
I. Title
DS318.S85 1981   955'.053   81–14052
ISBN 0-393-01516-5   AACR2

  W. W. Norton & Company, Inc. 500 Fifth Avenue, New York, N. Y. 10110
  W. W. Norton & Company Ltd. 37 Great Russell Street, London WC1B 3NU

                    1 2 3 4 5 6 7 8 9 0

Contents

Contents

Photographs appear between pages 150 and 151

Preface

The revolution that deposed the Shah of Iran in 1979 was one of the major political events of the second half of the twentieth century. Its full consequences for the world at large are not yet clear, but it has already altered the strategic balance between the Soviet Union and the United States. The ordeal for the American political conscience that resulted from the Iranian seizure of official American hostages will have long-lasting effects. The weaknesses in the formulation and execution of United States foreign policy that were exposed by Washington's ineptitude in the face of the revolution continue to be subject to public scrutiny.

For all these reasons, a number of books have been and will be written on various aspects of the revolution. Some of them will be scholarly and objective works. Others will be works of apologia or advocacy, with little regard for scholarship or accuracy.

This book fits neither of those categories. It is a subjective narrative of my service as United States ambassador to Iran from June 1977 to April 1979, during the span of the revolution. It attempts to illustrate, through anecdotes drawn from that time, the forces at work in Iran and the reactions of the United States to those forces.

It is not a diary and does not attempt to give a precise chronological ordering of events. It recounts those episodes in which I personally participated which, in my judgment, had some bearing on the events involved in the revolution. I have been persuaded to record them now, while they are still fresh in my mind, because they may be useful to those attempting to analyze an historical event.

Before I went to Iran in 1977, I had had no significant experience in that part of the world. However, I had been a foreign-service officer for thirty years and an ambassador for thirteen years. Moreover, I had worked for a number of years in the upper reaches of the foreign-policy bureaucracy in Washington. In short, I was an old hand in a new situation.

Therefore, the turmoil to which I was exposed in Tehran was not unfamiliar, even though the personalities and the culture were alien to my previous experience. What was new was my inability to exert any constructive influence over Washington policy decisions. I still do not understand all the reasons that underlay our policy failures at that time, and I will not attempt, in this book, to examine them. I will try to illuminate their consequences.

MISSION TO IRAN

1

Assignment to Tehran

Baguio is a hill station on the island of Luzon, north of Manila. During the American colonial period in the Philippines, before the days of air conditioning, it was, for three months of the year, the summer capital. Roads were built from the plains, tortuously climbing into the hills to a pine-filled valley where the thick-walled government structures rose among the scattered small villages of the mountain people. In 1935, when the Philippines became a commonwealth, the governor general's mansion was turned over to the Filipino president, and a new residence was built for the American high commissioner. After independence, that white-walled, bougainvillea-bedecked villa became the summer home of the American ambassador.

During my four years as ambassador, we used this residence far too seldom. Most of the year, I turned it over to members of my staff and their families for their vacations from the heat and turbulence of Manila. During the Christmas season and on occasional weekends, my wife and I managed to slip away to this retreat perched on a promontory ridge, overlooking the gold mines deep in the ravine below.

In the early spring of 1977, after the elections that had

brought President Carter into office, the pace of diplomatic activity between the United States and the Philippines slowed down. The negotiations on military bases, which had occupied much of my time in 1976, were in suspense. The Filipinos were awaiting the policy line to be adopted by the new administration, and I was expecting reassignment to some other diplomatic post. Consequently, in late March we arranged a long weekend in Baguio and flew there early on a Friday morning.

While we were changing into our golfing clothes, the "hot line" phone from the embassy in Manila rang in our bedroom. Molly Stephens, who had been my secretary for several years, had a keen understanding of which things were truly important. When I heard her voice, my first instinctive reaction was therefore to assume that some crisis had arisen that would require me to return to Manila. Instead, she told me that the word we had been awaiting about a new assignment had finally arrived.

The Carter administration had taken somewhat longer than usual to name its new diplomatic representatives. A presidential commission had been appointed to assist in their selection. This commission, which was headed by Governor Reubin Askew of Florida, had several members, such as Dean Rusk and Averell Harriman, who were well known to me. Their task was to evaluate and screen the various candidates, both from the career service and from other walks of life, who were nominated to become ambassadors in the principal world capitals. Given the fact that I was among the most senior career officers available and that I had spent many years in East Asia, I expected to be named to an Asian capital. At the same time, I rather hoped the commission might make an imaginative move and name me to the one post I truly coveted—Mexico City. Instead, the post being offered to me came as a complete surprise. Tehran.

The nearest I had ever served to Tehran was in Calcutta nearly thirty years before. I had never lived in the Islamic world and knew little about its culture or its ethos. While I recognized the importance of Iran, the proposal did not make me jump for joy. I told Molly that my wife and I would play eighteen holes of golf and call her back in a few hours.

Our golf that day was less than satisfactory. Neither of us felt much thrill at going to a country that enjoyed a generally poor reputation in the United States and where I had no particular qualifications. At the same time, I recognized Iran's strategic significance, the serious nature of the diplomatic problems that faced us there, and the fact that the presidential commission doubtless believed it to be one of the major challenges for any career officer. The old habit of duty therefore asserted itself, and I called Molly that afternoon to dictate a decidedly restrained acceptance of the nomination.

The next two or three weeks were taken up with the rituals of departure from our friends in the Philippines, the packing and shipping of household effects, and arrangements for our return to Washington. We had enjoyed our tour in Manila, but I had not accomplished many of the goals I had set when I took the post in 1973. The revision of our military base agreements was incomplete. We had not been able to negotiate a trade agreement to replace the inequitable treaty that had lapsed. Because of the martial-law regime and human-rights issues, relations between Washington and Manila had remained decidedly cool.

Perhaps the greatest disappointment concerned events that were only peripheral to the Philippines and were centered in Vietnam. I had played a key role in negotiating the agreements that terminated the war in Vietnam. One of the provisions of those agreements was that the United States and North Vietnam would open diplomatic relations and exchange ambassadors. The North Vietnamese had been informally advised that I would be the first American ambassador in Hanoi.

The plan was that I should assume this function concurrently with my assignment to the Philippines. Dual accreditations of this type are not unusual, but this scheme was planned in order to give us maximum flexibility in handling the tricky problems of Vietnam. It was intended that I should spend limited periods of time in Hanoi, commuting back and forth in a small military jet stationed at Clark Air Force Base in the Philippines. Daily operation of our Hanoi embassy would be left in the hands of the chargé d'affaires, assisted by a small staff, all of whom would be resident in Hanoi.

This plan never became a reality, because Hanoi did not carry out the terms of the Paris agreements. Its crass violations, particularly of the military provisions, made it impolitic for the United States to open diplomatic relations with Hanoi. More seriously, the violations led to the collapse of the whole structure of peace that we had negotiated and, ultimately, to the elimination of the Republic of South Vietnam. The debacle that Americans had fought for years to avert took place in 1975. Those fleeing the tragedy came first to the Philippines, either through Subic Naval Base or Clark Air Force Base or by helicopter—literally through the front yard of our embassy.

The shock wave that swept over Southeast Asia and much of the rest of the world seriously affected the nature of our last two years in the Philippines. This entire confusion was then compounded by the Watergate affair, which brought the United States government close to paralysis and seriously impaired its official representation in Manila. It was consequently something of a relief to me to be leaving the Philippines, despite the attractions that it offered in normal circumstances. I looked forward to working for a new administration in a new atmosphere and in a new post.

We left Manila on April 25, 1977, and flew by way of Tokyo to Honolulu. There I performed the last of my official functions as ambassador to the Philippines and the last of my official duties in the nearly thirty years I had spent in East Asia and the Pacific. These functions consisted of debriefings and consultations with the United States military headquarters in Honolulu, which was responsible for our military policies and presence in the entire Pacific area. Most of the senior officials in this command were men I had known for a number of years, going back to the Korean war and the extended conflicts in Southeast Asia. It was a congenial meeting, but not a particularly optimistic one, as we faced the consequences of the loss of American military prestige in Indochina. Nevertheless, the briefings were conclusive in that we believed there was opportunity for a stable balance of power in the western reaches of the Pacific that might last for a long period of time and preclude the possibilities of further wars into which the United States might inevitably be dragged.

The Pacific command also had certain responsibilities extending into the area of the Indian Ocean and Persian Gulf, and it therefore touched on my new assignment in Iran. From the discussions in Honolulu, I learned more about the military facilities at Diego Garcia, about the deployment patterns of the American navy in the Indian Ocean, and about the nature of the Soviet military and naval presence in that part of the world. I could see that in my new post I would not entirely lose contact with the Hawaii military-command structure. On the completion of my consultations, we resumed our trip toward Washington. I had been forewarned that there would be no prospect of home leave, despite the fact that we had spent the last two years in the Philippines without any leave. The post in Tehran had been open since December 1976, when the preceding ambassador, Richard Helms, had resigned. There was, as a result, considerable urgency on the part of the new Carter administration to put an ambassador in place in Tehran as soon as possible. Thus it was not going to be part of the scheme of things to have a period of rest before I took up my new duties. I therefore flew straight to San Francisco.

While my family went for a brief visit to Mexico, I flew across the country to Washington and plunged into preparations for Tehran. Since I was innocent of any detailed knowledge of Iran, this meant first reading basic background books. The Department of State library provided me with a half-dozen, which I managed to read on weekends and during the evenings and which gave me at least a working knowledge of the fundamental facts concerning the country. The books available were, however, not all that extensive or all that relevant to the needs of an ambassador who had never served there, and I required considerably more detailed briefing from various specialists who were available in the Washington bureaucracy.

Before turning to them, however, I began my rounds of meetings with the senior officials of the new administration. First on the list was Secretary of State Cyrus Vance. Cy Vance is someone whom I had known for more than ten years and for whom I had the greatest respect. I was delighted to see him installed in the office of the secretary of state.

In my first meeting with him, I asked why I had been selected to be the ambassador to Iran when I knew nothing of the country or of the region in which it was such a significant feature. The secretary told me that it had been decided to send a professional who had had considerable experience in dealing with authoritarian governments and with leaders who were forceful personalities. The issues of area knowledge and specific acquaintance with the culture of the region were considered secondary qualifications for this post. Although this rationale may have explained my selections, it still left me painfully aware of my shortcomings in experience and knowledge related to Iran.

Therefore, I sought out as much guidance as I could obtain from talking with those who knew the country, the region, and the issues. Roy Atherton, then the assistant secretary of state for Near Eastern affairs, had joined the service at the same time I had, and we were old friends. Iran fell under his supervision in the Department of State. Roy gave me some sound advice, but he was preoccupied in those days with the issues of the

Arab-Israel conflict and was unable to provide much more detailed consideration.

My tutelage, therefore, fell largely into the hands of Charles Naas, who was Iran desk officer. Charlie had spent a good portion of his professional career in and around Iran. He had served twice in Tehran, once in Afghanistan, and once in Pakistan, and had become the Department of State's leading expert on Iranian matters at that time. Through him I met all the other experts in the various Washington bureaucracies dealing with Iran. He also arranged a seminar for me to meet the leading academic experts on Iran, who came to Washington specifically to brief me. Moreover, I met a number of other personalities, such as Kim Roosevelt, who had been an active participant in the events of 1953 that restored the shah to his throne after his regime had been badly shaken by the actions of the Iranian parliament.

I then began to call on the senior members of the new administration, starting with the cabinet officers and the cabinet-level officials—among them Admiral Turner, head of CIA —who had interests in Iran. Next I met with the Joint Chiefs of Staff, most of whom I had known for some time, and obtained their appreciation of the military situation in the Persian Gulf. Finally, in the Pentagon, I met with those officials, both civilian and military, who administered the enormous military-sales program under which the Iranians were procuring much sophisticated military equipment from the United States. When I had finished all these rounds, I considered it appropriate for me to seek an appointment with the president.

Somewhat to my surprise, the officials in the Department of State who normally arrange visits between new ambassadors and the president told me that things were going to be different in this administration and that the president did not really wish to meet with the ambassadors who were going to be representing him abroad. They said that he had established a very limited quota of ambassadorial appointments with whom he would meet and that it had already been filled for that particular time. Although I found that somewhat strange, particularly in the case of an ambassador going to a post as sensitive as Iran, I had learned to accept the different behavior patterns of American presidents, and I prepared to limit my White House contacts to the officials on the National Security Council staff.

Accordingly, Charlie Naas made appointments for me to meet with Zbigniew Brzezinski, the assistant to the president for national-security affairs, and members of his staff dealing directly with the Middle East and Persian Gulf region. In the course of these discussions, Brzezinski asked when I was making my call on the president; when I informed him that no such appointment had been made, he moved immediately to correct this omission.

Despite the injunctions under which officials in the Department of State were operating, I thus received an appointment within the next two or three days to meet with President Carter. This would be my first meeting with a man whom I had observed only on the television screen and in press accounts of his political campaign during the time I was in the Philippines.

My call on the president was somewhat delayed because he was holding a press conference in the Executive Office Building next door to the White House. However, at the appointed time Zbig Brzezinski and I were ushered into the Oval Office to wait for him. While we waited, I was able to reflect on the changes I had seen, not only in the physical characteristics of the Oval Office, but also in the personalities who had occupied it over the past several years. I had first been in this room during the presidency of Dwight Eisenhower, and, despite the easy formality of the Eisenhower personality, I had been enormously impressed by the prestige of office that permeates that rather small oval room.

I had seen it often during the short presidency of John Kennedy, and much more often during the presidency of Lyndon Johnson. During the Nixon years I had been in it very seldom, since the few meetings I had had with President Nixon were in other parts of the White House or while he was traveling overseas.

My first look at the office under the Carter administration indicated that it had been redecorated in somewhat lighter colors and that it contained fewer mementoes and gadgets than had been there in other years. It seemed a more spartan room.

These vagrant thoughts were soon interrupted by the entrance of the president into his office. My first reaction was one of surprise to see how small and slight a man he was. He gave the impression of tightly coiled energy under very close control. He had just come from a press conference, yet he seemed to have left all that behind as he bounded forward, shook my hand, and invited me to pose with him for photographs. These photographs showing an ambassador with the president are much prized by the publicists of our embassies abroad, since they demonstrate the personal association of the ambassador with the president and therefore place a cachet on his personal representation of the chief of state. The photographers flocked in for the usual "photo opportunity." There must have been twenty of them, and they jostled each other in the normal manner of the White House press corps. What struck me as unusual, in contrast with previous photo opportunities in which I had been engaged in the Oval Office, was that each photographer also carried a tape recorder; some of them even had assistants with microphones on long booms, presumably so that they could pick up any indiscretions that might occur in the small talk between the president and the other officials being photographed.

When the photographers had finished and were herded out of the room, the president invited Brzezinski and me to take seats, and he moved rapidly into an overview of his policy toward Iran. Given the fact that he had just come from a press conference, that he had no notes, and that his mind must have been cluttered with a number of other more pressing issues, I was strongly and favorably impressed by the way he approached his subject. He clearly had done his homework and gave an orderly presentation of his views.

The president made clear that he regarded Iran as strategically important to the United States and our allies. He also warmly endorsed the shah as a close friend and a trusted ally, and stressed the importance he placed on the continuing role of Iran as a force for stability and security in the Persian Gulf region. He outlined traditional attitudes toward the problems of oil pricing and several other matters of a bilateral nature between our two countries. He then asked whether I had any questions.

Because the new administration had not really shaken out its policy options on various critical matters of interest to us in Iran, I had come away from my executive-branch briefings with a number of questions. I addressed three of these to the president.

The first concerned the level of our military-equipment sales to Iran. Under previous administrations the Iranians had been permitted to purchase any amount of weapons they felt they could handle and, in most categories, ones just short of the most sophisticated. They had on the table for discussion with us a significant list of additional military equipment they wished to acquire. I knew the president was introducing a memorandum to the executive branch restricting arms sales in general, and I asked him how he wished to apply this to Iran.

His response was quick and specific. He wished to be quite generous with the Iranians, and there was nothing currently on their shopping list under consideration that he felt it necessary to deny them. This specifically included the AWACS aircraft that were still being introduced into the United States Air Force. On other arms sales, the president indicated that his memorandum, to be published in the near future, would give me guidelines for handling the quantities and types of equipment we would be willing to sell to Iran.

My second question concerned the Iranian government's desire to acquire nuclear-power plants from the United States. The shah had embarked on an ambitious program to install a significant generation capacity of nuclear power in his country before the end of the twentieth century. This program was designed to provide Iran with a continuing source of cheap energy once its petroleum reserves had been exhausted. Iran had already arranged to buy some reactors, of American design, from the Germans and the French. They were now pressing for acquisition of later-model American reactors.

Again the president was precise and affirmative. He saw no problems, he said, in providing nuclear-power plants to the Iranians on the condition that they accept appropriate international safeguards concerning their use and the disposition of spent fuel. He also indicated a willingness on our part to reprocess spent fuel in the United States and to return the product to Iran for further use in the generation of power. It was a categorical endorsement of American exports of nuclear energy to Iran.

My final question was somewhat more sensitive. I pointed out that we had had a long-standing collaboration between the CIA and SAVAK, the Iranian intelligence organization. I alluded to the fact that SAVAK had, over the years, become a political-police organization as well as an intelligence organization. In view of the emphasis that the Carter administration was placing on human rights, and in view of the reality that SAVAK had a poor reputation as far as human-rights observance was concerned, I asked the president whether he wished to continue the intelligence collaboration in its current form.

The president again answered promptly, indicating that he had examined this issue and reached the conclusion that the intelligence which we received, particularly from our listening stations focused on the Soviet Union, was of such importance that we should continue the collaboration between our two intelligence agencies. He qualified this general endorsement only by indicating that he expected me to try to persuade the shah to improve the human-rights performance of his government in all its aspects.

By this time my meeting with the president had extended some fifteen or twenty minutes beyond the time scheduled, and at least one note reminding him of a waiting appointment had been passed during our conversation. However, my training in meeting with a chief executive had always taught me that I should leave only when the president so indicated. After we had finished our questioning and he had wished me—very graciously—a good tour in Tehran, the president rose and showed Brzezinski and me toward the door. It had been a most satisfactory meeting from my point of view and had filled me with considerable respect for the intellectual abilities, the candor, and the grace of our new president.

Back at the State Department I went immediately to see Philip Habib, the undersecretary of state, who was a close and longtime friend. I told him with some enthusiasm of my meeting with the president and of the policy guidance I had received on three delicate issues with which the bureaucracy was still struggling. Habib was delighted to have such clear guidance from the chief executive and asked me to dictate a memorandum that he would then distribute to the appropriate offices in the bureaucracy, informing them what the policy was on these three issues and removing any further necessity for the preparation of position papers seeking a presidential decision. I dictated the memorandum and left feeling that the policy-formation process in this new administration seemed to be much more easily resolved than I had known on previous occasions.

I discovered a few days later, however, while discussing some of the points the president had made with other members of the Department of State at the assistant-secretary and deputy-assistant-secretary levels, that they were totally unimpressed that the president had established positions on the three matters I had raised with him. They continued to grind out their position papers, some of them totally at variance with the president's position. When I pointed out to them that under our Constitution the president made foreign-policy decisions and that they should consider themselves fortunate to have had the decisions taken for them, they scoffed at the idea. They took the view that the president had not really examined these matters in depth and that the bureaucracy would continue its work and then advise him more cogently on what attitudes he should take.

Although I did not recognize it fully at the time, these attitudes reflected problems that would later emerge as major internal weaknesses of the Carter administration. The fact that subordinates in the Department of State and elsewhere did not respect the president's decisions concerning major policy matters derived from the circumstance that they had been selected from members of political factions in the Democratic party who held no personal loyalties toward Carter and who felt that he, in turn, gave no particular loyalty to them. It was a curious situation.

2

Preparations in Washington

Having been out of the United States for much of the period preceding my nomination as ambassador to Iran, I did not have a precise idea about the way that country was perceived by Americans. I was aware that the presence of large numbers of Iranian students in the United States was becoming known to many Americans who lived near colleges and universities. I was also aware that most of these students seemed opposed to the shah's regime and had become increasingly vociferous in stating that opposition. I knew that they had adapted the techniques of Vietnam-protest movements to their own cause and had mounted numerous political demonstrations in several states.

It seemed to me that most Americans, even those who had been sympathetic to or tolerant of anti-Vietnam protests by our own students, were less than enthusiastic about foreign students who protested against their native country in the United States. Not only were they vexed by the disruptions and violence that accompanied these protests, but they found something unseemly in the fact that much of the abuse in these protests was directed against the United States, the country that was their host.

At the same time, I understood that the stridency of the protests and the multiplier effect created by those young Americans who supported the Iranian students had introduced a new picture of the shah to much of the American electorate. He had always been presented in this country as an enlightened and benevolent ruler who, while autocratic, was leading his nation out of the squalor and misery of the past. Now he was being condemned as a despot who was ravishing the wealth of his people and crushing their political, religious, and cultural aspirations.

Both pictures of the shah coexisted in the United States at large. In Washington, particularly on Capitol Hill, the more benign view was in favor. Many senators and congressmen, especially the more senior ones, had made several visits to Iran. They had been lavishly entertained by the shah, they had been briefed on his programs for "the White Revolution," and they admired his forthright friendship for the United States. They had met him many times on his visits to Washington, and they regarded him as a valuable force for stability and progress in a turbulent part of the world.

Much of the favorable image that Iran enjoyed in Washington was also due to the assiduous efforts of the shah's ambassador to the United States, Ardeshir Zahedi. His reputation as the most energetic and effective diplomatic representative in the capital was widespread. He enhanced it by spectacular party giving, by shrewd association with worthwhile charitable causes, and by the role he had played as a successful mediator in a Black Muslim terrorist action that had startled Washington a few years earlier. I looked forward to meeting the man.

My first meeting with him was in a call that I made on him at his office, accompanied by the Iran country director from the State Department, Charles Naas. We were received, somewhat to my surprise, at an office in the first floor of his residence rather than next door in the chancery. (I was later surprised to attend a glittering dinner in a large dining room in the chancery, rather than in the residence.) I found him tall, ruggedly good-looking, and energetically athletic. I was fascinated by his speech. He spoke rapid, fluent English, but rather heavily accented and filled with perceptibly deliberate foreignisms of the type that mid-American matrons find charming. He rarely finished a sentence and often left verbs to the listener's imagination.

He talked with enthusiasm of his work in the United States and dropped a long series of significant-sounding names to suggest the range of intimate influential friends with whom he worked and consorted. His tone, when he spoke of the shah, was one of reverence, and he took pains that I perceived how close he stood to the throne and the Pahlavi family. His only deliberate indiscretion was when he spoke of the prime minister, Abbas Amir Hoveida, whom he disliked and denigrated. It was an interesting introduction to my counterpart.

My second meeting with Zahedi was at a small dinner party given for us by the deputy assistant secretary of state, Sidney Sober, whose jurisdiction included Iran. On that occasion, a balmy spring evening, I had a chance to hear Zahedi talk with less theatrical effect. He described how he, the son of a general (who was later to be prime minister) had gone off to be educated in the United States, had studied dry-land farming in Utah, had roamed around the country as a student, and had become a fervent admirer of things American. He spoke of his early days with the U.S. Point IV program in the economic development of Iran, and of his rather rapid advancement through the Iranian bureaucracy.

Finally, he talked at length of his association with the CIA in the countercoup, led by his father, that returned the shah to the throne in 1953, and of the resultant close associations he had with the shah. These led to his marriage to the shah's only daughter, the progeny of the brief prearranged dynastic liaison between the Pahlavi family and the Egyptian ruling family of King Farouk. He later introduced us to his only daughter, the shah's only granddaughter, who was a student at Princeton.

Zahedi did not strike me as what the French would call a "serious" person. He spoke often in broad philosophical terms, heavily tinged by his open profession of faith in Islam. Whether this covered a razor-sharp mind or whether it was a screen for less than met the eye, I could never really determine. My conclusion ultimately was that Zahedi was shrewd, able to determine where the main interests of his country and his future lay, and masterly at manipulating Americans. However, I do not believe he had a brilliant, analytical mind or the capability to conceptualize much beyond the guidelines that were laid out to him from Tehran.

On my third meeting with Zahedi, I saw him in his most accomplished element. He invited my wife and me and our two daughters to a formal dinner that he was giving to honor the new secretary of agriculture, Robert Bergland. The dinner was held in the chancery building next door to the embassy residence. The guest list was studded with senators and congressmen and their wives, with journalists, with members of what passes for the jet set in Washington, and with a number of attractive young ladies from Washington official society. Unfortunately, because I had returned from a visit to New York that evening, we arrived late at the dinner and did not meet many of the guests. However, we were there in time for the main course and for the speechmaking that followed the dinner. The main course was a fine rib of beef served with Idaho potatoes garnished with Iranian caviar. It may not have been the most exquisite culinary discovery of the century, but it certainly was unique and did form an appropriate gesture, which Zahedi could use as background to his speech toasting the secretary of agriculture. After dinner, I watched Zahedi operate among his guests. He was always attentive and charming, lavishing dessert and drinks on them although drinking nothing himself, and was particularly gallant with the ladies. He was assisted in this operation by a staff of handsome young Iranian couples, who were the junior officers of the embassy and their wives. As a professional, I admired the entire effort and saw how effectively the shah's government was represented in a city that places much emphasis on personal attention rather than the substance of events.

In addition to the education I received from government officials and the academic community, I sought out whatever information I could obtain from the American business community associated with Iran. In 1977 thirty-five thousand Americans were living in Iran, and the overwhelming portion of them—all but two thousand—were employed by private American firms. It is true that many of these firms were engaged in the sale of military equipment and technology, but they were private employers rather than government agents.

The first of these employers with which I became acquainted was the Bell Helicopter Company. It was part of the Textron conglomerate and manufactured the Huey helicopter, which had been widely used in Vietnam. A number of Hueys had been sold to Iran, and Bell was also selling other models —larger and more sophisticated—to the Iranians. Because of this and because the Iranian armed forces needed training in the use of this equipment, Bell had become the largest single American employer in Iran. Shortly after I arrived in Washington, the president of the company indicated he wished to see me.

Before seeing him, I obtained as much information as I could about Bell contracts and operations in Iran. The information from the Departments of Defense and State made the Bell operation seem almost open-ended. Not only were more helicopters being sold and more Americans being deployed to Iran, but there existed plans for the manufacture and assembly of other helicopters in the country, with no indication when the entire operation could be phased out and turned over to the Iranians to run. Much concern had already been expressed in a report from the United States Senate about the possibility that American employees of military-equipment companies would become, in effect, mercenaries in the structure of the Iranian armed forces. The pattern Bell was developing in Iran seemed to give substance to that concern.

Consequently, when the Bell president called on me, I spread a number of charts on the table and indicated that they seemed to have no effective termination point. It looked to me as though Bell was planning to stay permanently in Iran and indeed to meet much of its operating budget from the Iranian enterprise. Although the Bell president did not counter this observation, he seemed offended that I should be concerned about it and became quite defensive. Our meeting went from bad to worse and ended with my strong suggestion that Bell had better pull itself together by fixing some appropriate deadline when it would pull out of Iran and turn over the functions it had created to an exclusively Iranian management.

My second meeting with a purveyor of military equipment to Iran hardly went much better, although it was a far more civil session. The president of Northrop Aviation came to call and explain something about the nature of Northrop operations in Iran. The Iranians had purchased the F-5 aircraft some years ago and had subsequently received later models of this fighter-interceptor. From all indications—which were later borne out—they had been able to absorb the aircraft into the air force, fly it, maintain it, and generally manage its operations effectively. It was the sort of military-sales program I would have liked Bell to emulate.

However, the current problem facing Northrop was that it had developed a new plane, the land-based version of the navy F-18 fighter, which the shah wished to purchase from the United States. Under the new presidential directive limiting arms sales, it was stipulated that no aircraft could be sold abroad that had not already been purchased by the United States armed forces. The F-18L had not been sold in the United States and was being developed exclusively for export. The new presidential directive expressly prohibited that sale. The president of Northrop was deeply frustrated by this turn of events, but there was nothing I could do to relieve his problem in any direction.

Other representatives from other military-equipment firms came to call on me, several of them retired military officers whom I had known in East Asia and elsewhere. Their function, to maintain liaison with United States government officials, was one that had been accepted as a general pattern by the military even though it had been often criticized in the Congress and by the press. Most of these callers had nothing they particularly wanted to sell at that moment; they merely wished to leave their cards, renew acquaintance, and otherwise establish their mark.

Most American business operations in Iran did not center on military sales. As a result, most of the senior executives of the corporations engaged in business in Iran were not located in—and did not often visit—Washington. The bulk of them had their corporate headquarters in New York. Through an organization that has served as an intermediary between business and government, I scheduled meetings in New York to consult with the senior executives of companies concerned with Iran. I called on some of these executives in their offices and met members of their staffs; however, the principal meeting was one that took place in the boardroom of the Pan Am Building over Park Avenue.

Here more than thirty senior executives of major New York–based corporations assembled to give me their views of American business interests in Iran. For the first half hour or so, I listened to them tell me in rather glowing terms about the business opportunities as they saw them and the economic future they forecast for the country. They seemed to be universally optimistic, and all of them indicated that their Iranian business was highly profitable. I detected one common feature, however: very few of them had made any significant equity investment in Iran. Most were operating under service contracts or arrangements in which the services they provided constituted their partnership or their equity in the Iranian corporations with which they were associated.

Since I had just come from the Philippines, where I had been acutely aware of the problems resulting from imbalances between labor and capital, I could not bring myself to be quite so optimistic about the future of the Iranian economy. In the Philippines there had been an enormous surplus of well-educated labor but an acute shortage of liquid capital. In Iran the opposite seemed to be true. The country was earning twenty-two to twenty-three billion dollars a year from oil revenues but had practically no skilled labor and only limited resources of unskilled labor. I doubted that the economy could ingest the rapid industrialization programs that the shah was pressing forward. I expressed these views in the form of a question to my business interlocutors around the Pan Am table.

Walter Levy, an oil consultant whom I had known for many years, immediately leaped forward to expand upon the doubts I had raised. He not only entertained the same doubts but had a number of other negative things to say about the nature of the Iranian regime, the prevalence of corruption, the unrest in the labor force, and the generally unsound economic conditions. This observation touched off a cascade of contradictory comments from the other participants. All of them excoriated Levy's analysis and cited their own experiences to demonstrate that things were going well, that the industrialization program was being absorbed, that Iran was meeting its payments and obligations, and that the industrial and labor peace had never been better. Levy did not counterattack, and we left the issue where it lay. Although Levy had something of a reputation as a Cassandra, my own instincts in this particular instance paralleled his, and I left that meeting feeling disturbed. It struck me as abnormal that a group of sophisticated American businessmen who approached market opportunities hardheadedly was unanimously certain about something on which I entertained doubts and Levy obviously harbored strong negative convictions.

On my return to Washington I began the final stage of the pilgrimage that must be made by every person nominated an American ambassador. The march to Capitol Hill.

The congressional liaison staff of the Department of State had arranged for me to call on appropriate committee chairmen and members in both the Senate and the House of Representatives. Many of these men were good friends whom I had known over the past thirty years. Most of them were of my generation, and we had grown up together amid certain patterns and convictions about the world. Some were newer and younger and held different points of view. They were more closely attuned to the younger generation, which reflected the dissidence of Iranian students and their American sympathizers. They warned me and their colleagues about growing political problems in Iran as well as a growing apprehension among many Americans about continued support for the shah's regime. In sounding out the more senior members of the House and the Senate, I found that they, too, were aware of these rumblings but tended to discount them because they had heard them on several previous occasions in the long regime of the shah.

The staff members of the Senate and House committees were even more alert to the political dissidence reflected in the actions of the Iranian students and to the possibility that this could embroil the United States disadvantageously. Several of them had visited Iran and were in direct contact with dissident groups underground in that country. It has always been interesting to me to note that the members of the Congress and

their staffs are usually far more sensitive to political potentiali-
ties than are the bureaucrats in the executive branch or the
journalists of the national press. It was, therefore, useful for me
to hear these points of view from people who were going to
have a direct effect on the future policies of the United States
in Iran.

My primary purpose in going to Capitol Hill, however, had
to do with the inevitable procedure of confirmation by and
with the consent of the Senate of the United States. Presidents
may nominate ambassadors, but they can be sworn in only after
the Senate has confirmed them. I therefore had to prepare for
my hearings before the Senate Foreign Relations Committee,
which were a prelude to the confirmation process.

The Foreign Relations Committee at that time was under
the benevolent chairmanship of Senator John Sparkman of
Alabama. Senator Sparkman had acceded to that position only
recently, with the departure of Senator Fulbright, and was not
to hold office much longer himself. He and most of the members from both parties on the committee were well known to
me, and I had often appeared before them in regard to many
subjects. Moreover, in the years when I had served as ambassador abroad, I had entertained most of them in our home and
knew them as personal friends.

Therefore, despite the political sensitivity that was begin-
ning to emerge on the subject of Iran and despite the fact that
I had spent a number of years involved with Indochina issues,
I anticipated no problems in the confirmation process.

Shortly before my hearings were scheduled, I was informed
there would be two adverse witnesses—a professor from
Princeton who would testify against me because of my previous
involvement in Indochina, and a professor from Georgetown
University who would testify against the idea of sending any
ambassador to Iran since he opposed the shah's regime. The
Georgetown professor was accompanied by fifty or so students
who wore masks to disguise their identities but who claimed to

be Iranians. The Capitol police would not let the masked students enter the office building where the hearings were to be held; it required them to stand across the street.

In the event, the hearings were uneventful. I was called first, made a short statement, and was questioned briefly. I was then dismissed so that I did not have to stay in the room to hear the negative testimony of the two professors. When I left the building, I walked across the street toward the Iranian students to test their temper and determine their attitudes. As I approached them, it became clear to me that they had no idea who I was, and they merely parted to let me pass through. In view of that reaction, I did not stop either to identify myself or to engage them in dialogue to learn just who they were or where their interests lay.

Within the appropriate few days, the committee reported my name favorably to the full Senate and I was duly confirmed. According to the records, one senator, Dick Clark of Iowa, voted against me. I was astonished to learn this, since I had never met Senator Clark and since he had not been present at my hearings. Therefore I asked the congressional liaison people in the Department of State to arrange an appointment for me with the senator so that I could determine why his vote had been in the negative and what it was that troubled him about my appointment. After some signs of embarrassment, the word came back that the senator's vote had been cast in error by one of his aides and that the senator had no particular desire to meet with me.

These formalities over, I arranged to be sworn into office discreetly in the office of the chief of protocol and made preparations to leave Washington as soon as possible to take up my post in Tehran.

3

Arrival at Post

Because of the large numbers of military personnel assigned to my mission in Iran and because of the significance that military-sales programs assumed in our general relations with Iran, I accepted an invitation from the United States military command in Europe to visit with them en route to Tehran. This command had nominal responsibility for the logistics and personnel servicing of the military detailed to the Military Assistance and Advisory Group in Iran. It also performed such vital functions as providing for the health services, the commissary supplies, and many of the other amenities that were used by the official American community in Tehran. Therefore, my wife and I decided to interrupt our trip at Frankfurt, where we would be met by a military escort and taken to the United States military headquarters in Europe, located at Stuttgart.

In Frankfurt we were greeted by a young escort officer who bundled us and our baggage across the field to the military terminal at Rhein-Main Airport. There a small T-39 liaison aircraft was awaiting us for the flight to Stuttgart. As we approached the plane, we realized that the pilot looked familiar. He stood at the bottom of the ramp with his hand in a crisp salute but with a large grin spread over his face. He had been one of the pilots assigned with similar T-39 aircraft to fly me around Southeast Asia in the days when I was ambassador to Laos and had to keep in communication with our officials in Saigon, Bangkok, and Phnom Penh. It was therefore a familiar face and a comfortable flight to Stuttgart. When we arrived, the pleasure was doubled as the aircraft was met by the commander of the liaison squadron, who was another veteran of the Southeast Asian T-39 group.

We were hustled off during the late-spring dusk to the home of the senior American military officer in Stuttgart, who bore the title of deputy commander for United States forces in Europe. This rather awkward title was necessary because the nominal commander was the supreme allied commander—that is to say, the head of the NATO forces, who had his headquarters in Belgium. The operating headquarters in Stuttgart and the staff for United States unilateral force functioned under his command. The supreme allied commander in Belgium was General Alexander Haig, with whom I had worked closely during his years in the White House, and the deputy commander in Stuttgart was General Robert Huyser of the United States Air Force, whom I had never met.

On arriving at the Huyser residence, we discovered it was a solid old German burgher home of the type built by prosperous Stuttgart merchants earlier this century. It was comfortably appointed but not pretentious, and it was amiably run by a household staff that seemed used to having everything function on time and in appropriate military order.

General Huyser was a large, rough-hewn man who was completely without guile. He was straightforward in his approach to all issues and we got along well from the beginning. We were guests that evening at a pleasant dinner that he and his wife gave in our honor, bringing in some of the senior members of their command, a few German residents of Stuttgart, and the United States consul general and his wife who were located in

that city. After dinner, Dutch Huyser and I discussed some of
the problems we saw in the operation of a military outpost in
Iran, so far removed from the central structure of the United
States headquarters in Europe. But it was not until the next day
that I received my formal briefings from the Stuttgart headquarters command.

There were no surprises in the briefings, and the staff seemed
smoothly professional. It was clear that we could work together
at long distance without difficulties. Thus reassured, my wife
and I climbed back onto the T-39, returned to Frankfurt, and
caught the next flight into Tehran.

We arrived over Tehran in the early hours of the evening,
after darkness had fallen on the city. After having passed many
wastelands in the eastern parts of Turkey and the northwestern
parts of Iran, we found spread out below us the glittering slope
of the Elburz Mountains where the five million inhabitants of
Tehran lived. The city's elevation reached nearly seven thousand feet at its northern limits, and went gradually down to
about four thousand feet at its southern limits. The airport, to
the west of the city, was about halfway between these two
altitudes and boundaries.

On arriving, our plane was met by the Iranian chief of
protocol and the chargé d'affaires of the United States embassy. We were immediately whisked off to the VIP lounge
where the senior officers of the embassy and their wives were
assembled. It was a group of twenty or so, a few of whom I
knew from other parts of the world. They all seemed congenial
and pleased to have a new ambassador after having been six
months without one.

As soon as we could gracefully make our departure, we shook
hands all around and bundled into our armored car behind the
protection of a police escort to make the trip to the embassy
residence. Our driver was a pleasant, squat Armenian whom I
came to appreciate greatly over the course of the next two
years. His name was Haikaz Ter Hovenissian, and he had been

driving for the American embassy for over twenty years. I had heard of him and his skills, because he had saved the life of one of my predecessors during a period of violence a number of years before. On that occasion an assassination team had attempted to kill Ambassador Douglas MacArthur II, but it had been foiled by Haikaz's courage and driving skill. He was a man of great wisdom, with a cheerful sense of humor and an amazing amount of knowledge about events taking place in the city of Tehran.

We drove through the dark broad streets of Tehran, down Eisenhower Boulevard, straight into the junction with our own road, and reached the embassy in fifteen or twenty minutes. This was possible because the traffic in the evening in that part of town was not heavy; in daylight it would have taken anywhere from three-quarters of an hour to an hour to make the same transit. Tehran looked impressive in the darkness. I had been there only once before for a few days and had thought it a rather drab city, but during the night, with the illumination of the street lights and the lighting in the store windows, it looked deceptively modern and clean.

On arriving at our embassy compound on the corner of Roosevelt Avenue and Takht-e Jamshid, we were whisked through the large iron gates, along a pleasant drive through the trees, and pulled to a stop at the front door of the embassy residence.

The residence itself had been designed by American architects with certain Persian flourishes. Although the combination did not quite succeed architecturally, it was nevertheless a comfortable dwelling and extremely well built. Our household staff met us on the outer steps. They consisted of four Pakistanis, two Iranians, one Bangladeshi, and the Italian chef, Luigi. Luigi had for twenty years been in the service of the American ambassador to Iran and, like Haikaz, was a living legend, well known throughout the foreign service. He and Haikaz were close and inseparable friends.

With this professional staff and the well-furnished embassy residence, we needed to waste no time on household arrangements. Our personal effects from the Philippines would arrive in a few days, but the equipment already in the residence made them unnecessary for basic creature comforts. Consequently, I was ready to begin work the day after we arrived.

My first order of business was to become acquainted with the embassy staff, to find out what their work programs were, and to obtain some sense of the direction in which I wished the functions of the embassy to proceed. There was a system for this that I had developed in other posts and that was more or less standard throughout the service. I would take a day with each section, meeting with its officers, discussing the programs they were working on, walking through their space in order to meet not only the secretarial staff but the Iranian employees as well, and then moving on to the next section until I had completed the program for the entire mission.

Tehran was a big mission, even though not quite as large as the one I had just left in the Philippines. All told, including the members of the various echelons in the military mission, over two thousand Americans were assigned there, and their families brought that total to close to five thousand. The Iranians affiliated with the embassy in all its manifestations also numbered about two thousand. It thus took me some time to work my way through this entire operation and determine what its various members were doing. They were, of course, engaged in all manner of activity, as happens when two countries work as closely together as did the United States and Iran. By far the largest contingent was in the military mission, and most of those were people who were on one-year tours of duty, without their families, to assist in the training of Iranian military forces and to prepare them for the absorption of the sophisticated military equipment that the United States was selling to the Iranian armed forces. Otherwise we had the normal political, economic, consular, informational, and administrative services.

Naturally, also connected with these various groups was a large contingent of intelligence personnel working in close affiliation with the Iranians.

As I completed my survey of the embassy personnel, the one thing that disturbed me was how few of those serving in Iran had had previous experience in the country. Only a limited number spoke Farsi or knew the culture of the country well. In inquiring why this was so, I came to the conclusion that most officers and their families who lived once in Iran had no great compulsion to go back. It is a rather forbidding country, and its culture is not all that congenial to foreigners. Moreover, until recent years there were real problems of schooling, public health, and the other conveniences that attract career officials toward longer or repeated stays in a foreign country.

The other thing that struck me was the number of Iranian nationals working for the embassy who were Armenian Christians. Very few of the senior positions among the Iranian staff were filled with Muslims, and those few were of a specialized character. Later on, in discussing this phenomenon with other ambassadors stationed in Tehran, I found that they had the same experience. It seems that the Islamic Shi'as did not find working for foreigners very congenial. In fact, most of them found the discipline of work as required in the Western ethic somewhat offensive to their mores. Therefore, more than in any other country where I had lived and served, I felt myself insulated from and alien to my environment. I determined that I would learn Farsi as soon as possible in order to make some breakthrough in understanding the Iranian ethos.

My general conclusions after having become acquainted with the embassy personnel and their work programs were that the mission was professionally organized and run, that its personnel were competent, and that it had few administrative weaknesses. I was pleased that Jack Miklos, my deputy, who had acted as chargé d'affaires for the six months following the departure of Ambassador Helms, had held the organization together well and kept it on a solid footing.

There were, however, two areas that I wished to investigate more thoroughly and to revise. The first had to do with the general manner in which we handled the question of military sales. Our military mission had been built up during the period of almost unlimited military sales that characterized the early 1970s. In that period, the military-advisory group acted primarily as purchasing agents for the Iranians. The Iranian authorities laid out their requirements, and the military-assistance group undertook to acquire them in the United States from funds supplied by the apparently unending cornucopia of Iranian oil money.

Not only did this procedure have to be changed because of the president's directive on arms sales, but I also felt that the military-assistance group owed the Iranians somewhat more in the way of advice concerning their capability to absorb the weapons they were acquiring, to service them, to maintain them, and to utilize them effectively. From what little I saw in my first observations, I believed that we would render the Iranians a constructive service if we took greater action to cost for them the continuing obligations that they incurred in their purchase of sophisticated military equipment.

The second area that I wished seriously investigated concerned the future of the shah's industrialization process in the context of the entire Iranian economy. The doubts that had first arisen in my mind about this industrialization program when I talked with the American business executives in New York had become compounded as I looked further into the economic equations for Iran. I therefore wanted some studies in depth concerning the ability of the Iranian economy to cope with the enormous industrialization program that the shah was pressing on the country. This meant an examination of the capacities of the Iranians to manage and to provide skilled labor for programs that were already on the books. The economic section of the embassy, which spent most of its time attempting to assist American businessmen, who had flocked to the country like bees to honeysuckle, threw up its hands in collective despair when I levied this requirement upon them. We therefore had to ask Washington for special assistance in the form of researchers to come out and help with this particular project. Unfortunately, although it became an obsession with me and I was constantly riding the economic officers to complete it, I never did get the information I sought.

One other feature of embassy life in Tehran that was new to me, despite my thirty-three years experience, was the centering of all our principal activities in a single compound. This meant that I was able to avoid the frustrations of Tehran traffic in commuting to and from the office, since I merely walked through a small grove from my residence to the chancery building in order to be at work. It also meant that I could indulge my favorite practice of a noontime swim in the residence swimming pool when I did not have to attend some official function in the middle of the day. But it inevitably resulted in having embassy business always with me, and the chancery code room only a few steps away. The compound had formerly been on the northern edge of the city, but the city had grown around it, and the twenty-three acres that we held, walled in by a thick brick barricade, were now dominated on three sides by ten- and twelve-story apartment and office buildings, and on the fourth side, to the east, by a large stadium where football was played most evenings.

Other features that I had been used to were present in a form somewhat different from the one I had experienced elsewhere. For example, we had a large American school, located well to the north of the city in a compound made available by the Iranian armed forces. The buildings, which were constructed for the three thousand or more students in the American school, were eventually going to become an adjunct to the Iranian military academy. We also had a small American hospital staffed by United States army doctors, complete with the most modern equipment for a twenty-five bed unit. In addition, we had something unique to Tehran—a community-services center that had been established to assist the American community with problems endemic to service in Tehran. These were problems resulting from the frustrations of cultural shock and from the difficulties many family members had in adjusting to the alien atmosphere. These problems manifested themselves in alcoholism, drug abuse, and psychological strain. The clinic was manned by a full-time American psychiatrist, assisted by two trained psychiatric workers and a staff of therapists. It was sustained financially not only by the United States government but by contributions from the various American business concerns operating in Tehran.

All in all, therefore, the mission in Tehran was complex and required a considerable span of management. In addition to our people in Tehran proper, we also had consulates in Tabriz, Isfahan, and Shiraz. Moreover, our information service had Iran-American Society branches in Meshed, Ahwaz, and Hamadan. Over the first few months of my assignment in Iran, I would attempt to visit all of those places, and through those visits acquire a broader knowledge of other aspects of the American interest in this rather strange and challenging country.

But at the outset I had to observe the rituals of diplomacy by presenting my credentials to the shah, calling upon the appropriate senior officials of the Iranian government, and meeting formally my colleagues in the diplomatic corps. Because of Iran's prestige as an oil producer and as a regional power, there were better than seventy ambassadors in the city and I was expected to exchange calls with each one of them.

4

Shah Mohammed
Reza Pahlavi

The presentation of an ambassador's credentials to the head of
the government to which he has been accredited is accompanied by ceremonies typical of the host country's culture and
society. In general, republics tend to make the ceremonies as
simple as possible (in our own case, the president of the United
States receives half a dozen ambassadors at a time, and the
presentation of credentials is a rigidly austere ceremony). However, in some of the monarchies—such as the British—the
ceremonies are rather impressive, featuring gilded coaches,
horsemen, outriders, and considerable pomp. In the case of
Iran, which has an imperial court, the ceremony on which I was
about to embark was formal and dignified but not particularly
pompous.

The evening before my credentials were to be presented,
senior members of my staff and I went to the palace to rehearse
the little pageant in which we would participate. It would
essentially consist of a brief presentation, in which I would give
the shah the letters of recall of my predecessor accompanied
by a letter of credence signed by the president of the United
States. I would then read a brief statement that I had written

concerning the policies that the United States entertained toward Iran, and would listen to a brief reply from the monarch, delivered extemporaneously. After that I would present the senior members of my staff to the shah, following which he and I would withdraw for a brief conversation in his library.

After the rehearsal I returned to the embassy residence and mulled over for some time what I had recently learned about the country in which I was to serve and the monarch to which I was to be accredited. This information was not particularly sophisticated, since I had read only somewhat superficially concerning the history of the country, the nature of the people, and the substance of their culture.

The Iranians are descended from the ancient Persians, a people who 2,500 years ago, under the leadership of Cyrus the Great and Darius, had created the first real empire state in recorded Western history. That state stretched from what is now the southern part of the Soviet Union all the way down to Egypt. The shahs of that era had introduced concepts of jurisprudence, of fiscal responsibility, and of general centralized administration that had been unknown before then. Even after the collapse of their empire, Persians served as civil administrators in most of the area, working for the successor states of the region.

Because of this illustrious past, Persians have long held a somewhat romanticized view of their past and have felt that history has somehow or other cheated them out of their just desserts. They have believed that there ought to be a renaissance of their ancient domination in the region, and they have always entertained a sense of superiority with respect to their neighbors, particularly their Arab neighbors. They have thought of themselves as a nation that deserves a better place in the sun than recent events have accorded to them—and as a people that will one day revive some of the glories of Persia's past.

The Persian people, over the years, have been conquered by

the Greeks, the Romans, the Seljuk Turks, the Mongols, the Arabs, the British, and the Russians. Despite these successive waves of invasion and control, they have somehow managed to maintain their national identity.

Some observers have argued, however, that this identity has been retained only at a price. They suggest that history indicates that the Persian people accommodated themselves to their various conquerors and adopted a course of political expediency. They point out that through this expediency, Persians became adept at determining which faction or nation was in the ascendancy so they could attach themselves to that rising power. By the same token, Persians are reputed to have been able to discern who among the leaders—or the nations—was losing power and to detach themselves rapidly from that authority.

One other aspect of Persia's past that I found instructive concerned its history in the nineteenth century. At that time Persia found itself at the nexus of the struggle between the two superpowers of the period: the Russian empire, moving down from the north, and the British empire, moving out of its Indian possessions to the east. As these two superpowers contended with each other in the "Great Game" that they played across the sweep of Southwest Asia, the Persians became pawns to the ambitions of empire.

Persia at that time was a country in name only. The writ of the Qajar shahs extended little beyond the capital of Tehran. The rest of the country was ruled by tribal leaders, regional chieftains, and religious authorities. More often than not these lesser satraps were manipulated by the British and the Russians. They accepted bribes from one or the other and were prepared to place their limited authority at the disposal of the imperial rivals.

In fact, by the end of the nineteenth century and in the early part of the twentieth, the situation had become so demoralizing within Persia that law and order throughout the country were no longer maintained by Persian authorities. Instead, in the northern regions the constabulary forces were made up of the Cossack Brigade, a military organization that recruited from local and tribal sources but, as its name implies, was officered by Cossacks seconded from the czar's imperial armies. By the same token, in the eastern and southern parts of the country law and order were maintained by the Persian Light Rifles, which were local troop levies, but officered this time by British officers seconded from the British Indian army.

To the average Persian, then, it was clear that very little authority emanated from Tehran. Instead, almost all decisions affecting the daily life of the ordinary citizen came either from Moscow or from London. This experience ingrained itself into the political consciousness of all Persians, and even to this day the belief exists that unseen foreign hands are somehow manipulating the daily lives of Iranians. This attitude of suspicion, coupled with a xenophobia derived from the incursions of the imperial powers on Persian soil, has made it difficult for foreigners to communicate in a straightforward manner with Persians. Through my own brief reading on this subject, I came to the conclusion that the problem extended from the lowliest peasant all the way up to the shah himself.

The shah was the son of Reza Shah, who had founded the Pahlavi dynasty in 1925. Reza Shah was born in the nineteenth century in a northern region of the country near the Caspian sea. As a young man he was a tall, strapping, athletic figure and had a quick mind and a commanding sense of authority. He chose to go into the soldiering trade. In the part of the country in which he lived, becoming a soldier necessarily meant joining the Cossack Brigade.

In the Cossacks the young man rose rapidly through the Persian ranks, and by the time the Communist revolution took place in Russia, he was known as Reza Khan and was the senior Persian serving under the Russian officer cadre. Consequently, when the revolution occurred and the Cossack officers left,

Reza Khan succeeded to the command of the Cossack Brigade.

The British, sensing the opportunity that was presented to them by the collapse of the Russian presence in Persia, moved rapidly to try to establish their total hegemony over the country. General Ironside, who was the senior British officer serving in Persia, suggested to Reza Khan that he bring the Cossack Brigade down from the north to the outskirts of Tehran and place pressure on the Qajar shah to accept a British protectorate.

Reza Khan did bring his brigade to the gates of Tehran and did put pressure upon the Qajar dynasty. But his goals were not those of the British. He wished to force the Qajar shah to abdicate, and to create a republic.

In this ambition he was following the course of Kemal Atatürk, who, in next-door Turkey, had moved in the wake of the collapse of the Ottoman empire to establish a republic in Ankara and to set out on a course that would modernize, westernize, and secularize that ancient Islamic empire. This was the role that Reza Khan also saw for himself.

Over the period of the next few years, in which he maneuvered with respect both to the British and to the Qajar dynasty, Reza Khan eventually placed himself in a situation in which he was able to overthrow the Qajars and to assume a position of power for himself. By this time, however, largely at the urging of the senior members of the Shi'a clergy, Reza Khan had abandoned his idea of establishing a republic. The Shi'a clergy, who were enormously influential in the country, preferred to retain a monarchy. In 1906 they had joined with other elements in the country, particularly the merchant class, to force a constitution upon the Qajar shah that contained a number of provisions they found congenial. For example, the constitution stipulated that Shi'a Islam should be the official religion of the state. Moreover, it provided for the establishment of a council of mullahs that would have the authority to review actions taken by the parliament in order to determine whether or not they were in conformity with the teachings of the Prophet as recorded in the Koran. If they were not, the council had the right to veto these actions of parliament and to declare them null and void. Because of these and other considerations, the Shi'a clergy prevailed upon Reza Khan to proclaim himself a shah rather than to establish a republic.

Accordingly, in 1925 Reza Khan established the Pahlavi dynasty and proclaimed himself Reza Shah. The state that he inherited was in a shambles. While the Russians had abandoned their imperial incursions into the country, the new Soviet regime was attempting to stir up revolution in the northern provinces bordering the Soviet Union. Similiarly, although the British had been frustrated in their efforts to place Persia under their formal protection, they nevertheless wielded a pervasive control over the economy of the country and had begun to recognize, as a result of the navy's needs during World War I, the importance of the petroleum reserves that had been discovered in the southern part of the country. Interlaced with these problems faced by the new shah were the open rebellion and separatism of a number of tribal areas.

For the first fifteen years of his reign, therefore, Reza Shah spent most of his time attempting to consolidate his control over the country and to restore the authority of Tehran in the various provincial regions. Usually at the head of his own troops, he engaged tribal leaders and their forces in military action, conquering them one by one or forcing them into exile.

At the same time, he moved against the remnants of the old Qajar aristocracy and of the feudal landholders who had been their allies. He expropriated the lands and other properties of the Qajars in the best tradition of Persian dynasties. These lands and properties formed the basis for the Pahlavi fortune that was in later years to assume such prominence in the annals of Iran.

In order to secure the support of the peasant population, Reza Shah also instituted sweeping land reforms. He took away enormous holdings that had been run by feudal families and limited feudal control to a single village for each such family. The remaining lands and villages were given to the peasants who actually tilled the soil.

During these same years, Reza Shah worked on his original plan to modernize and westernize the country. He built railroads, installed basic infrastructure in the country, widened roads, erected modern buildings, and attempted to give the cities the appearance of Western civilization. He introduced the public-school system and attempted to bring modern education to the ancient institutions of higher learning.

Above all, he strengthened the armed forces. He was a man of the army, and the army was his principal instrument in establishing his control over the country. He provided well for his loyal officers and established an arms industry with the assistance of foreign advisers. He developed a civil service that was responsible and loyal to him, and he carried out constant inspections to be certain that the measures he had set in motion were being pursued. He was the very model of an enlightened despot attempting to bring his country out of the ancient slough of ignorance, poverty, and disease. At the same time, his political regime became more and more authoritarian, and the 1906 constitution was ignored regularly by the practices he instituted, particularly with respect to the parliament. In short, he eventually brought the country under his personal control. But as he developed this control, it became clear in the 1930s that there was only one institution that effectively resisted his domination. This was the institution of Shi'ism, the state religion of Persia. Shi'ism had a dominant position among the Persian population. It was a branch of Islam that had become popular in Persia largely as a mark of resistance to the Arab conquerors, who espoused the Sunni branch of Islam and believed that their supreme clerical authority was vested in the caliph of Baghdad. The Shi'a religion, by contrast, holds that the supreme clerical authority in Islam has descended through the family of the Prophet, particularly through those who were martyred because of their schism with the larger Arabized institution of Sunni Islam. This religion has chosen as its leaders a series of imams who could trace their lineage directly back to the Prophet and who, for the most part, had eventually been resident in the territory of Persia. The last of the living imams disappeared in A.D. 874, and it is the belief of the Shi'a faithful that he has gone into occultation and will return one day to establish his authority over the Islamic world.

In the Shi'a religion there is a greater concentration of authority in a hierarchy than there is in other branches of the Islamic faith. This hierarchy is headed by a group of ayatollahs that is self-perpetuating and chooses its membership in an obscure, informal manner. The ayatollahs of Shi'a Islam have, over the centuries, exerted great authority in Persia through their control of the madrasseh, schools that train young men for the clerical life. Through the mullahs and the preachers in the mosques, these clerical dignitaries have been able to enjoy an inordinate degree of authority among the clergy and faithful.

Therefore, when Reza Shah confronted the institution of Shi'ism in Persia, he was taking on a formidable opponent. In the 1930s, though, he became convinced that Shiism was an obstruction to the accomplishment of the modern secular state into which he hoped to make his country. Accordingly, he chose the confrontation and chose it on grounds that would perhaps command the greatest degree of popular support.

Although his confrontation was relatively broad in its spectrum, its focus fell upon the Shi'a dress code for women. Under the decrees of the Shi'a clergy, Persian women were required to wear the chador, a long black seamless garment that covered them from head to toe and through which they could peer only because they were permitted to leave exposed their eyes and upper portion of their faces. This ungainly garment handicapped a woman's movements and made it difficult for her to be a constructive member of a modern westernized society. Reza Shah contended that this excessive modesty was not decreed in the Koran and that it was beyond the province of the Shi'a ayatollahs to enforce it upon the women of Persia.

This confrontation between the shah and the ayatollahs grew in bitterness and burst into violence at several points throughout Persia during the 1930s. As that decade drew to a close, however, the internal struggle became overshadowed by foreign developments.

War clouds were gathering in Europe, and it soon grew apparent to Reza Shah that a conflict would erupt. Viewing the situation shrewdly from the Persian perspective, he was concerned that hostilities would bring Persia's ancient nemeses, the British and the Russians, into close collaboration again. He feared that these two historical enemies of Persia would move as they had before to dominate and partition his country.

Reza Shah began to cast around for some nation to serve as a counterpoise to this renewed imperial threat. He found a ready and willing candidate in Nazi Germany. The Germans, keenly appreciating the value of Persian Gulf oil and seeking to frustrate the ambitions of both the British and the Russians, were quite happy to be offered an opportunity to gain a foothold in Persia. They began in the late thirties to move into the region in significant numbers. They helped Reza Shah develop his infant arms industry and train his armed forces in modern warfare, they built heroic new structures in Tehran to house the Persian government, and they improved the railroads and other infrastructure that the shah's government had begun.

Their influence was more than merely military; they also had a certain political and psychological effect on the shah. In fact, in the late thirties, in order to emphasize the Aryan nature of Persian origins, Reza Shah changed the name of his country from Persia to Iran, a name that was intended to signify the Aryan aspects of his people and his regime. It was Reza Shah's futile hope that by siding with the Germans in the coming conflict, he would not only protect himself against the incursions of the British and the Russians but also be associated with the ultimate victor.

Perceiving this and recognizing the significance that a German presence could have for their allied interests in the Persian Gulf, the British and Russians both reacted nervously to the increasing German presence in Iran. Consequently, when the Germans attacked the Soviet Union in 1941 and scrapped the Molotov-Ribbentrop pact, British and Russian planners set in motion measures that would extirpate the German presence from that region.

On August 25, 1941, British and Russian military forces moved once again into Iran. The Russians occupied and controlled the northern part of the country; the British did the same in the south. Reza Shah was arrested and sent into exile, eventually finding his way to South Africa, where he died. On the throne in his stead was placed twenty-one-year-old Mohammed Reza Pahlavi, Reza Shah's eldest son, who had been trained as crown prince to inherit this power eventually from his father.

Thirty-six years later this man, known universally as "the Shah," stood waiting to receive me in the large reception hall of the summer palace in the northern outskirts of Tehran. When I was shown into the room, I found him placed at the far end of two lines of court officials, all resplendent in braided uniforms and facing each other to form a narrow corridor leading to their monarch. The shah himself was dressed in full court regalia and was situated in the brilliant sunshine that streamed in from a tall window at his back. The net effect was to make him look particularly refulgent and to cause the visitor, standing in the shadows, to squint at the imperial presence. It was great theater.

I performed my little ceremony, handed over my letters, read my brief statement, and presented the senior members of my staff to the shah. All in all it consumed about five minutes, including the time allotted for the shah's answer. He then gestured to me to follow him off to the right to his library, and left my staff officers to converse with the court officials. The normal practice was for the conversation with the shah to last fifteen or twenty minutes, after which the shah and the ambassador would emerge to mingle briefly with the others before the embassy group took its formal departure from the palace. In this instance, however, our conversation went on for an hour and a half.

When we entered the library, the shah gestured me to a couch and slumped unceremoniously into a chair. He immediately unhooked the neck of his stiff tunic and settled back for an informal chat. After an exchange of pleasantries, he entered into a half-hour monologue in which he gave his view of the international situation. It was a rather pessimistic picture that he painted. He saw the Soviets encircling the Arabian peninsula, establishing footholds in the Horn of Africa, making inroads into Central Africa, and maneuvering to seize eventual control of the Persian Gulf oil resources. He saw them establishing at the same time nuclear parity with the United States while building up their conventional forces to a level that would eventually overwhelm Europe. It was clear in all of this that the shah felt the position of Iran was of key strategic importance and required the closest friendly attention from the United States.

These observations were conducted in impeccable English with a moderate, almost casual tone of voice and an obvious sincerity. They reflected a keen mind and a serious study of international events. The shah's discourse also demonstrated a good appreciation of history and the role that he and his country had played over the entire postwar period. I found him quite a different personality from the one I had imagined. There was no pomposity, no arrogance, and only limited acerbity. He seemed to be a man who had reasoned out most of his conclusions in solitary fashion and presented them almost tentatively, looking for confirmation or contradiction. When I replied to some of his observations with bits of information that apparently were new to him, he pursued them eagerly. Since I had spent so much of my time in East Asia, he was especially keen to have further views and facts concerning the situation in that part of the world. The conversation therefore continued on well beyond the scheduled time and touched on many broad areas of general interest to our two countries. He particularly wanted to know as much as I could tell him about the new administration in Washington and the policies that President Carter intended to pursue toward Iran. When I gave him a general summation of the instructions I had received from the president, he seemed enormously pleased and relieved.

This first exposure to the shah was most enlightening. From the briefings I had received in Washington and the "psychological profiles" I had read concerning the monarch, I expected a rather arrogant man, masking his insecurity in pompous pronouncements. The man I met was anything but that. He spoke in a quiet tone, maintained a modest demeanor, and was quite candid, almost tentative in the manner in which he presented his conclusions, and rather gentle in his courtesies. We parted with an exchange of messages from mutual friends, and I left his library feeling much more pleasantly disposed than I had anticipated toward this legendary modern figure.

When I emerged from the library, I discovered that all of the courtiers and my staff, with the exception of the chief of protocol, had given up waiting for me and had dispersed. Accompanied by the chief of protocol and my usual carload of police bodyguards, I returned to the residence in order to extricate myself from the confines of white tie and tails.

That evening I contemplated what I knew about the shah in an effort to relate that information to the personality I had just met. I knew that as a young man he had stood in great awe of his father. His father had taken a personal hand in his early training and had treated him very much as if he were a young cadet almost from the day he could toddle out of nursery school. He had been trained first in a special tutelage at the palace and then, as a young boy, had been sent off for further schooling in Switzerland. On returning from Switzerland, he had attended and graduated from the Iranian military academy and been commissioned into the Iranian military forces. During the few years that remained to him before his father was deposed, he had acted as an aide to the old shah, observing something of the zeal that the old man had for reforming his country and learning something of his constant driving attention to detail.

However, according to observers, the young shah did not have that same inner conviction and singularity of purpose that drove his father. Instead he was reported to enjoy a good time and love a good party. He spent much of his time in the postwar years traveling in Europe and the United States. He was a superb athlete who enjoyed skiing in Switzerland, kept a large stable of horses, and loved to drive fast cars and fly airplanes. Indeed, as a younger man he had an international reputation for being something of a playboy.

On the other hand, he was reported to be a man of courage. He had twice escaped assassination attempts. On one occasion a bullet had passed through his lip and another had entered his shoulder. In both instances he seems to have escaped miraculously and to have kept his composure.

On the other hand, in the chronicles concerning the political crises of 1953, he appeared to be an indecisive man. His confrontation with Prime Minister Mohammed Mossadeq was not in the same mold as the confrontations that his father had had with his political enemies. The old man had been indomitable in his will and decisive in his actions. Mohammed Reza Shah indicated a fateful sort of indecision and an absence of conviction in crisis.

To many observers these traits were the result of his youthful subordination to his father. It was suggested that, because of the old shah's stern ways, the young man had lost the courage of his own convictions and had not learned to take decisions on his own responsibility. Others pointed out that he had only partly completed his training for the throne when his father was deposed. Still others have suggested that his exposure to a Western education and to the democratic culture of Switzerland left him ill fitted to assume the authoritarian role that the culture of Iran demanded from its shahs. In any event, over the months in which I observed him and during critical periods when I saw him under stress several times a week, I came to the conclusion that the external image of the haughty autocrat that had been cultivated by his court and promulgated by his critics was not an accurate one. He was not truly cast to be a leader of men or the nation in time of crisis.

These thoughts bemused me as I remembered the reason that had been given me to explain why, despite my ignorance of Iran and the Islamic culture, I had been chosen to be ambassador to this country. My previous experience in dealing with "hard-nosed leaders" had conditioned me to recognize a tough customer when I met one. The man to whom I had presented my credentials certainly did not fit into that category.

5

The Diplomatic Rounds

Having presented my credentials to the shah, I was transformed by this diplomatic alchemy into an official personage
in Iran. This meant that as the representative of the United
States, I had to make a number of ritual calls and undertake
a number of obligations that were expected of me. The first
calls, on which my wife accompanied me, were on the shahbanou, the shah's wife, and other members of the royal family.
We were quite taken with the shahbanou, finding her a handsome, graceful, educated woman with a nice sense of humor
and an appreciation for both Western and Iranian culture. She
was the shah's third wife, and the first to bear him a male heir
to the throne. She was considerably younger than he and came
from a prominent merchant family in Tehran. Other calls in
court circles were on the shah's sisters and half brothers. These
gave us an insight into the way in which life-styles, personalities, and character can be affected by living in the shadow of
an absolute monarchy.

Then came the calls that I had to make on the cabinet
ministers and other government officials. In general, I was
more impressed by the ostentation of their offices than by the

capabilities of the individuals who occupied them. The two exceptions were the prime minister, Abbas Amir Hoveida, who was a delightful boulevardier with a razor-sharp mind and a politican's personality, and the head of the single political party, Jamshid Amouzegar, who was later to replace Hoveida as prime minister.

The other man who impressed me but who was already dying of cancer when I met him was the minister of court, Assadollah Alam. I wish I had been able to know more of this interesting man before he died.

In moving around the city to make these various calls, I became acquainted with some of the inconveniences that would afflict our lives in Iran. First, I discovered that I could not go anywhere without a significant bodyguard. There had been assassination threats against two of my predecessors, and in the two years before I arrived in Tehran six Americans associated with the embassy had been murdered by terrorists. The American ambassador was therefore provided with a small army of Iranian national police as security protection. Seventy policemen were assigned to this task; thirty-five of them lived on the embassy compound and were on duty at any one time. This contingent was in addition to the fifteen United States marines who guarded the chancery and the entrances to the compound.

The duty of these Iranian national policemen was to patrol inside the embassy grounds in order to preclude assassins from approaching the ambassador's residence. Moreover, whenever I went out of the compound gate, I was accompanied by one police officer who rode in the front seat of my limousine, and followed by a chase car with four other policemen armed to the teeth. On some occasions when there were terrorist alerts, my car would be preceded by another armored car containing another four policemen.

The old Cadillac limousine, which was only partially armored, was seldom used. Instead, I rode in a fully armored, unmarked, and undistinguished Chevrolet that looked much like many of the other vehicles on the streets of Tehran. My car did not fly a flag and my driver did not wear a uniform. The precautions taken included the avoidance of certain streets that were often too congested and the constant alteration of routes so that no driving pattern could be established by continual observation.

All of these security features, however, did little to improve the pace at which I could make my way through the traffic of Tehran. Although we had entered the city on our first arrival from the airport in the late evening, and driven home in fifteen minutes, I discovered that it would often take three-quarters of an hour to move from my embassy compound to the foreign ministry less than two miles away. Moreover, since most of the streets in the northern part of Tehran were mere expansions of village alleys that had existed there until a dozen years before, the congestion in the movement toward that part of the city was extreme. The Iranians are cavalier drivers; their streets are narrow, cluttered with horse-drawn carts, camels, and an occasional small herd of sheep; their pedestrians are reckless and unheeding of traffic signals; and all the major urban roads are lined with deep drainage ditches that trap errant vehicles with frustrating regularity.

Compounding these circumstances was the way in which the city of Tehran was laid out. It stretched down the slope of the Elburz Mountains for several miles from north to south. The southernmost portion of the city consisted of slums in which the newly arrived workers and would-be workers were housed. This was an area that had grown up at random as an outgrowth of urban prosperity in the industrialized city. Immediately to the north of these slums lay the old city, which had previously been enclosed by walls and which consisted of a number of neighborhoods that had been melded together over the years. In this area, government buildings and palaces, mosques, modern apartment buildings, department stores, theaters, boutiques, and old bath houses all mingled together in an architectural and sanitary monstrosity. Our compound was just at the northern limits of this old city. Beyond us to the north were the new suburbs that had been built since the arrival of petroleum prosperity in Iran. In these areas, luxury apartment buildings, sumptuous private villas, and a few palaces jostled the ancient mud-walled villages off the mountain slope. The aristocracy, the nouveaux riches, the diplomatic corps, and most of the foreigners lived in the northern part of the city. Most of them had never visited its southern region.

We regularly made pilgrimages to these northern suburbs. Partly this was for meetings or dinners with our colleagues from the diplomatic corps. Partly it was to meet and become acquainted with the leaders of the American business community. On most Saturdays during the better part of the year, it was to get in a weekly round of golf at the Imperial Country Club.

The diplomatic corps was an odd mixture. The British and Soviet ambassadors were senior members of their service and well experienced in this part of the world. Both of them headed large embassies in sprawling compounds and drew on a long tradition of their national interests in Iran. The Soviet embassy was made up very largely of intelligence agents who had no apparent diplomatic functions in the country and who seemed to emerge from the walls of their establishment only after dark. The Indian and Pakistani governments were well represented, but most of the European missions were concerned primarily with the commercial aspects of relations between their countries and Iran. Tehran offered my first exposure to Arab diplomats in large numbers, and I found them a rather amusing lot. They were surprisingly uninformed about most of the factual details of life in Iran but seemed capable of picking up the most extraordinary rumors, particularly those that might have scandalous implications. They were constantly communing with each other, happily passing on totally erroneous information, exchanging it for frivolous banalities. The outstanding exception to this pattern was the Kuwaiti ambassador, an engaging young sheik from the ruling family of Kuwait who had been in Iran for nine years and was the dean of the diplomatic corps. Perhaps the best-informed but least-conspicuous of my colleagues was the Israeli representative. He was a senior official who did not, however, enjoy formal diplomatic status in Tehran. The relations between Israel and Iran were intimate, but because Iran was an Islamic country, the shah preferred to keep them on an unofficial level. However, since there was a large colony of eighty thousand Jews in Iran who penetrated into almost every aspect of Iranian life, the Israelis enjoyed an information network that was second to none.

Finally, there were the Iranians. They have been described by some observers as "the ring around the embassy." For the most part those Iranians who knew the Americans and wished to be associated with them socially were people who had had some long affiliation with the United States. Many of them had been educated in the United States, and, partly because of that Western education, had prospered significantly in the modern Iranian society. Many others were from the old aristocracy or from families that had grown prosperous in times of British ascendancy, and they wished to maintain an affiliation with the new dominant power in the Western political spectrum. Almost all of them were wealthy, handsome, gracious, and entertaining. A number of them provided interesting salons where an ambassador or members of his staff could meet political personalities, but for the most part they attempted to emulate the international jet set and were not particularly productive from a professional point of view.

My first reaction on encountering this phenomenon was one of some annoyance that our embassy officers spent so much of their social time in these sterile surroundings. The affluent Tehranese of the northern part of the city provided a comfortable escape from the harsh realities of the daily traffic jams, the southern slums, the constantly failing utilities, and the unfailing rudeness of the average Iranian merchant or clerk. Many of their households were staffed with British butlers, Spanish or Filipino maids, and Italian cooks. They lived in opulent villas and entertained lavishly. In view of seductive diversions like these, it is easy to understand why foreign diplomats in Tehran did not see more of those people who were enjoying less material prosperity under the shah and who felt more negatively about the nature of his political regime. On the other hand, when I sought to meet people of that type I discovered how suspicious they were of foreigners, particularly Americans. I recall being in the rather modest home of one Iranian intellectual who had never before met an American ambassador and who seemed genuinely surprised that I was essentially a human being who had a rather liberal outlook on political and social matters. By the end of the evening, he had made it clear to me that in general he did not care for Americans and that he thought I must be a rare exception to the conceptual image he had of all my countrymen. As a consequence of this and other similar experiences, I found it difficult to define in exactly what measure of affection and respect we Americans were held in Iran. The adulation, emulation, and generous hospitality we received from that small section of the Iranian society that cultivated our favor did not seem to reflect the general reception that was accorded us by those whom we casually encountered in commerce or occasionally met in other circumstances.

6

The Iranian Economy

Once I had settled into the routine of the embassy and had generally gotten on top of all pending problems, I turned again to the issue that had bothered me from my earliest briefings on Iran. That was the nature of the economy and the consequences of the shah's industrialization program. Iran, which is bigger than Alaska, is a country that has been capriciously endowed by nature. The Elburz Mountains to the north, which border on the Caspian Sea, provide a barrier against the cold, wet climate of the Russian landmass, but also serve as a cloud trap that prevents moisture from reaching most of the central Iranian plateau. The net result is that the best agricultural regions in the country are on the northern slopes of the Elburz or else down in the ancient valleys of the Tigris and the Euphrates. Most of the rest of the country is very dry and hence can support crops only with sophisticated irrigation systems. In its earlier days Persia was able to survive as an agricultural country because people lived in the fertile valleys and grazed their sheep and cattle in the grassy mountain regions. However, as the population grew and the cities began to spread across the arid plateau, the country became less self-sufficient.

The limited amount of arable land lay in the area in which the feudal society of Persia had its strongest grip. When Reza Shah instituted his land-reform programs and broke up the old feudal holdings, he struck a blow for greater economic independence for the peasant farmers, but he also broke up an agricultural system that had been successful for centuries. By destroying the link between the capital supply that the feudal landowners could provide their peasants and the marketing network that they controlled, the shah's reforms introduced a vastly more inefficient agricultural operation. Although his intentions were good, he failed to complete the reform process by arranging for credit to the farmers, for fertilizer supplies, and for an efficient marketing system.

The net result was that the problems for agriculture, which had already begun to assert themselves because of the pressure of population on arable land, became compounded as that arable land was farmed less efficiently. Families living in the farming areas began to recognize that they could not support themselves with the resources available, and it soon became standard practice for younger male members of the family to leave the farms and seek employment in the cities.

The shah's industrialization program added to the pressures for migration. The availability of attractive jobs in the infant industry in and near the cities provided an additional impulse that complemented the pressures that were forcing young men off the land. But not even this great migration, which accelerated in the late 1970s, could keep up with the demand for workers.

Iran is a country of fewer than forty million people; in 1977 it probably had about thirty-six million inhabitants. One-half of these were under the age of fifteen, and, because of the compulsory education system introduced by the Pahlavis, they were not permitted to enter the labor force and were required to remain in school. One-half of the population was female, and, given Islamic taboos against women in industrial positions, they were also unavailable to Iran's potential industrial machine. To recruit labor for his industrialization scheme, the shah was down to a resource of only nine million people. One-half of those lived in the agricultural and rural sectors and had no desire to move into the industrial area. Moreover, most of them lived in small settlements removed from the monetarized sector of the economy; they were conservative, semiliterate villagers.

This meant that the labor pool for industrialization programs in Iran was at best four and a half million people, of whom one and a half million were already in the armed forces and the civil service. As a consequence, only three million Iranians were available to undertake the ambitious program that the shah set in motion after the oil boom of 1973.

Because of that boom, Iran began to earn about twenty-two billion dollars a year in hard currencies from selling its crude petroleum overseas. The shah determined that he would plunge almost all of that back into the industrialization of his country, so that by the year 2000 it would be "the fifth-largest industrial entity on the face of the earth." He moved ahead with this ambition unrelentingly. He decided, for example, to anticipate the depletion of cheap petroleum resources for energy and to build a network of nuclear- and hydroelectric-power plants. He undertook to build a large petrochemical industry so that the oil that did remain after the completion of the new energy system would be converted to highly profitable chemical and plastic products. He sought to induce manufacturers of automobiles, tractors, and trucks to establish manufacturing plants in Iran and, together with Iranian entrepreneurs, to establish a protected market for their products. In a massive "turnkey" project, based on a contract with the Soviets, he expanded the size of the Iranian steel mills. He also attempted to begin a copper industry and to build adequate infrastructure in the way of railroads and ports to serve this new industrial domain.

It was patent to anyone who did the basic arithmetic that all this could not be accomplished with a mere three million people in the industrial labor force, and that the quality of those laborers was inadequate to the task that the shah was setting for them. He was fully prepared to bring in foreign technicians at enormous expense in order to install the industrial plants and to train Iranians to handle them. He was willing to accept the fact that his forced methods cost more than would otherwise be the case, since he felt that those costs would soon be overtaken by inflation if there was delay in order to construct the enterprises in a more orderly and less urgent fashion.

However, it seemed to me that he failed to take into account a number of other considerations. First were the human consequences that flowed from the nature of his industrialization efforts. Bottlenecks inevitably developed in the effort to construct enormous industrial enterprises without adequate preparation. These bottlenecks usually involved some confrontation with the bureaucracy. In the time-honored Persian way, the bureaucracy's confrontations always seemed capable of being surmounted if adequate bribery was involved. Given the nature of the programs, the amounts of money involved, and the costly consequences of delay, the bribes became huge. Moreover, the corruption that was entailed by them reached into the highest levels of government and indeed into the precincts of the imperial family itself. The corruption that came from this forced industrialization was, in my judgment, a major liability to the shah and his regime.

The second problem arose from the young male workers who had been attracted from the countryside to work in the new industries. By and large they came from conservative rural backgrounds and were educated in the strict Islamic tradition. When they came into the modern westernized cities, they saw things that were uncongenial to them and that offended their basic sense of propriety. Moreover, although they were getting a far greater income than they had ever anticipated in their lives, they could find no satisfactory way to spend it. They saw huge high-rise luxury apartments being built for speculation and standing vacant, while they lived ten and twelve to a room in the slums in the southern part of Tehran. They saw civil servants and middle-class Iranians riding about the city in chauffeured Mercedes-Benzes, while they struggled for a place in the totally inadequate public-transportation system. Their frustrations were legion, and their sources of relief were very few. Many of them became actively involved in drugs, and many others gave vent to their hostility in senseless hooliganism. Thus the additional human cost of industrialization was affecting a critical sector of Iranian society.

Besides these considerations, I was concerned about the ultimate purpose of the Iranian industrialization program. The Iranian market itself would never be large enough to sustain industrial plants of adequate efficiency to be competitive. Any industrialization plan would therefore have to assume that there were markets for Iranian products outside of Iran. In the petrochemical industry, this might conceivably be possible, because the integration of the industry into nearby sources of petroleum, and the highly automated plants being built by the Japanese for this industry, could perhaps make up for other potential inefficiencies in the industry. In all other aspects of the industrialization program, however, I could see no hope for Iran's achieving competitive efficiency or production that could move profitably in international trade. Therefore, while the shah's general program of substituting cheap energy for dwindling petroleum supplies and installing industrial plants that could provide substitutes for expensive imports reflected astute planning, I was not convinced that the way in which he had chosen to execute his program was sound.

In response to my concern, the Department of State sent a research expert to Tehran to assist in examining the industrialization program in an effort to reach some factual conclusions.

Unfortunately, however, the department bureaucracy, having heard of this project, then attempted to adorn it with a number of other features, such as an examination of the Iranian ability to absorb military equipment it was purchasing and the political consequences of the entire Iranian economic program. These adornments made the project so complex as to render it infeasible, and the study, to the best of my knowledge, was never completed. In the absence of satisfaction from the State Department, I then asked the Central Intelligence Agency analysts to undertake an examination of the industrialization program. They sent an officer who spent several months in the embassy attempting to accumulate information for a study along the lines I had proposed, but I never saw the results of that effort either.

In the meantime, proceeding on instinct and without the benefit of a good, solid statistical analysis, I began to ask Iranians questions about their industrialization program. On one occasion I had the embassy economic counselor invite ten prominent Iranians to a stag working dinner at my home. At this dinner, at which I was accompanied by my deputy, the economic counselor, and the commercial attaché, I laid my concerns out on the table and asked the views of the Iranians present. These included the minister for economic affairs, the minister of finance, the head of the Central Bank, the head of the National Planning Organization, and a handful of other senior Iranian economists. When I was explaining my concern, I noticed a considerable nervousness around the table and a number of my interlocutors averted their faces. When I finished, there was a general silence and all the Iranians turned toward the minister for economic affairs.

The minister, in a rather impassioned defense of the shah's wisdom, rejected all my observations and defended the industrial program in its entirety. He denied the existence of corruption, except for petty bribe taking by minor officials, assured me that all bottlenecks were in the process of being resolved, and defended the competitive nature of the Iranian projects. After he had finished, there were two or three comments supporting his remarks from other senior officials in attendance, but by and large it was clear that most of them wished not to pursue the subject further. I made one or two futile efforts to challenge the minister's position; it soon became apparent, though, that there would be no deviation from his thesis on the part of those around the table. Consequently, I broke up the working aspect of the dinner, retired to the library with my guests, passed around brandy and cigars, and finished off the evening with small talk.

However, as the evening broke up and the guests left, I walked with each of them to the front door, beginning with the economic minister. To my astonishment he pulled me aside as he was retrieving his coat from the cloakroom and told me that my remarks were absolutely well founded and that he agreed with everything I said. He confided, however, that he could not, in that company, afford to be critical of the shah or the shah's program. As he phrased it, he had to set the right example.

One by one, as each of my Iranian guests left, he made substantially the same remarks, and more than half of them urged me to discuss my reservations about the program directly with the shah.

After I had seen the Iranians off and returned to the library with my American colleagues, I told them what had happened. Jack Miklos, my deputy, shook his head and said that the performance was inevitable. Not one of those around the table knew who among them might be a SAVAK agent who would report adverse remarks to the shah. Therefore, in a company such as I had assembled, each felt compelled to support the shah's position unswervingly. If it had been reported back to the palace that any one of them had deviated from the official position, I was assured, he would be out of a job tomorrow.

The results of my effort to question the shah's industrialization program were depressing. At the same time, encouraged by the candid relationship I felt I had established with the shah, I began to take seriously the idea that I might act on the advice of my Iranian interlocutors and raise my reservations directly with him. Accordingly, in the course of the next audience I had with him, I turned to the subject of the industrialization program. As I laid out the general observations and reservations I had about the program, he became quite defensive. He listened very intently and then responded rather querulously. He did not raise his voice, but he asked a number of somewhat petulant questions. He slumped lower in his chair and seemed to react peevishly. He permitted himself a little rancor by pointing to the economic difficulties that were currently besetting the United States and the industrialized world, but in general he attempted to brush off my questioning of his industrialization program as irrelevant. Knowing what I now know about his mental processes, I am sure that deep inside he was asking himself with the usual Iranian morbid suspicion just why it was that the United States was seeking to frustrate his industrial independence. Toward the end of the audience, the shah shifted the subject to other, more congenial matters of mutual interest, and by the time I left he had completely regained his composure.

Following the audience, however, I became aware that the conversation had touched more deeply than I had appreciated at the time. In the normal course of events, the shah would ask to see me about every ten days. Sometimes he had a matter of substance that required decisions in Washington, but often he called me merely to exchange information and to permit me to pass his observations on the international scene back to my government. After our conversation on the economy, there was a long gap in which the shah did not initiate any contact with me; I assumed that this was a sort of banishment that reflected his annoyance that I had chosen to raise an awkward subject with him.

During this period, however, I began to hear reports from the embassy officers and from Iranians associated with the economic scene. It seems that the shah had called his economic ministers for a complete review of the industrialization program and other aspects of economic policy. This review went on in a series of meetings with the economic cabinet over a period of three or four weeks. At the end of that time, the shah let it be known that some changes were in order. Shortly thereafter the cabinet resigned, and the prime minister was made minister of court. Jamshid Amouzegar, the former head of the single political party, was brought in to be prime minister and to introduce a program of austerity that cut back sharply on the industrialization investment and that also limited significantly the generous credit rules that had buoyed the economy into high inflation. Such measures as crackdowns on corruption and bribery were also announced. Unfortunately, much of this was done in such an abrupt way that it caused repercussive shocks in the business community. The bazaar merchants, who had come to depend upon easy credit terms, were particularly hard hit. Therefore, in making his economic corrections to address some of the political problems growing out of his industrialization program, the shah succeeded only in raising new frustrations and creating a new area of dissidence among the merchants of the bazaar.

I did not know exactly what cause and effect there was between my conversations with the shah and the actions that he subsequently took to revise his economic programs. I frankly preferred not to find out, because the implications of it troubled me. It suggested that the shah had no really well articulated economic program and that a brief word of concern from a friendly outsider could alter significantly the course of his nation's economic future.

7

The Iranian Armed Forces

During the reign of Reza Shah, the armed forces became the principal instrument of his support and in many ways the principal articulation of his authority. He took great pride in the army, from which he himself had emerged, and made a place in the officer corps the sinecure of his reign. In the debacle that occurred in 1941 when the British and Soviet forces invaded Iran, the army collapsed in the face of over-whelming military arms, and during the war it was reduced to acting as a subordinate constabulary for the occupying forces. It was only after the war that the armed forces began to be rehabilitated. When they reoccupied Azerbaijan and swept aside the feeble resistance that the Soviets had abandoned there, their place in the new regime of Mohammed Reza Shah was assured.

In 1953, when the shah had chosen to retreat and fly to Italy after his confrontation with Mossadeq, it was essentially the armed forces, rallied by General Zahedi, who put him back on the throne. From that time on the armed forces became the principal support for the shah's government. They also became a major center of his interest, and he, like his father, lavished material goods on them.

After the collapse of the Soviet effort in Azerbaijan, at the beginning of the cold war, the United States took a great interest in the Iranian armed forces. From the late forties onward, United States military assistance was a key element in the rehabilitation and modernization of those forces. The United States military mission to Iran was unique. It was the first of the military-assistance groups that later flourished in other parts of the world, but it never changed its character as far as the Iranians were concerned. From their point of view the United States military personnel assigned to Iran were integrated into the Iranian forces. At the end of the shah's regime, all of those personnel with the exception of six senior officers were paid for and maintained by Iran. Their salaries, allowances, transportation, the schooling of their children, and all other incidentals were borne by the Iranian government. They wore arm patches indicating that they were members of the Iranian armed forces.

Because of this relationship, and because of the prevalence of the armed forces in the general functioning of the shah's government, I naturally took a keen interest in learning more about the Iranian military. Shortly after my arrival in Tehran, I made the appropriate calls on its senior officers and became acquainted with them and the structure of their commands. Having had considerable experience in dealing with military establishments in other parts of the world, I found the Iranian military somewhat unusual.

In the first instance, I discovered that each of the principal branches of the armed forces—the army, the air force, and the navy—was literally headed by the shah. Although there was a chief of staff for each service, he reported directly to the shah for all matters concerning the funding, the organization, and the military direction of his branch of the service. The shah deliberately saw each of these senior officers separately on a fixed schedule in order to maintain the integrity of his control over that service.

There was a single chief of staff of the armed forces, and he met with the service chiefs in a supreme military council, but he did not have the sort of authority that the chairman of the American Joint Chiefs of Staff enjoys, nor did the council function as a coordinated command structure with an integral staff of its own. The chief of staff, General Azhari, was a mild, intellectual, and loyal officer who had come up through the army and who had gained a great deal of respect and personal wisdom in the course of his career. He was, however, not the sort of fierce military commander one might expect to find in a regime based so heavily on military support.

The chiefs of the other services more or less reflected the branches they headed. For example, General Oveissi, the chief of the ground forces, was a solid, rocklike man who looked a bit like Mussolini and who never spoke much. He did not strike me as particularly imaginative, and the forces under his control were perhaps the most conservative in the nation. On the other hand, General Rabii, who headed the air force, was a dashing young man given to great bursts of enthusiasm and rather improbable political hypotheses. He was a fine active athlete. He and his attractive German wife were both well practiced in American air force slang. By contrast, Admiral Habibolahi, the head of the navy, was a serious intellectual who measured his words carefully and enjoyed conceptual discussions. His wife was a ballet teacher, something quite unheard of in Iranian society.

Because there was in Iran a constant coming and going of high-ranking American military officials and because such visits always occasioned social events, we saw a great deal of these senior officers and their families. On the whole we found them professionally competent men, dedicated to their services and fanatically loyal to the shah. They did not engage in much political analysis, and they enjoyed the perquisites of high military office in the shah's regime.

The two officers who did occasionally discuss political subjects were Admiral Habibolahi and General Gharabaghi, the
chief of the constabulary. Gharabaghi, who, unlike his colleagues, spoke no English, was not as well known to the American military officers as were the remaining members of the
military establishment. Moreover, since his forces were technically classified as police forces and since the Congress of the
United States had expressly prohibited any assistance or advisory role by our government with foreign police forces, our
military mission had little professional association with Gharabaghi. However, because I spoke French, he found it congenial
to talk with me on several occasions. He was an interesting
person.

He was among the few who had been chosen by Reza Shah
to accompany the crown prince, Mohammed Reza, during his
European education in Switzerland and to continue on with
him during his matriculation at the Iranian military academy.
Because of this association, Gharabaghi had always remained
close to the palace and was a personal favorite of the shah's.
He was a trim man who had been educated largely in the
French military tradition, and had absorbed the French military mannerisms. His wife was from a family that had close ties
with the Iranian religious establishment.

One other significant military officer whom I very seldom
met and with whom I cannot recall ever having had a social
conversation was General Fardust, the inspector general of the
realm. He, like Gharabaghi, had been one of that select group
chosen to be classmates and companions of the crown prince,
and he was now reputed to be closer to the shah than any other
officer; the monarch used him as his "eyes and ears." By making him inspector general, the shah fashioned an instrument
of loyalty in whom he had complete confidence and who could
act discreetly to check information he received from other
officials. General Fardust constantly made unpublicized trips
throughout the country, investigating not only military matters

but also civilian governmental activities. He was particularly respected and feared among the bureaucracy, because his reports could result in the rapid termination of a career or even in a criminal action that brought corrupt officials into disrepute.

The operating structure of the armed forces below the level of these senior officials was an interesting patchwork, reflecting the transition period of Iran from a feudal agricultural kingdom to a modern industrial state. The ground forces, for example, were made up about equally of professional cadre and conscripts. The cadre were men who had spent their lives in the military and had been pampered by the shah's regime. They enjoyed good housing, schooling and medical attention for their families, adequate allowances, and a secure life-style. The conscripts, on the other hand, were paid next to nothing, were given limited fundamental military training, were housed in barracks, and were required to perform the most menial tasks in the armed services.

It was never quite clear to me how decisions were made concerning the admixture of these two elements in the various field forces of the Iranian army. Some divisions, such as the imperial guard, were made up exclusively of professionals; others comprised a mixture of conscripts and regulars. In some few divisions only a small cadre were professionals, while the rest were entirely conscripts.

Although the army was posted throughout the country in a garrison deployment that was unchanged from the time of Reza Shah, the apple of the shah's eye was clearly its armored force. This force, equipped with British-built Chieftain tanks, was the primary striking force for the ground units and received first priority in the assignment of men and equipment. The navy, based along the Persian Gulf, was the smallest of the three military services. It consisted mainly of small patrol craft but did have a strike force composed of a couple of American-built destroyers and a handful of British frigates. One of its unique characteristics was a Hovercraft force based on the island of Kharg, the principal fuel-loading depot in the Persian Gulf. This force, which could react rapidly into the mouth of the Persian Gulf, effectively controlled the Strait of Hormuz.

The shah, however, had ambitions for his naval forces that went beyond the Persian Gulf. In their immediate composition, they could dominate any local situation and significantly outweighed their nearest competitor, the small naval force of Iraq. But the sea lanes in the Arabian Sea and the Indian Ocean were beyond their competence. Therefore, the shah wanted a blue-water navy that could control these approaches down to the southern limits of the Arabian peninsula. For this purpose he had contracted with the United States Navy to provision him with four Spruance-class cruisers, the most modern in the American inventory and perhaps the most modern in the world. He had also acquired two obsolete diesel submarines from the United States and was arranging to purchase half a dozen more from Germany.

Training requirements for an expansion program of this size were enormous. Consequently, great numbers of young Iranians, recruited out of high school and in some instances out of the universities, were studying for long periods in the United States to master the technology that would face them when they attempted to absorb these new ships into their naval inventory.

It was the air force, however, that primarily attracted the shah's concern. A skilled pilot himself, he was fascinated by the latest in aviation technology. During the period immediately following the oil boom, he had moved rapidly to enhance the capabilities of his air force. The F-5 fighter aircraft, which had been successfully absorbed into the structure of his air force command, were soon supplemented by the F-4 model. Although these F-4s were big and complex and although a significant number of American technical personnel were required to maintain them, the Iranian armed forces had by 1977 done quite well in absorbing them and extremely well in flying them. But the shah was not satisfied with these generations of aircraft. He sought, in addition, two much more sophisticated weapons systems for his air force. The first was the F-14, which had been perfected for the use of the United States Navy, and the second was the F-16, designed for our air force.

Based on military theories that he had developed himself, the shah concluded that he needed a force of one hundred and fifty F-14s to fly at high altitude equipped with the Phoenix missile, and a force of three hundred F-16s to act as protective screen for these F-14s, in order to protect his territory from all potential attackers. The Iraqis, with their modern Soviet-built and French-built aircraft, were of course his primary concern, but the potential capabilities of the air fleet he envisaged made it clear that he was also preparing to render the territory of Iran indigestible to the Soviets.

In order to deploy all this air equipment effectively, Iran required significant ground infrastructure. Accordingly, a series of airfields was being built around the country, and Eye Hawk ground-to-air defense missiles, to be manned by the army, were acquired to defend the ground installations. One great gap remained, however. Because of the mountainous terrain and the inaccessibility of many parts of the country, Iran had no satisfactory radar-defense screen. To establish radar stations on all the peaks necessary to cover all possible approaches to Iranian territory, it would have been necessary to spend untold billions of dollars. Therefore, when the United States Air Force developed the airborne warning system called the AWACS, which was mounted on a Boeing airframe, the shah was convinced that he needed such equipment for the air defense of his territory. A United States Air Force team, after surveying the relative costs involved in the acquisition of AWACS and in the installation of ground radar, generally agreed with him. Therefore, he placed an order for ten of these new systems with the American government. This order was later to produce considerable political turmoil both within the United States and in its relations with Iran.

In addition to all these elements of the Iranian armed forces, the shah had taken special pride in developing an airborne-cavalry system. This concept, borrowed from the United States experience in Indochina, would require a great number of helicopters. These, to be supplied by Bell Helicopter, were well beyond the capability of the Iranian ground forces to operate and maintain. Nevertheless, they were introduced into the country, and at the same time an air-cavalry organization was brought into being to operate them. The result was a large presence of American training and maintenance personnel, introduced into the southern-central plateau at Shiraz and Isfahan. Since most of these Americans were recent by-products of the Vietnam War, and since many of them came equipped with Vietnamese wives and habits acquired in Vietnam, they proved to be a particularly disruptive element in United States–Iranian relations. However, if the air-cavalry concept could have been effectively introduced into the Iranian armed forces, it would have given the shah a potentially potent weapons system to use in almost any local military incident in the Persian Gulf area.

Much has been written about the ambitious Iranian military program and the nature of its contribution to the downfall of the shah's regime. While I believe that many of the shah's plans were overly imaginative, and while much of the equipment he purchased could not be used immediately, because of the low technical competence of the Iranian armed forces, I do not believe that the military-purchase program in itself was a major contributor to the revolutionary turmoil in Iran. It was certainly not a question of money being diverted to these purchases that could have been better used for social purposes in the country. Iran had a surplus of liquid financial assets, and the acquisition of military equipment at least served to sterilize some of those funds rather than add them to the appalling pressures for inflation. From a strictly financial point of view, therefore, the country could well afford the equipment that it was purchasing. Moreover, particularly after the acquisition program had been scaled back to a reasonable balance in 1978, a justifiable case could be made for the equipment on order if Iran was to achieve independent self-defense capabilities. The most telling complaint against the weapons-acquisition program was that it diverted the best human resources away from social and economic programs and concentrated them on a sterile military purpose. The young men who were brought into the armed forces from the secondary schools—for example, the homofars, who were trained as air force technicians—clearly had the best intellectual potential for handling the shah's misbegotten industrialization program and for grappling with the forgotten problem of agricultural reform.

Moreover, the way in which the weapons-acquisition program was conducted led to some of the most flagrant cases of corruption and bribery. The United States was not alone in supplying military equipment to Iran. The British provided the bulk of the tracked vehicles, including Chieftain tanks, the French supplied many of the smaller patrol craft for the navy, and the Germans were scheduled to provide the submarines. The Russians contributed most of the wheeled vehicles, including armored personnel carriers and some artillery and antiaircraft weapons. Except for the new naval program, the United States confined itself primarily to the provision of equipment for the air force and to artillery for the ground forces. The Iranians produced their own small arms, ammunition, and a number of specialized items of equipment. All of this was built on the arms industry that the Germans had developed for Reza Shah shortly before World War II. Ironically, much of it was subsequently modernized, adapted, and specialized by a close collaboration between Iran and Israel. General Toufanian, the vice-minister of war whose special charge was weapons procurement, maintained a close association with the Israeli armed

forces. He and his technicians, often assisted by Israeli technicians, experimented constantly with various types of military
equipment intended to be of use both to Iran and to Israel.

When I first began making my visits around Iran, I naturally
wished to meet with those officers of the United States military
mission who were stationed in air fields and garrisons in the
far-flung parts of the country. On my first trip outside Tehran,
to visit our consulate in Tabriz, I accordingly made arrangements through the MAAG chief to have such a visit take place.
When I got to Tabriz, however, I discovered a great deal of
confusion. Although arrangements had been made through the
American military chain, no parallel authority had moved
through the Iranian chain of command. Instead, the officers in
charge of the military installations were operating under their
standard rule, which did not permit any foreigner to enter their
gates. (This rule was one of the reasons the Iranians had decided to integrate members of our military-advisory group into
their own military-force structure.) As a result of this embarrassment, a major flap ensued in Tehran, with the net result
that the matter was taken directly to the shah. He decreed that
from then on I had carte blanche to enter any Iranian military
installation at my request, assuring his military that he could
safely stonewall any parallel request from other ambassadors,
including the Soviet.

After that, in my visits around the country, I regularly called
at Iranian military installations. I found the officers commanding these bases professionally competent, and their forces
usually in an impressive state of discipline. They were proud to
show off what they were doing and were particularly pleased
to demonstrate the physical amenities that had recently come
their way. These included good, solid housing as well as schooling and medical care for their dependents.

One of my most instructive visits was to a military target
range in the desert, to the southeast of Tehran. I was invited
to visit there by the chief of staff of the air force to witness a

"flyoff" between Iranian and American aircraft. The American aircraft, which had participated in a CENTO maneuver in the Persian Gulf, were stopping off in Iran to conduct joint maneuvers with the Iranians on their way back to Europe. The "flyoff" would consist of bombing, strafing, and rocketing runs to be made by aircraft from the two air forces, in a competitive spirit.

On the morning of the event, the chief of the military-aid group, his chief of the air force section, and I flew down to the desert in an Iranian air force transport plane with the senior members of the Iranian military establishment. We landed on an improvised strip in the middle of a desolate part of the country. This strip was later to achieve worldwide renown as the place where the American rescue mission, seeking to extract the hostages, came to an ignominious end in 1980.

There, out in the middle of nowhere, the senior officers of the Iranian military forces, the American ambassador, and two American air force generals stood and looked at the sky. In due course a second plane appeared. At this stage one of the Iranian military arranged for all of us to fall into a reception line. I was asked to stand at the head of the line with the Iranian minister of defense, the rest of the participants stretching beyond us, moving from four-star rank down to the more junior officials. A convoy of gleaming new vans approached across the desert and drew up alongside the strip. The next transport plane landed, with the shah at the controls. After he had parked his plane, shut off his engines, and emerged from the aircraft, the shah walked across the strip to where we were standing. He ignored the rigidly held salutes of the senior military officers and, strolling directly toward me, shook my hand and asked how the flight had been. He then gave a cursory snap of his hand to the minister of defense and the senior brass broke off their salute. He then invited me to accompany him in his van, and together we bounced off across the desert, trailed by a long convoy.

Eventually we reached an area where a bleachers had been erected; an air-conditioned trailer stood nearby. The shah asked me to join him in the trailer while the rest of the company moved toward the reviewing stand. Once inside, he unhitched his tunic, relaxed, and talked in his usual easy, gracious way about a number of things. Eventually there was a knock on the door, and an adjutant indicated that the airplanes were approaching and the air show was ready to begin.

With a sigh the shah straightened his tunic, stood up, and performed a small act that embedded itself in my memory. From the gracious, easy, smiling host with whom I had been talking, he transformed himself suddenly into a steely, ramrod-straight autocrat. This involved not only adjusting his uniform and donning dark glasses but also throwing out his chest, raising his chin, and fixing his lips in a grim line. When he had achieved this change to his own satisfaction, he thrust open the door of the trailer and stalked out across the few remaining steps to the reviewing stand.

I have often thought that that small vignette offered an interesting insight into the shah's life. As a rather timorous person, and one who enjoyed informality, he had been required since early childhood to assume the role of king of kings. I imagined that the military martinet I had just watched develop before my eyes was the shah's best effort to emulate the impression he always carried in his mind of Reza Shah, his father-tutor and constant critic.

8

Shi'a Islam

One of the earliest trips that my family and I took from Tehran was to Meshed in the northeastern sector of the country, up near the Afghanistan frontier. It was known as the holy city of Iran because of its shrine housing the tomb of the Imam Reza, the eleventh imam of the Shi'a sect, who had died in that city and been succeeded by the twelfth imam, who went into "occultation." It was a city of pilgrimages for Shi'a faithful from all over the region. It was also a city of some culture and an interesting past.

Although we in the West think of Persian literature, and particularly of Persian poetry, very largely in terms of the *Rubaiyat* of Omar Khayyam, Iranians consider that example of their literary past to be second-rate at best. They far prefer to commemorate such lyrical poets as Hafiz and Sadi and, above all, to cite the great epic poem *Shah nama.* This epic, in the manner of the *Iliad,* is the Book of Kings that gives a romanticized prehistory of Persia. Firdusi, who is credited with its creation, lived in a small village not far from Meshed, and one of our first tasks on arrival was to visit his tomb, sign the book, and acquire some of the magnificent fruit grown in that region.

The high point of our visit, though, was the shrine of the
Imam Reza, housed in one of a group of mosques near the
center of the city. Approaching from the air, we were surprised
to find that these mosques stood apart in a circular park, which
had been landscaped in a modern Western pattern and which
was obviously extremely well maintained. Later we discovered
that the park was of recent origin, having been created by
bulldozing the ancient bazaar and the clutter of small inns and
hostels for pilgrims that had been built around the mosques
over the centuries.

Although we had known that we would visit the mosques,
we did not, since we were foreigners, expect to be taken to see
the tomb itself. We were therefore unprepared when the
young, American-educated vice-governor of the province told
us that special arrangements had been made for us to go down
into the crypt where the tomb of the Imam Reza was located.
In addition we were being taken to see the library containing
a remarkable collection of Korans that had been donated to the
shrine over the years. Hand-illuminated, many of these Korans
were centuries old and had been copied by Islamic notables.

When the time came to visit the tomb, my wife and daughter were provided with black chadors; they tucked into them
so that only their eyes and the bridge of their noses were visible.
Carefully clutching these unfamiliar garments around them,
they joined me, the vice-governor, and a small platoon of wardens from the shrine who took us down a private stairwell into
the crypt. There we were hastily led off to one corner facing
the shrine itself. The tomb was set in a cagelike structure and
was surrounded by gold filigree. This structure reached from
the floor to the ceiling of the crypt and was perhaps twenty feet
long on a side.

Inside that cage was the actual sarcophagus containing the
relics of the imam. A steady stream of turbulent humanity
moved into the room from the left and exited to the right.
They came down a corridor only a few feet wide, wailing,

crying, and beating their breasts as they entered the room. They could be heard at least a hundred feet back up the corridor as they alternately shuffled and surged ahead. As soon as they reached the room, they rushed forward and threw themselves against the grillwork of the tomb. Many of them hurled money through the grill into the space surrounding the catafalque. All of them grasped the metal filigree and beat their heads against it, and some scratched their faces and shoulders in order to bleed on the spot.

A squad of solemn wardens, dressed in dark Western clothes, hovered constantly around the pilgrims as they performed their obeisances at the tomb. If any lingered too long, they were gently detached from the railing and moved away from the tomb toward the exit. If any were overzealous in beating their heads or producing a flow of blood, they were also carefully extracted from the rest and pushed onward. We stood watching this spectacle for about fifteen minutes. It was fascinating to me to see how zeal suddenly afflicted the pilgrims as they entered the crypt, spent itself so furiously on the tomb, and then apparently evaporated as they shuffled quietly out the door to the right.

It was the first time I had truly observed the frenzy of the Islamic religion at close quarters. In Calcutta, after the partition of India, I had seen Hindus and Muslims fight in the streets and had observed from a hotel balcony the fury with which the Muslims threw themselves into the fray. I had read in the Philippines about the persistence of Moro attacks against superior numbers and the martyrdom that the Moro soldiers had sought in battle against the Christians. But until I had observed the mass frenzy of this file of pilgrims in the crypt of the Imam Reza, I had not fully understood the meaning of the zeal of Islam.

When we emerged from the crypt into the upper regions of the mosque and thence out into the courtyard, I was told by the young vice-governor that this performance by the pilgrims took place twenty-two hours a day, three hundred and sixty-five days a year. The crypt was closed between 2:00 and 4:00 A.M. to permit the area to be cleaned and to enable the wardens of the shrine to remove the money and other valuables that were thrown through the grill toward the sarcophagus of the imam. At all other times, no matter what the weather, the human pressure of the pilgrims prevailed. Sections of the filigree work had to be replaced from time to time because they were torn loose by human hands or actually destroyed by the beating of human heads against them. Replacement sections were always available, and they were of thick metal not easily damaged by casual mishandling.

As I left the tomb, I realized that I needed to know more about this religion. I had read what I could about Islam itself and particularly about the Shi'a branch of the Islamic religion, and had been informally tutored on several occasions by the Pakistani ambassador, who was a scholar of history and a Shi'a himself. I had asked questions of many Iranians but had never really captured the true meaning of the force of Shi'ism in Iran.

Consequently, when I returned to Tehran I examined more carefully the nature of the embassy's associations with the institutions of Shi'ism. I discovered that we had one or two contacts in the hierarchy of the Shi'a ulema but that they were generally "tame" mullahs who were very much responsive to the government. I wanted a far broader access and asked the embassy officers to pursue that in greater detail.

Before returning to Tehran, however, we saw to another aspect of our visit to Meshed. This was a luncheon provided by the governor, who was also designated deputy trustee of the shrine. After the lunch, he showed us film of the bulldozing of the area surrounding the shrine, depicting the resistance that had been mounted against the clearing project, and told us with great pride of his accomplishments.

Then, to my surprise and consternation, he produced gifts for all the ladies present. My wife received a set of jewelry that contained a necklace, earrings, and a ring, all in solid gold with turquoise stones surrounded by diamond chips. She immediately protested that she could not keep these items, but the governor persisted and she appealed to me. I then told the vice-governor that it was contrary to our law and regulations for my wife to accept such valuable presents and that we would have to return them to the governor. He said he understood and would explain that to the governor but asked that in the meantime, in order to avoid embarrassment to the other guests, we take them with us and arrange to return them later.

This action set in train a series of efforts over a period of several weeks to return the jewels to the governor, only to have them come back immediately into our hands. Eventually, I had to send them to Washington and tell the Department of State to put them in the vault reserved for state gifts which subsequently are sold at auction by the General Services Administration. In the course of this futile effort to return the gifts, I was repeatedly told that the shrine was so wealthy in terms of jewelry, rugs, and other precious possessions given to it by the faithful that the jewels my wife returned, though worth several thousand dollars, were in the eyes of the shrine "no greater than a cup of coffee."

It was clear from what little I had seen that there was significant tension in Meshed between the civil officials of the government and the faithful for whom the shrine was a sacred precinct. Not only was the civilian governor the deputy trustee of the shrine, who controlled such matters as disposing of its material possessions and bringing outsiders into the most holy regions of the crypt, but he was also the man who had defied religious tradition and the resistance of the faithful to clear a park area around the shrine in order better to attract tourists. This struck me as a rather cavalier approach by the government toward a force that clearly commanded much authority among the population.

Over the following months as I occasionally discussed Islam

and the Shi'a ulema with the shah, I detected in him a similar contempt for the leaders of the Shi'a religion. While he himself professed to be a strict Muslim and while he said his prayers and never touched alcohol, it was clear that he differentiated this piety from his attitude toward the Shi'a hierarchy. In private conversations with me, he often spoke of them as "ragheads" and told how corrupt and venal they were. He felt that they stood in the way of his country's progress and that their obstruction of many of his programs was based on their personal greed and their desire to hold on to the remnants of their secular power.

Despite the assaults that Reza Shah had made on the Shi'a hierarchy, they continued to exercise considerable authority down into the period of the shah's regime. Indeed, in the first few years of his regime, while he was too weak to assert his own authority, the Shi'a clergy reacquired many of the prerogatives they had lost under Reza Shah, particularly in the small villages. Once again, especially in the field of education, they had to be confronted by the younger Pahlavi and pushed back into the areas of faith and morals that he had reserved for them. The ulema themselves never accepted this, contending that Islam was a religion that concerned itself with all aspects of human existence, well beyond the limits of religiosity.

In 1953 the clergy had played an ambivalent role. In the beginning they had joined with Mossadeq to challenge the authority of the shah and particularly to seek a restitution of the 1906 constitution, which had been largely ignored by the shah and by his father. However, as the Mossadeq rebellion became more and more associated with the Communist Tudeh party, the Shi'a hierarchy began to draw away from the extremes to which Mossadeq pushed his political action. When the shah left the country and it appeared that Mossadeq might establish a republic in league with the Tudeh, the Shi'a clergy shifted once again and strongly backed the restoration of the shah to his throne.

During the 1950s a sort of truce prevailed between the Shi'a institutions and the monarchy. However, in the early 1960s the shah took the offensive once again.

On this occasion he began to push his land-reform program to include not only the feudal lands owned by large secular landholders but also the lands owned by the Waqf, which was a sort of trust from which the revenues of the Shi'a hierarchy were derived. It was apparent that if these lands could be taken over and distributed to the peasants who tilled them, the Shi'a hierarchy would be deprived of its independent income and have to rely instead on the tithings of the faithful and handouts from the crown. The astute members of the clergy perceived this and undertook to resist the government's action.

The resistance of the clergy was led primarily by a senior mullah named Ruhollah Khomeini, who was one of the senior theologians in the country's theological center at Qum. Khomeini attacked not only the shah's plan to impinge on the independence of the Shi'a institutions but also a number of his other actions, including the granting of juridical immunity to the American members of the army mission in Iran. The resistance grew, confrontations became sharp, and considerable bloodshed eventually occurred. As a result of this, Khomeini, who had been belatedly named an ayatollah by his coreligionists, was arrested and sent into exile in Turkey; ultimately he settled down in the deserts of Iraq at another sacred Shi'a site in Najaf.

With this action, observers generally conceded, the shah had broken the back of Shi'a resistance to his regime. The shah himself felt that he was now free to move ahead on his programs of modernization, westernization, and secularization without significant Shi'a resistance. He tempered these conclusions with the assumption that his government must always preserve the official obeisance of the state to the Shi'a religion and must always hold Shi'a precepts in official high regard. Most observers shared the shah's view of his dominance over the clergy. I recall, for example, that when I made my official call on the Soviet ambassador and was discussing with him the political situation in the country, he answered my inquiry about the forces of Islam by asserting that the Shi'a institutions were of no political significance and would never recover from the blows they had been dealt by the shah's regime.

My efforts to penetrate further into the mysteries of Shi'ism were constantly frustrated. It was clear that, in the minds of the Shi'a authorities, Americans not only were directly associated with the shah's policies but were their inspiration. Except for the few tame mullahs to whom we had access, I could not produce any useful contacts for embassy reporting. Neither our political officers nor our intelligence officers were able to satisfy my interest in obtaining further insights into the workings of the Shi'a mind.

Eventually an American businessman who acted as a consultant to one of the larger American corporations in Iran, and who had had nearly thirty years experience in the country, came to my assistance. When I was complaining to him about our inability to understand Shi'ism better, he offered to put our officers in touch with a prominent member of the bazaar who, in turn, was a liaison between the *bazaari* merchants and the Shi'a ulema. This contact, which was successfully pursued by our political officers, produced our first real insights into the attitude of the Shi'a authorities.

What we learned from those contacts suggested that, contrary to the conventional wisdom, the Shi'as did not consider themselves crushed by government actions. On the contrary, they had begun over the years to develop a sort of political idiom in the language and teachings of the Koran. They had their own political philosophers, particularly a young man named Ali Shariati, who had died of cancer in London only a few years before. Our officers attempted to read and understand his writings in order to gain a better understanding of the Shi'a mind. They also developed further contacts with some of the intellectuals among the Shi'a faithful who had built a research center founded on the writings of Ali Shariati and who had attempted to transform the wisdom of the Koran into precepts for modern government. All of these contacts served us in good stead when the Islamic revolution developed later during my tenure in Iran.

But none of them ever served to alleviate the suspicions with which the Shi'a clergy and the Shi'a faithful eventually viewed the United States and our representation in the country. The most extreme members of the Shi'a faithful had formed themselves into terrorist organizations that were determined to fight for the primacy of Islam against the secularism of the state. The most effective of these, the Mujahadeen, had become an urban terrorist movement that concentrated on assassination as its method of operation. Over the two years before my arrival, the Mujahadeen had assassinated six Americans and a number of Iranian officials. An intensive SAVAK operation to control and eliminate them was a major effort in the shah's security program.

Neither I nor the embassy was ever able to make much progress in comprehending the mind set of the Shi'a hierarchy or in obtaining sympathetic consideration from them for the United States. Although we had a tenuous acquaintance by the time the revolution came along, this was heavily overlain with the suspicions and accusations that had been engendered over the years when the embassy and Islam had remained aloof from each other.

9

SAVAK

From the times of Cyrus the Great, Persian shahs had always been served by organizations that acted as their "eyes and ears." These institutions functioned in many ways to preserve and protect the authority of the throne. They were usually clandestine in nature and involved agents who traveled around the kingdom in various disguises.

One of their functions was to submerge themselves among the general citizenry and learn what it was that most concerned the man in the street. In this way, the shahs could determine where public interest lay and could take measures that would make them popular with the masses.

Another function was to observe the work of the shah's officials in order to ascertain which among them were competent and effective. At the same time, they were able to report to the shahs which officials were incompetent, unpopular, and corrupt.

Above all, they were deputed to find out which officials, feudal lords, religious leaders, or tribal chieftans were disloyal to the shahs. The occupants of the throne were always uneasy about the possibility that revolts or plots were in process against their authority. Given the turbulent history of the region, they also had good reason to be suspicious that their neighboring states were plotting with some of their citizens, seeking to subvert Persian authority and dominate Persian territory.

In order to assert authority and to command respect for the power of the shahs, these organizations acted with stealth, zeal, and brutality. Secret arrests in the middle of the night, abductions and imprisonment, and, above all, torture were the marks of their profession. They tried to establish methods of operation that inspired among the general populace an awe for their ubiquitous presence and knowledge, a fear of their harsh retribution, and a deference to their final authority. Over the centuries, this system served the shahs and sustained their dynasties.

Reza Shah, although employing such a system, was not particularly dependent on it for his authority. He was fearsome enough in his own right, he was constantly on the move as his own eyes and ears, and he had at his command a far more respected organization in his precious army. However, when he left the throne and when his army collapsed, there was little in the way of an invisible institution to serve the new young shah, Mohammed Reza. Indeed, during the period of World War II, while Iran was under Allied occupation, he had very few "eyes and ears" of his own.

It thus came as a considerable shock to him and to his government to discover, in the aftermath of the Mossadeq assault on the authority of the throne, that the Soviet Union, during its occupation of Iranian territory, had built up a large espionage organization that reached deep into the upper echelons of the Iranian armed forces. In reacting to this, he sought assistance from his American friends in establishing a modern intelligence organization that would guard against the technologically proficient KGB and GRU organizations that were functioning under Soviet direction in Iran.

In 1957, after considerable organizational effort by the CIA, the United States government devised for the shah a framework of a modern intelligence system and helped him establish it. It was given the name Sazman-e Ettela'at Va Amniyat-e Keshvar (Iranian State Intelligence and Security Organization) and, from the initials of this title, soon became known by the acronym SAVAK. Recruits who were designated for this new service were given training in intelligence and counterintelligence methods in the United States and, later, in Israel. They were trained not only in fundamental police work but also in the analysis of Soviet techniques and, above all, in the detection of sophisticated Soviet electronic espionage.

At its beginning, SAVAK had a structure not unlike that of most Western intelligence and counterintelligence organizations. Although we never know exactly how many full-time professionals the structure embraced, our best estimates put the total somewhere in the vicinity of six thousand. At its later peak, this number was augmented by many part-time informers and hangers-on, who were able to enhance status or their local reputations by acting as "eyes and ears."

In the 1960s, especially after the rebellions led by Ayatollah Khomeini in 1963, SAVAK became something considerably more than an intelligence organization. In a reversion to the instincts of the earlier shahs, Mohammad Reza permitted his SAVAK chiefs, particularly the notorious Bakhtiar (uncle of the last Pahlavi prime minister, Shahpour Bakhtiar), to expand the functions of the intelligence organization to include those of a political police force. This force, again tending toward atavistic Persian models, began to revive the practices of torture, of arbitrary arrest, of capricious imprisonment, and of other abuses in order to combat the terrorist organizations that were spawned by the events of the 1960s. But, once the practice began, it was not confined to terrorists.

All political activity was suspect. Not only the Communists and the Islamic extremists, but also the Social Democrats, the old aristocracy, and the regional political leaders were victims of SAVAK repression. Student organizations were especially watched and infiltrated. SAVAK informants were myriad on the university campuses and used the techniques of accusation and incrimination to settle all sorts of rivalries.

During this period, particularly in the late 1960s and early 1970s, there was a sort of reign of terror in Iran. Most prominent politicians, many westernized families, and persons from all over the realm were affected by it. There were mysterious disappearances, murders in the prisons, and the generalized use of torture. Ironically, all this was taking place at about the time when the shah began his "White Revolution," which was a generally enlightened effort to free his country from the ancient curses of poverty, disease, ignorance, and famine. Although the incidents of SAVAK brutality were not as widespread as the postrevolutionary propagandists in Iran alleged, they were nevertheless a very real dimension of life in Iran.

By the mid-1970s, SAVAK had fairly well succeeded in bringing much of the terrorist apparatus under control. The shah was eager to improve his international reputation, and the shahbanou, in particular, was sensitive to the anachronistic police practices of the regime. For these various reasons, the most brutal of SAVAK practices were abated during those years. By the time the Carter administration came into office, there was no evidence that official torture was still being used in the Iranian prison system.

SAVAK, nevertheless, retained an unsavory reputation, both in Iran and abroad. President Carter's decision to retain the CIA liaison with SAVAK was not an idle one and obviously involved a careful searching of conscience on his part. That liaison, it should be stressed, had never involved official United States complicity in the political-police aspects of SAVAK behavior or in the use of torture, arbitrary arrest, or murder, as many critics have alleged. Unhappily, the Persian heritage of brutality has left most modern Iranians quite capable of devising their own actions in this regard, as the postrevolutionary practice has demonstrated. *Liaison* was a word the CIA used to describe the interchange of intelligence of mutual interest to the two governments, particularly intelligence having to do

with the subversive activities of the Soviet Union and its satellite nations in Iran.

In order to acquaint myself with this aspect of our official
representation in Iran, I was thoroughly briefed at CIA headquarters before I left the United States. In Tehran, I was
further briefed on operational details of CIA activity by the
station chief. Finally, I asked to call on General Nassiri, the
head of SAVAK, in order to learn something about him as an
individual. I had read much about him—how he had delivered
the shah's order of demission to Mossadeq in 1953, only to be
arrested when that fiery old prime minister defied the shah and
tried to stay in office; how he had personally challenged and
disarmed a hijacker who had taken over an airplane at Tehran
Airport; and how he ran his organization with an iron hand.

Nassiri received me in a magnificent villa, which was the
SAVAK guest house. It was set in a quiet garden, surrounded
by a high wall, and removed from the general traffic flow of
Tehran. It was the house that was usually used when senior
Israeli officials quietly visited Tehran.

He was a large, powerfully built man in his early seventies,
obviously used to authority, and very much at ease in his
opulent surroundings. He spoke in Farsi through a bright
young interpreter. Although he was not exactly pompous, there
was something about him that tempted me to pull his leg.
Accordingly, I asked him a few questions about *The Crash of
'79,* a novel concerning Iran in which he was rather scurrilously
portrayed. The questions embarrassed the interpreter enormously, but seemed to confuse Nassiri, who appeared genuinely ignorant of the book's existence. All during our subsequent conversation, he kept coming back to the book and to
my earlier questions. I finally undertook to send him a paper-
back copy of the novel, which was formally acknowledged but
which neither of us ever raised in conversation again.

Nassiri was subsequently relieved of his duties with SAVAK
and sent as ambassador to Pakistan. His successor was General

Moghaddam, a scholarly military officer who ran the office of military intelligence. Both of them were brutally executed after the revolution. Nassiri was severely beaten and his windpipe crushed before his trial. I will always remember seeing him in that condition, being interviewed on television, blood oozing down his face from his bandaged head, and aspirating his words with great difficulty through his shattered throat.

The quality of intelligence that we received from our relations was not of the highest professional caliber. The Washington analysts usually considered it of the Chicken Little variety. A Communist sky was always falling on our joint interests. Iran was always under siege by evil external forces. It therefore became easy, perhaps too easy, to discount SAVAK information. This happened, unfortunately, in the case of Afghanistan. The Iranians constantly alerted us that Communist plots were widespread against the neutralist government in Kabul, and, all through the early months of 1978, they warned us that a potentially successful coup was being organized. Our experts in Washington and our observers in Kabul disagreed. Too late, they had to accept the fact that Iranian information was better than our own.

Whatever the quality of the information exchange, our intelligence collaboration with Iran was more than justified, in Washington's view, by Iran's willingness to let us position two major listening posts on Iranian soil overlooking the rocket- and missile-launching facilities that the Soviets maintained in their central-Asian republics. From these stations, we could monitor every electronic activity at those facilities, as well as Soviet military activity in the whole arc of territory facing toward the Persian Gulf. They were essentially simple antennae with tape-recording devices, manned by civilian technicians who lived in barren isolation, but their product was the most sophisticated compendium of military intelligence in the entire watching brief that we maintained on the Soviet threat.

10

Merchants, Oil, and Scholars

One other institution of Iranian life that fascinated me was the bazaar. The trade of the country had been carried on for centuries out of these centers of commerce. I remember that in my first visit to Iran some years back I had been taken to an enormous covered bazaar in Shemiran, north of the city of Tehran. It was a primitive structure, crowded with small booths and stalls in the manner of any Asian market. However, I had never seen quite such a variety of goods on display in such quantities and so many different brands. It was clear that the merchants who controlled the trading channels that brought these goods from all over the world to these small outlets in Iran operated a sophisticated system of commerce. In everything I had read about Iran, I discovered that the bazaars had been the center of political intrigue, of finance, and of social reform during much of the country's existence. I also read that the bazaars formed the financial foundation for most of the mosques and that the association between the *bazaari* and the Shi'a clergy was an intimate one.

It was disappointing, therefore, to discover that our embassy had less than adequate associations with the bazaars. I knew that in the past those ties had been quite close. Kim Roosevelt, former CIA representative in Tehran, had boasted to me that in 1953 his people had been able to turn out the *bazaari* in the streets to confront the Communist forces and overwhelm them in favor of the shah, but whatever contact we may have had at that time now seemed to have disappeared and our sources of information in the bazaar were not significant. One reason for this was that many of the *bazaari* with whom we had been closely associated as an embassy in years past had branched out from the bazaars, had taken over banks, and were now wealthy industrialists who controlled great conglomerates in the country. Unfortunately these people had also lost touch with many aspects of the bazaar.

When we visited Tabriz in our first expedition outside of Tehran, we found the bazaar thriving and humming just as it had been many years ago. A large portion of the merchants in this northwestern city were Armenians and seemed particularly friendly to us as we visited with them on our expedition there. The situation in Meshed, however, was quite different. When we went into its newly built bazaar, which had been erected to replace one that had been bulldozed in the clearing project for the shrine, we were preceded by a wedge of policemen. The crowds in general scattered as we came along, and the bazaar merchants looked anything but inviting. It may have been the heavy hand of the governor, but I got the impression that foreigners, and particularly Americans, were not at all welcome in the bazaar of Meshed.

When I spoke about visiting the bazaar in Tehran, my security officer came to see me in some consternation. He said that the Iranian police would find such a visit impossible to control. They feared that the prospects for assassination in the old Tehran bazaar were greater than they could handle and that if I insisted on going there they would first have to clear out most of the patrons. Faced with those considerations, I decided not to press the issue and hoped instead to learn more about the bazaars in Shiraz and Isfahan. However, in those two cities I found the police equally nervous and therefore resiled from my intention to gain further firsthand acquaintance with the bazaars.

At the same time, I wanted the embassy to inform me as much as it could about attitudes and thinking in the bazaars. Again this proved difficult. The *bazaari* were not interested in meeting with Americans or being seen with them. Part of this reluctance may have stemmed from their feeling that they would be observed by the SAVAK in any meetings with Americans and would be subjected to retaliation on grounds of the general suspicion that they were expressing dissidence to us. Part of it, on the other hand, may have come from their antagonism toward the United States. Unhappily, I never found out the real reasons, because, during the course of my tenure in Iran, we never did establish satisfactory relations with the leaders of the bazaar. We were, therefore, unable to judge the true political ferment that permeated the bazaars by 1978 and that brought the enormous crowds out into the streets later that year in support of the revolution.

* * *

Oil is the lifeblood of Iran. Located in the southwestern region along the northern stretches of the Persian Gulf, the oil resources of the country were first developed by the British early in the twentieth century. The oil fields that they discovered and explored were enormously productive. During World War I, after the British navy had converted from coal- to oil-burning ships, these fields acquired significant strategic importance to the British and were one of the motivations for the British occupation of Iran during the war. Even before the war, however, oil had been a continuing source of contention and conflict between the British and the Iranians, who complained, with considerable justice, that the British were providing them far too little return for the resources they were depleting from

Iranian territory. This dispute smoldered into the post–World War II years and eventually erupted into a full-scale confrontation in 1951 and 1952.

In those years the National Front government led by Mohammed Mossadeq nationalized the oil industry, and the British, supported by all the other members of the oil producers' cartel, boycotted Iranian products and brought the economy of Iran to a standstill. It was against this background that the deposition of the shah and his subsequent return to the throne in 1953 took place.

Also as a result of these circumstances, the United States government intervened to negotiate a settlement between the British and the Iranians that would permit the resumption of Iranian production and the flow of Iranian petroleum products into the international markets. This settlement accepted the premise of Iranian ownership of the oil resources and the nationalization of the oil industry. However, it also established a consortium of oil producers that then acted as the agents of the National Iranian Oil Company in the exploration and exploitation of the oil fields. Based in London, this consortium was, for reasons of political comity, largely staffed by Americans in Iran and in the offshore regions of the Persian Gulf.

During the years immediately after the settlement, the international sale and distribution of the Iranian product was handled exclusively by the major oil companies that made up the consortium. As time went on and as these agreements were renegotiated, the National Iranian Oil Company itself began to move more and more into the sale and distribution of its own products. To most Iranians, the relationship between the National Iranian Oil Company and its consortium colleagues was viewed as a confrontation between David and Goliath. Even after the facts had altered this relationship subsequent to the formation of OPEC, Iranian xenophobia continued to look on the picture of oil production and distribution as one of constant confrontation with the West.

Under the shah's general policy, Iran began to turn away from its past practice of being exclusively a producer of primary products and to look increasingly toward the refining and petrochemical industries as a major element in the Iranian oil picture. The oil refinery at Abadan, which had originally been built by the British and subsequently been expanded by a number of American contractors, was the largest in the world, with an average daily throughput of nearly 700,000 barrels of oil. Most of this product was consumed in Iran or within the immediate regions of the Persian Gulf. In 1977, when I arrived in Iran, refineries were also either in production or under construction in Tabriz, Isfahan, and just south of Tehran. This increment to the refinery capacity served partly to diversify Iranian sources of refined products away from their concentration in Abadan but also to keep pace with the increased use of refined petroleum products in the country as prosperity multiplied automobile ownership and increased consumption of energy.

The shah was greatly interested in petrochemical manufacture as well. He was not able to induce many American chemical companies to become engaged in this production, because most of them saw the petrochemical field as already overbuilt. One American chemical company, Du Pont, did enter into an equity arrangement with a local private industrialist and built a medium-sized polyester plant that was uneconomical from its inception. Other American companies became actively engaged in the construction of other plants working downstream from the Iranian production process. However, they were, by and large, contractors who had no equity investment.

The only large investor in the petrochemical field in Iran was the Mitsui Company of Japan, which undertook the construction of a huge three-billion-dollar petrochemical complex on the Persian Gulf. Given the significant dependence of Japan on Persian Gulf oil and the high cost of transportation of crude oil from the gulf to Japanese ports, this enterprise probably made commercial sense in the long run. However, it would appear that in the short run the complex would be less than competitive internationally if its product was to be sold in the world petrochemical market.

I began my acquaintance with the Iranian oil industry by making visits first to Abadan, then to Ahwaz, and finally to Kharg Island. In Abadan I was impressed by the size of the refinery and by the fact that it was run almost exclusively by Iranian engineers and managers. Indeed, at the time of my visit, there were only twelve foreigners in the work force, all of them engaged as instructors in the NIOC technical-training school colocated with the refinery. The refinery itself, despite its huge size, was not one of the world's most efficient. All the old elements were significantly outdated in a technological sense but continued in production even as modern catalytic crackers were added to the complex. All in all, however, it was interesting to note that, despite the predictions of the British in 1951 that the Iranians could never operate their own oil industry, they had succeeded in taking over the entire British installation, including the palatial old residences that had been built along the Shatt al Arab.

In Ahwaz, however, it was a different story. There, at the headquarters of the OSCO (Oil Supply Company), the atmosphere was decidedly American. Although there were Iranian "counterparts" for every echelon in the management of this production group, it was clear that the work was being done almost entirely by the Americans. They were, however, an unassuming lot who did not appear to rub their Iranian colleagues the wrong way and who were accepted largely because of their industrial expertise. Most of them were from Texas, Oklahoma, or the Louisiana region, men who had grown up in the oil fields of the American gulf regions and learned their production techniques the hard way. They lived in Iran much as they had lived in other oil camps around the world. Their tastes in life were modest, their pleasures simple, and their habits homespun.

In the deserts, marshes, and shallow waters of the Persian Gulf, these men had worked some remarkable engineering miracles. In Iran, oil does not have to be pumped from its reservoirs, as is the case in most of the world. It is under such intense pressure that a shaft drilled into the well produces automatically unless the valves are shut off at the "Christmas tree" above. On the other hand, these wells were losing their pressure over the years, as their supply became exhausted, and complex engineering systems were being installed to permit secondary and tertiary recovery by the capture and introduction into the wells of the associated gas, which was being separated from the crude oil product. This enormously expensive undertaking was designed to extend the lifespan of Iranian production considerably beyond the years previously forecast for its exhaustion.

On Kharg Island, facilities had been built to make the island the primary loading depot for the oil produced out of the southwest Iranian fields and the Persian Gulf offshore rigs. Here another facet of the oil industry was apparent. The Kharg Island facility had become so automated that very few personnel—of either nationality—were stationed on the island. The oil, moved by pressure out of the wells, flowed by gravity down toward the pumping stations on the mainland near the island, and was then boosted to reservoir tanks on the higher surface of the island itself. When the supertankers pulled up to the piers, valves were opened and the oil flowed freely into their holds. It was probably the most economical production, transport, and loading system existing anywhere in the world.

This petroleum industry had an installed capacity in 1977 of about 6.2 million barrels of production a day. During 1977, nearly 5.8 million barrels were actually produced, and about 5 million barrels of that oil moved into international trade. Iran, therefore, was the second-largest exporter of oil in the world, coming only after Saudi Arabia. The income derived from this industry reached nearly twenty-four billion dollars a year in 1977 and constituted Iran's principal economic activity, in terms of both its gross domestic product and its foreign exchange earnings. As the agricultural sector of the economy had been permitted to degenerate, the oil industry's earnings made up for that lapse by subsidizing the importation of foodstuffs from the rest of the world. Iran was, for example, the largest purchaser in the world of American rice and also bought significant quantities of feed grains from our country. At the same time it was a major importer of Australian and New Zealand live lambs and of dressed lamb flown in daily from the East European satellite countries. Oil revenues also purchased the military equipment that the shah had ordered, and, by permitting the Iranian Central Bank to maintain an artificially low rate of exchange for the rial, they subsidized the daily import of almost any consumption item brought into the country.

The men who controlled this vast enterprise were a small and privileged breed. When I first arrived there, the president and chairman of the National Iranian Oil Company was a former physician, trained in France and married to a French wife, who had operated on the shah the first time he had been hit by an assassin's bullet. Because of his close association with the shah, his Western education, and his loyalty to the imperial household, he was awarded the plum of heading the NIOC. He was a man of enormous vanity and clear intelligence. However, I was never able to ascertain how much he really knew about running an oil industry.

Through the embassy's petroleum attaché, I met a number of other Iranians at middle levels in the oil industry who clearly were technically competent in handling their jobs. They were people who had been largely trained in the United Kingdom and had worked previously for the old Anglo-Iranian Company. Some of them were American-trained engineers, and many had business training in the United States. Through them I gathered the impression that the company more or less ran itself and that it stood as an institution apart from the rest of Iranian society. The shah naturally took a direct and personal interest in the operations of NIOC and met regularly with its chairman.

Because of its critical importance to the United States, I kept as close a watch as I could on the operations of this giant industry and was able to gain useful insights into its functions and those of its subordinate, OSCO. These insights proved additionally useful because of the role NIOC played in the turbulent times that were to come.

*   *   *

The final institution with which I tried to become acquainted as I began my task as an ambassador was the Iranian university system. Tehran University, the center of this system, had been created by Reza Shah in an effort to introduce Western learning into the modernizing process of the Iranian state. Located on sumptuous grounds in the western part of the center of Tehran, the university was built on a French model and had at its inception employed largely French academic staff. While most of the foreign instructors had long since disappeared from the campus, its chancellor and its general system were still heavily influenced by the French tradition.

In a sense this introduction of European learning into the Iranian system was ironic. Centuries before, European scholars had traveled to the Persian university center of Hamadan where Abu Sena (Avicenna) had presided. His system had been renowned throughout Europe and formed the basis for much of the modern institutional framework that eventually became the European universities. Nevertheless, since all of this learning had been allowed to lapse during the intervening centuries, it was essential that a whole new body of modern scientific and secular knowledge be introduced into the universities if the new state of Iran was ever to sustain its modernization process.

Naturally, during the years following World War II, with

the pervasive influence of the United States in Iran, more and more of the Iranian educational system had become Americanized. New college campuses had been constructed in Tabriz, Shiraz, Isfahan, Kerman, and near Meshed, at the center of learning made famous by the poet Firdusi, chronicler of the shahs. Almost all of these had direct associations with the United States, either because their faculty was made up largely of graduates from American institutions or because they had cooperative contractual arrangements with American universities. Many of them had been founded with assistance from the United States during the period when we provided economic aid to Iran. Although most of them carried on their instruction in a system that was effectively American, they nominally fell under the general guidance of the Tehran University system and under a ministry of education that had a bias toward the French method of instruction. A significant exception to this rule was Pahlavi University in Shiraz, which had been established by a contract with the University of Pennsylvania and at which all courses were actually taught in English.

Because of this extensive American association with the university system, I made an effort to visit as many of the campuses as I could. Although in most instances I was graciously and even ostentatiously received by the chancellors, I noticed that I was shielded carefully from the student body and that the security protection afforded me on the campuses was very heavy. I also observed that a number of the campuses showed evidence of physical damage—broken windows, smashed furniture, and on occasion indications of a fire in some of the buildings. I had been told that university campuses were traditionally hotbeds of political activity, but it seems to me that my briefings on this subject had been understated. In the case of Tehran University, I was never able to penetrate more than a few yards into the campus, and my visits were consistently held in buildings that were accessible to the broad boulevards surrounding the institution.

Since many of the faculty members were Americans, I inquired further into the nature of the disorders on the campuses. These Americans, who had come from American campuses during the Vietnam disorders in our country, did not seem particularly surprised or upset by the violence that surrounded them. They said that the university students were infallibly polite and respectful to them and exempted them from the direction of their political activities. These activities were conducted against the shah and his political system, which the students consistently described as undemocratic and repressive.

Similarly, the consular officers and the United States information officers in the university cities did not find the activity on campus particularly out of the ordinary. They expressed the opinion that student protests were a way of life not only in Iran but at European universities and that the occasional outbursts of violence were mere exuberance that had to be expected in these circumstances. The same general theme was advanced at the various Iran-America Societies I visited. These societies were organized under the sponsorship of our information service but were sustained by local subscription. They largely paid their way by offering language instruction in English at nominal fees. The instructors were mostly "world travelers"—dropouts from American campuses or American university graduates who were taking a year or two in the far corners of the world before settling down to the mundane business of earning a living back home. Since Iran was directly on the route to Nepal, one of the havens for these restless young products of the sixties generation, it made sense for many of them to stop off for several months to earn a little spending money by teaching English to their Iranian clients. Most of the students of English were either studying at universities or aspiring to do so.

Despite the rapid growth of the Iranian higher-education system, it could still accommodate only about 130,000 new students a year. A great number of Iranian students who were qualified to enter universities and whose parents could afford to send them were thus without means of obtaining advanced education. Since American universities enjoy the reputation of being the best in the world, and since many of the Iranian middle-class instincts reached out toward the United States, Iranian university applicants exerted constant pressure to obtain visas for the United States.

This pressure happened to coincide in time with the end of the baby boom in the American university system. Consequently, as Iranian students sought to enter the United States, some American institutions were actively recruiting them in Iran. As a result, the provision of immigration forms attesting to admittance to an American university (a prerequisite to the issuance of a student visa) was more than abundant. The visa officers began to complain.

We were, they told me, admitting to the United States on student visas applicants who barely qualified either in terms of their academic preparation or of their ability to handle the English language. They believed that the issuance of immigration forms by some American recruiters was clearly fraudulent. They wished to assert a tighter control over those who could receive visas, therefore cutting down significantly on the flow of Iranian students into the United States.

After carefully considering their arguments, I decided against them and permitted the issuance of visas to continue much as before. I did ask the Department of State and the Immigration Service to examine carefully the instances of possible fraud and to suspend the privilege of immigration-form issuance by some institutions whose abuses seemed flagrant in this regard. Overall I reasoned that Iranian students who were exposed to the United States in an effort, however feeble, to obtain an American education eventually became better able to understand our society and consequently could, in the future, be assets for friendly relations between our two countries.

Balanced against this, of course, was the fact that the Iranian students in the United States were being particularly obstreperous in their demonstrations against the regime of the shah and against United States policy in Iran.

On the whole, I believe that my decision was correct and that in the long run those who came to this country for an education will be of constructive significance to the future relations between our two nations.

The political dissidence on the university campuses was somewhat difficult to track. Some of it was Marxist in its inspiration and clearly enjoyed support and agitation from abroad. Some of it was the result of exposure to more democratic forms of government and society, such as those the students had experienced in the United States and Western Europe. However, another and perhaps the most significant strand of dissidence came from a strictly Iranian source. This was an indigenous effort to try to blend the culture of Islam and the teachings of the Koran with the strains and stresses of modern society.

The most prevalent and prominent efforts to synthesize these two essentially opposing abstractions began with an Iranian scholar called Ali Shariati. Shariati, who had been educated in Iran and France, had developed a philosophical case that reconciled in his mind the teachings of the Prophet as recorded in the Koran and the social justice of distributed welfare as espoused by social democrats. He specifically eschewed Communism and the dialectical materialism of Marx. However, he was able to blend the theories of modern socialism with the communal practices of the early Islamic communities. He enjoyed a great vogue, particularly at Tehran University, and when he died of cancer in London in 1977 the usual rampant Iranian xenophobic imagination ascribed his death to a collaboration between the agents of SAVAK and the interests of the British petroleum concern.

Despite the association of the American educational institutions with the Iranian universities, the student agitations on campus took on an increasingly anti-American coloration, particularly as they reflected the demonstrations that were taking place in the United States. The accusation was regularly made that the United States was the principal supporter of the shah, and indeed that the shah was a puppet of the United States. Therefore, more and more of the campuses became areas that were difficult for officers of the embassy to know and evaluate. However, two or three of the officers successfully continued to teach courses at some of the smaller universities even into the more violent days of the revolution that were to follow.

11

AWACS and OPEC

The first major crisis to develop between the United States and Iran during my tenure came in the summer of 1977. The issue: the proposed sale of AWACS aircraft to Iran. It will be recalled that in my first meeting with President Carter he indicated he was prepared to sell the AWACS despite the fact that he was introducing a memorandum to limit the sale of sophisticated weapons systems overseas. To my surprise, however, he was not able to enforce his decision in its entirety within the bureaucracy.

The human-rights activists who had come in with his administration, particularly in the State Department, chose the issue of AWACS to make a stand against the human-rights practices in Iran. They took the view that providing the shah with a sophisticated new American weapons system would enhance the repressive capability of his government and would, in effect, reward him for a program of repression that they found anathema.

Although their distaste for the Iranian political system was understandable, the logic of their opposition to the AWACS was questionable. These were unarmed aircraft whose prime purpose was to act as flying radar screens to assist in the air defense of Iranian territory. The link to the repression by the shah's regime was tenuous at best.

Opposing the stance of the human-rights activists was the view of the United States Air Force. Not only did the air force conclude that the AWACS were far more economical and efficient for air defense in Iran, but it also espoused the sale because an increased production and sales rate on this system would lower the unit cost to the Pentagon of those aircraft that the air force wished to acquire from Boeing for its own use. Eventually the dispute within the executive branch was settled by the president himself; he opted to sell a reduced number of aircraft to the Iranians—seven rather than ten. This made it possible for the Iranians to operate an effective air-defense system but gave them fewer spares for ground time and maintenance work.

Having lost their case within the executive branch, the human-rights activists did not rest there. They used their close association with the staffs of individual members and appropriate committees on Capitol Hill to provide additional information to the Congress, so that the sale of the planes could presumably be blocked by congressional action. The debate that followed became a classic example of the role that the Congress had grown to play in the latter stages of the Indochina conflict, when its committees attempted to make decisions that had normally been reserved to the executive branch. In this case the problem was exacerbated by the inept relationship that the Carter administration had developed with the Democratic leadership in both houses. In fact, one of the prime elements in the debate had nothing to do with the intrinsic merits of the case for AWACS sales; rather, it had to do with White House insistence on determining a calendar of actions to be taken by the Senate before its adjournment, despite the vigorous objections of the Senate leadership.

The consequence was a rather wild, uninformed, rhetorical

debate in both houses of Congress that repeatedly attacked the shah personally and scored the nature of his regime. It was so badly handled that, despite a close victory for the sale of the aircraft in the House of Representatives, the Senate actually voted against it.

The shah was furious. He instructed General Toufanian to cancel the request for the aircraft and to inform the United States military-advisory team that he would look elsewhere for his air-defense system. Since this made no sense either from the Iranian or the American point of view, I put off General Toufanian with various stratagems and sought some constructive repair work from Washington.

At this point the professionals from the Pentagon moved in and worked out a compromise with the congressional leadership. That compromise required certain substitutions of equipment—particularly encryption equipment—and certain other modifications on the AWACS aircraft before the planes could be sold to Iran. With this compromise in hand, and with General Toufanian briefed on the subject, I asked to see the shah.

At the time, he was vacationing in one of the small palaces his father had built along the Caspian. Accordingly, I flew in our small embassy aircraft over the mountains to his reported location. I was met by an official of the palace who told me that the shah had gone to another, even smaller palace along the coast, having an even smaller airfield. It seemed he was test-driving his new Cadillac Seville.

When I landed at the new location, I was again met by palace officials and taken to a small marble residence set in an orange grove above the town of Ramsaar. I was ushered into a reception room by a rather nervous retired general and told that His Majesty was expected shortly.

In a few minutes, I heard the crunch of tires on gravel as a car sped up to the palace door and stopped. The retired general returned, ushered me toward the porch facing the Caspian, and then backed laboriously away. On the porch, I found the shah, dressed incongruously in black silk pajamas, looking rather vexed.

When I told him why I had come, he began a long, pained monologue about the fatuity of the United States Congress, the treachery of the American press, and the ordeal that seemed to result from being friendly to our country. I let him get it all out of his system and waited until he seemed ready to discuss airplanes and radars.

At that point, I put the proposed compromise before him. He understood perfectly what was involved as far as the technology was concerned. He recognized that the changes in equipment would not degrade the system significantly. But, he was offended by the indignity of having to accept the appearance of degradation in order to qualify as a client.

Although he resisted for another two or three rounds of discussion, he finally threw up his hands and accepted the inevitable. The audience was over, and I withdrew quietly to leave the wounded sovereign sulking on his orange-scented terrace, in his black pajamas, above the bright-blue Caspian Sea.

* * *

In the summer of 1977, as persistent inflation gripped the American economy, it became clear that the price of oil was a significant factor in the economic and political realities of our country. Since Iran was one of the major producers of oil and since the shah had been one of the primary proponents of increasing the price of oil, the focus of American official attention on the shah's attitude toward oil prices became more intense. During the preceding administration, the shah had been singled out for criticism particularly by William Simon, the former secretary of the treasury, who once referred to the shah as a "nut." The shah had resented this and had often told me the rationale that lay behind his efforts to have the price of oil increased. According to his line of reasoning, oil was too precious a commodity to be wasted by burning it profligately in the internal-combustion engines of American and West European automobiles. He felt that, as a wasting resource, it should be preserved for its unique qualities, such as forming the base for petrochemicals, and that other forms of energy should be found for the most essential Western industrial requirements. He was particularly high on nuclear energy and had become something of an amateur exponent of fusion technology, which in his judgment would relieve the world of its dependence on oil for energy.

In many of the discussions I had with him, we used to run over his view of world energy problems in great detail. It was his feeling that countries like Iran, which rested their economy on the fragile and evaporating value of their oil resources, should ensure their own futures by shifting to other forms of energy, particularly nuclear energy. He felt that in the long run, once basic industry had been established in his country, it should be premised on the residual value of petrochemicals. He wanted other countries in the world similarly to shift away from oil so that oil resources could be used for purposes that he considered far more productive and, of course, far more profitable. He contended that Iran, Saudi Arabia, and other oil-producing countries had been defrauded of their just economic benefits by the international oil companies over the years and that their return on a barrel of oil had been far less than they deserved. He argued that his action in leading OPEC toward higher prices had merely been a rectification of past practices and that the OPEC level of oil pricing was not out of line with the economic benefits that oil could command on the world markets.

Since OPEC had formed the practice of meeting twice a year, the attitude of the United States in the late summer and early fall of 1977 toward the OPEC meeting that was to take place in December of that year became more and more frantic.

Economists and commentators pointed to the balance between world demand for petroleum products and world supply to suggest that the time had come when OPEC could desist from its upward pressure on oil prices and recognize an equilibrium not only in the supply-and-demand equation but also in terms of price. Considerable pressure was therefore exerted on the Carter administration to press its friends in OPEC for some moderation of price prospects and to achieve a moratorium in price advances.

Although I had no instructions on the subject from Washington, I used my regular audiences with the shah to discuss the relation between the advance of his economy in Iran and the stability of prices in the United States. He would regularly complain to me about the increased cost of the military equipment he was acquiring from us, and I would just as regularly attribute the increases to the inflationary effect petroleum prices were having on the American industrial-price structure. In these several discussions, I felt I had brought the shah around to a point where he recognized the direct relation between the costs of petroleum sold on the world market by the OPEC nations and the costs of those products that the OPEC nations were demanding in ever greater amounts in order to enhance their rapid industrialization.

Unfortunately, just as this general consensus was gradually being achieved, the deputy secretary of the United States Treasury, Anthony Solomon, gave a speech that repeated many of the old charges that former Secretary Simon had leveled against the shah. The speech, while well received by an American audience, was certain to exacerbate the problems we had earlier had with the shah on the question of oil pricing. I consequently sent off a sharp blast to Washington complaining about "the ghost of Simon clad in the robes of Solomon," as an effort to steer the United States government away from the sort of sterile lecture that would do us no good in achieving our objective of OPEC price stability.

Because of the tone of the cable, there was considerable resentment in the Treasury Department at my rebuke, but both Mike Blumenthal, the secretary of the treasury, and eventually Tony Solomon took the criticism in good grace.

A few weeks after this speech, Blumenthal and Solomon arrived in Tehran to talk with the shah concerning OPEC prices. It was part of a swing they were making through other OPEC countries, including Saudi Arabia and the United Arab Emirates, to anticipate the OPEC meeting in December. Although we had some rather joshing interchanges about the speech and my cable, we also had some serious discussions about the manner in which the shah should be approached on the subject of oil prices. While Blumenthal's initial instincts were to be fairly blunt and to confront the shah directly, he eventually accepted my suggestion that the matter be discussed in somewhat less confrontational terms, on the grounds that the shah was already predisposed toward price moderation. The meetings, therefore, went well, although there was a marked coolness on the part of the shah toward Solomon. This was understandable, perhaps, even though Solomon had spent his wartime years in Iran as a young Department of Defense civilian laying the foundation for the technical assistance that the United States eventually gave to the Iranian government under President Truman's Point IV program.

The shah's reaction was also, in my judgment, influenced to some degree by the fact that he had accepted an invitation by President Carter to go to Washington in late November and that he wished to avoid turning that visit into an episode that would focus primarily on oil prices rather than on the broader issues on which he sought some mutual understanding with the new Carter administration.

12

State Visits

Over the years, state visits by the shah to Washington had become a regular feature of the American political scene. The stairwell of the chancery in our embassy was lined with photographs showing the shah in the company of every American president since Roosevelt. While these photographs had been taken primarily on visits the shah made to the United States, American presidents had also made return visits to Tehran. The relationship that these visits symbolized was one of an alliance that had grown closer over the years. The shah had become an accepted cornerstone of our policies in Southwest Asia and the Persian Gulf. He was generally considered by Washington to be an enlightened monarch, a reliable ally, and a congenial chief of state.

Therefore, when the shah was invited to visit Washington as one of the early state visitors in the new Carter administration, it was not an extraordinary event. Rather, it followed the pattern that had been set in other administrations, both Democratic and Republican, for the past thirty-five years. On the other hand, in the context of the Carter administration, there was something extraordinary about the visit. The Carter administration had made human-rights practices a touchstone for the nature of its relations with governments around the world. It was generally conceded that the shah's regime was not a democratic one and that it abused human rights. Therefore, although a general consensus existed at the top of the administration that a state visit by the shah was perfectly in order, many within both the administration and the Democratic-party constituency abhorred the idea of a visit by one of their least-favorite allies.

As an avid reader of the American press, the shah was keenly aware of this criticism, and it made him somewhat nervous. He questioned me regularly about the relationship of certain key individuals within the administration and the Congress with the president, and about their influence on eventual American policy. He felt he was not particularly appreciated in the Carter White House, and the problems he had encountered on the sale of AWACS aircraft left him less than reassured about his relationship with Capitol Hill. Therefore, he approached the idea of a state visit with considerably less confidence than had been his custom over the preceding two decades.

On the basis of the cables I had been receiving from Washington, I attempted to prepare the shah for the situation he would find. I pointed out that there were no pressing bilateral issues between the United States and Iran and that the question of human rights and the nature of his regime was something he would have to face squarely in his discussions with the president. At the same time, I said he would encounter a number of questions, either in the executive branch or in the Congress, and I suggested he be prepared to be responsive to those issues.

First was the price of oil. It was a subject he and I had discussed often, and I pointed to the Blumenthal trip as an indication of the seriousness with which the administration was prepared to pursue this issue. The shah nodded when I raised this point and seemed to suggest that he had all the answers necessary on that subject.

The second issue that I felt would confront him was the scale of Iranian arms purchases from the United States. I pointed out that we had already had an indication of the seriousness with which the Congress viewed this question in the course of the vote on the sale of the AWACS aircraft. I suggested that he be prepared to think in terms of a reduction in the weapons system he wished to acquire and that he work out some understandings concerning a long-range program for the acquisition of weapons, their maintenance, and their absorption into the Iranian armed forces. Again on this issue, while he was less comfortable than he seemed to be on the question of petroleum prices, he did not seem particularly disturbed.

The third issue on which I was certain he would be approached was the development of nuclear capabilities by the countries in Southwest Asia. I referred not only to the large-scale program that Iran had undertaken for the acquisition of nuclear-power plants but more particularly to the program Pakistan was pursuing for the construction of a facility that would permit the recovery of weapons-grade plutonium from the waste product of nuclear-fuel rods in power plants. On this question the shah was firm. He categorically renounced any desire to acquire nuclear weapons and said he would assist in attempting to dissuade the Pakistanis from such plans. In fact, he told me he had regularly attempted to dissuade Prime Minister Bhutto from an effort to balance the Indian acquisition of nuclear-weapons capability by pointing out how futile it was for him to waste scarce Pakistani resources in the development of nuclear weapons. He said he had asked Bhutto what he would do if he could acquire one or two nuclear bombs, and suggested that their only utility might be to be used as "suppositories." In view of this position, he felt strongly that Iran should be permitted to acquire nuclear-power plants from the United States, and he would press strongly in Washington to assure that the Westinghouse Corporation would receive licenses to export at least four reactors to Iran.

Finally, I indicated to the shah that I felt his assistance and support would be asked for the efforts being undertaken by the United States to arrange some settlement between the Israelis and the Arabs in the Middle East. On this the shah felt quite confident. His policy did, in fact, coincide closely with Washington's. He had good relations with Israel and a particularly close relationship with King Hussein of Jordan. He was therefore prepared to be reasonably forthcoming in any discussions with the Carter administration concerning the role he was prepared to play to assist in bringing about a constructive resolution of the Arab-Israeli issue. He also had a special relationship with President Sadat of Egypt, to whom his government had provided a considerable amount of economic assistance.

In the course of these preparatory discussions, and in response to the general summary of United States objectives that I had made, the shah indicated what his concerns were. First of all, he wished assurance of a reliable source of supply for sophisticated military equipment, particularly for his air force and navy. He did not want to have political considerations interjected into an arrangement he considered primarily a financial and business transaction.

Second, he wanted licensing for the export of American nuclear-power equipment to Iran. Third, he desired some understanding with the United States about our intentions regarding the threats he saw to the oil-producing regions of the Persian Gulf by Soviet actions in the Horn of Africa, in Aden, in Yemen, and in the approaches to the Indian Ocean. But most of all, he wished to size up the new administration, to understand the new president, and to assess how significant the obvious political differences we had in domestic terms would be for the strategic alliance that he felt was essential for the well-being of both Iran and the United States.

I reported these conversations in some detail to Washington and then, in anticipation of the shah's visit, flew home with my wife to be in Washington preparatory to the shah's arrival. It also was a trip that happily coincided with the opportunity to assemble our entire family for the Thanksgiving holiday and at the same time to help with and participate in the wedding of our oldest child. Our daughter Anne, a Washington lawyer, was about to marry another young lawyer who had been a member of Secretary of State Vance's law firm and who had come to Washington with the administration to become a government lawyer. The visit thus promised to be a thoroughly satisfactory one from the point of view of our official interests and also from our personal and family perspective.

The first indication that these happy prospects would not be entirely realized came when I was briefed by State Department security officials concerning information they and the FBI had accumulated about the shah's visit. A disturbing profusion of reports from radical groups all over the United States indicated they intended to converge on Washington to demonstrate against the shah's visit and the human-rights policies of his regime. Although a great number of the participants in these demonstrations would be Iranian students studying in the United States, it was also clear that many other participants would have no association with Iran. Many groups were Marxist, and there were indications that money was being funneled into the United States from obscure sources in Europe. At the same time, some reports suggested that pro-shah organizations were mobilizing supporters to come to Washington. All this evidence pointed to a possible confrontation in the streets of Washington between the shah's supporters and those who opposed his visit.

The numbers involved in these potential demonstrations were not of such a magnitude that they were particularly disturbing to police and security authorities in Washington. These authorities had, after all, survived the massive demon-

strations of the Vietnam period, and they felt capable of handling the expected groups. Armed with this reassurance, my
wife and I, together with State Department protocol officers
and representatives of the White House, drove off to Williamsburg, where the shah would arrive on his transatlantic flight
and where he would rest overnight before making the final leg
of his trip to Washington by helicopter.

The arrival at the airport was uneventful. As usual, the shah
was piloting his own plane and brought it to a halt in front of
the terminal. He and the members of his retinue disembarked
and moved immediately into the motorcade, and we were on
our way across the countryside to Williamsburg. Again, Williamsburg was surprisingly calm. We saw no signs of demonstrators, and there were reassuring numbers of Virginia state
police as well as Secret Service and FBI representatives. The
shah and his group moved into one of the restored historic
houses in Williamsburg, and several of us in the American
contingent moved into another. Then, as dusk began to fall
and we were dressing to walk over for informal dinner with the
shah and his party, a group of protestors slowly began to form
on the sidewalk across from the house in which we were staying. We watched them through the windows. They were a
composite of Iranians and Americans, their political coloration
being marked by their banners. Many of these banners were
directed exclusively against President Carter and the United
States (most carrying the hammer and sickle and the usual
Communist slogans). Another group of banners, however, bore
a portrait that has since become very familiar to the American
public—the portrait of Ayatollah Khomeini. These banners
were directed primarily against the shah. Many of them also
described the shah as a puppet of the United States and demanded, "U.S. hands off Iran."

Although I appreciated the role that Ayatollah Khomeini
had played in the struggle between the shah and the Shi'a
clergy, this was the first time I had seen his name and portrait

evoked in the struggle by the Iranian students against the shah's regime.

The demonstrations in Williamsburg were without serious incident. The police cleverly controlled the arrangement so that the protestors were drawn up in front of our residence while the supporters of the shah were assembled in front of his. The two groups were rigidly separated by a police cordon, and it is doubtful that the shah ever saw any of the anti-shah demonstrators during his Williamsburg stay.

The next morning, without event, we departed for Washington in two helicopters. Arrangements had been made for us to land on the mall near the reflecting pool and to be driven across to the south-portico entrance of the White House. As we approached our landing point, we could see the crowds drawn up on the ellipse. Several thousand people had assembled, and we knew from our security briefings that they, too, had been separated into pro-shah and anti-shah groups. However, there was a significant difference. In Williamsburg the demonstrators had been on two separate streets, with a large police force disposed between them. Here the two groups were separated only by light, collapsible fencing erected in a narrow space of not more than twenty yards. A mere scattering of park police moved in that twenty-yard stretch of no-man's-land.

The short drive was accomplished without incident, and when our official party arrived on the White House lawn, we were greeted in bright sunshine by President and Mrs. Carter. The shah and the shahbanou were led to a receiving stand while the rest of us took our appointed places in the ranks of the official welcoming party. Just as the twenty-one-gun salute boomed out and the band music resounded, a sudden surge of activity erupted on the ellipse. The anti-shah group had broken through the flimsy restraining fence, had overwhelmed the limited police force in the no-man's-land area, and had begun an assault on the pro-shah forces. In the confusion that followed, the park police unleashed tear gas to disperse the demonstrators and break up the fighting. Unfortunately, given the prevailing wind, the tear gas drifted gently across the White House lawns, arriving at the receiving stand just as the shah and the president began their speeches. The world was treated to the spectacle of the president of the United States and the shah of Iran dabbing at their eyes with their handkerchiefs, tears streaming down their cheeks as they made their formal presentations of respect. Under the circumstances, both chiefs of state retained their composure well and completed their statements as scheduled. The rest of us did our best to contain our tears and coughs as the ceremony moved to its completion.

The disturbances were quelled in a few minutes, but I am sure the anti-shah demonstrators felt their efforts were well rewarded by the inadvertent teargassing of their enemy.

After this unhappy beginning, the visit went extremely well. The president invited the shah to give his general assessment of the strategic situation in Iran's part of the world and then listened patiently and alertly as the monarch proceeded for nearly forty-five minutes to give his familiar prognosis of a Soviet pincer movement to encircle the Arabian peninsula and the Persian Gulf by activity in the Horn of Africa and the African continent on the one hand and by movement through and into Afghanistan and down toward the Arabian Sea on the other. It was a situation that obsessed him and that I had heard him address on many previous occasions. He was a convincing and well-informed advocate of this position, and it was clear that the president and his assembled advisors were impressed by the shah's performance.

We then turned to a discussion of the several points at interest between the two governments. This was first done in a large group that included several cabinet officers, and later in a smaller group of those more directly concerned with relations between the United States and Iran. In this latter meeting there occurred one incident that demonstrates the risks of summit-level meetings by chiefs of state. As he responded to the shah's earlier expressions of concern about Soviet operations in Ethiopia and Somalia, the president said that the United States felt this was a matter that should be, in the first instance, handled by the Organization of African Unity. The shah chose to reply quickly to this presidential statement.

Ordinarily the shah's command of English was impeccable, but occasionally he mispronounced some words, usually by putting the accent on the wrong syllable. In this instance he replied to the president by saying that he considered the Organization of African Unity to be impotent, putting the accent on the second syllable, so that it sounded like im*po*tent. The president, given his southern accent, immediately assumed the shah had said that the Organization of African Unity was *important.* He therefore quickly replied, "We consider the OAU to be im*poh*tant too." Two or three of us exchanged glances, aware of what had happened, but none of us interceded to correct the erroneous impression that two chiefs of state carried away from their conversation—that they had reached a meeting of minds on the value of the Organization of African Unity.

With this sort of minor exception, the rest of the meetings were highly successful. The shah was received on Capitol Hill by several senior members of both the House and the Senate and also had a meeting with a large number of leading American industrialists and bankers who had an interest in Iran. With exquisite timing, he gave a press conference shortly before the president's state dinner in his honor at the White House, in which he announced that Iran would take the lead against any increase in the price of oil at the December OPEC meeting. This message naturally attracted favorable publicity just before the White House dinner and set the stage for a well-televised exchange of toasts between the two chiefs of state to cap the visit.

Although demonstrations continued outside the White

House in Lafayette Park and elsewhere in the city, they were well contained by large numbers of uniformed police, who succeeded in avoiding any further disruptions to the state visit. Consequently, the shah left Washington the next morning with a feeling of great satisfaction that the visit had gone well and that his relations with the new Carter administration were on a firm and sound footing.

There were, of course, aftermaths of the visit, particularly with respect to the riots and demonstrations. Among these aftermaths were accusations in the Washington press that the Iranian embassy had interfered in United States domestic politics by recruiting and organizing the pro-shah demonstrators who had been brought into the capital for the occasion. However, these accusations never reached fruition in legal action consequent upon the visit.

It is the practice in international relations that visits by a chief of state are reciprocated. In the shah's case, this did not usually mean an exact symmetry in the number of such visits; indeed, the shah, like King Hussein of Jordan, usually came to the United States almost once a year. The president of the United States, on the other hand, usually went to Iran only once in four years. When, in his White House toast, the shah invited the president to Iran and the president accepted, most of us therefore assumed he would carry out this obligation sometime in the course of the next couple of years. He had already arranged an ambitious travel program for 1978, and it did not include Iran.

However, it soon became apparent in December of 1977, as the details of President Carter's travel plans were being worked out, that he had attempted to pack too much into one grand tour. He had planned to visit a number of European countries and then swing through Africa and Latin America on his return to the United States. As planning went forward for this enterprise, it became obvious that it could not be accomplished in one single trip without exhausting both the participants and the resources that had to be deployed to make one of these trips possible. The conclusion reached in mid-December, therefore, was that the trip should be broken in two, and that only half of it would be accomplished in the period beginning shortly after Christmas and ending shortly after the new year. Because some schedules were already locked in firmly, it was necessary to find a place where one day and one night could be spent between Poland and Africa. From the point of view of geography, politics, and the president's personal preference, Tehran seemed the logical place. I thus found myself in the early part of December seeking the shah's agreement to a short state visit by the president of the United States and his wife that would begin on the last day of 1977 and end on the morning of the first day of 1978.

The shah was thrilled at the prospect. It would not only demonstrate internationally that the close relations between the two countries continued; it would also show his critics in both the United States and Iran that the great American champion of human rights considered his regime worthy of a personal endorsement. The shah immediately accepted the proposal and attempted to persuade the president to make a longer stay. Since the visit would occur on New Year's Eve, he and his palace staff began to elaborate plans for a gala New Year's spectacular.

Once I reported this to Washington, the administration seemed pleased and relieved that a visit could be arranged on such short notice, but it also dashed cold water on the shah's plans for a gala evening. The White House specified that the shah's dinner should be informal, although the White House dinner had been black-tie; it indicated, too, that President and Mrs. Carter wished to retire from the dinner at 10:00 P.M. When I relayed this information to the palace, there was considerable chagrin. However, having been involved in the arrangement of state visits in other countries in similar circumstances, I was sure that some adjustment to this austerity would eventually be made.

Within a few days a White House advance team was prepared to come to Iran to lay on the details of the visit. When the telegram giving their names and passport numbers was received in order to facilitate their clearance into the country, the administrative officer brought it to me and asked whether I noticed anything striking about the list. On first reading, I had to confess that nothing concerning the composition of the team looked startling. Then he pointed to the right-hand column on the tabulation, which listed the dates of birth. Only one of the team members was over thirty. We wondered what sort of performance to expect from these young people.

We need not have worried. They all proved to be seasoned veterans of the Carter political campaigns, and "advancing" a visit was something they had done often and well. They were cool young professionals who knew exactly what they wanted and how they wanted it arranged. They found their Iranian counterparts also efficient in this sort of operation, since the shah's movements were usually staged with the theatricality of a political-campaign event as well. The two groups hit it off well, and the arrangements were easily adjusted—the dinner was converted to black-tie and the hour for its termination fixed at midnight rather than ten o'clock. Other features of the program fell nicely into place, but there was absolutely no extension of the time the president was prepared to spend in Iran.

Since the two chiefs of state had met so recently and since no new bilateral issues had arisen in the interim, little substantive preparation had to be made. However, because the president's attention was focused on Middle East affairs, particularly on attempting to reach understandings among Israel, Egypt, and Jordan, the shah saw an opportunity to advance some of the undertakings he had made to the president during his Washington visit. He quietly arranged for King Hussein of

Jordan to come on a private visit to Iran, thus giving him an opportunity to pursue one element of the Camp David agreements and carry it one step further. Those agreements provided that, after appropriate arrangements had been made between the Israelis and the Egyptians, Jordan would associate itself with the talks and presumably arrive at arrangements governing the West Bank that would ultimately resolve the Palestinian issue.

Because of these circumstances, the discussions in Tehran involving the chiefs of state concentrated primarily on the Camp David issues. In these, King Hussein participated along with the shah. The shah, who was a great admirer of Sadat and a close friend of Hussein, lent his efforts to try to persuade Hussein to join in the Camp David process. Hussein, however, beset not only by the radical PLO but by the conservative Saudis as well, was elusive about agreeing to join in these proceedings. Nevertheless, the conversations were conducted on a constructive note, and the three principal participants were reasonably well satisfied.

Once the substantive discussions were over, attention turned to the state dinner that the shah was to tender to President Carter. An amusing sidelight of this affair involved Hussein, who, although a guest of the shah, could not attend the dinner under Iranian protocol without being placed in a position senior to President Carter. This was not only because he had been a chief of state longer than Carter, but because, in monarchies, hereditary chiefs of state almost always take precedence over elected chiefs. Hussein therefore stayed away from the dinner, which became strictly an American-Iranian event. Even then I found the Pahlavi protocol amusing. Except for the places of President and Mrs. Carter, who were seated next to the shah and the shahbanou in the center of the long, horseshoe-shaped table, the prominent places of honor were all occupied by a long, serried row of Pahlavis—brothers, half-brothers, half-sisters, and so on—with the result that the secretary of state and other American dignitaries found themselves seated well below the salt.

The most memorable thing about this dinner was the toast that President Carter offered to the shah. In keeping with arrangements that attend state visits, the embassy had prepared a rather anodyne toast for the president to make. We were consequently amazed when he offered instead a fulsome little speech in which he cited the shah as being dearly beloved by his people and sustaining an island of stability in his part of the world. That toast would later come back to haunt the record of the Carter administration in subsequent days. At the time, though, the dinner was a great success. The two or three American correspondents who had been selected by the White House to attend were told at the end of the meal that the president's trip was being altered to include a stop in Aswan, where he would meet with President Sadat. This unexpected addition to the itinerary provided new excitement as the formal part of the dinner came to a close.

After dinner King Hussein was brought in to join the group. He, the shah and the president, and their two ladies, had a brief meeting in a drawing room off the main salon. Then most of the group proceeded to a room that had been arranged as a theater, where Iranian folk dances and singing were presented as the finale to the dinner ceremonies. During the course of that presentation, the shahbanou quietly prevailed on President Carter to extend his stay at the palace to see the new year in at midnight. Given in what she had obviously anticipated as a favorable presidential response, the shahbanou sent the young crown prince into the library to arrange for an informal New Year's celebration there.

Consequently, after the cultural presentation the group attending the principals was winnowed once again, and the remainder of us went into the library to help celebrate the advent of 1978. This was a particularly interesting occasion, partly because it appeared to be so impromptu. The crown prince had set up a stereo set on a balcony overlooking the floor of the library and had produced a number of dance records. The shah began by asking Mrs. Carter to dance, the president danced with the shahbanou, King Hussein and Princess Ashraf shuffled a bit in the center of the room, and the rest of us paired off to make as much merriment as decorum allowed. I particularly recall dancing at one moment with the wife of the prime minister, Mrs. Amouzegar, and watching Hussein and Ashraf, neither of them much over five feet tall, dancing mechanically and staring distractedly off into space.

One vignette of the evening was rather touching. The crown prince, barely seventeen, and his sister, who was sixteen, were both obviously bored by the music of the forties and fifties that had been selected. Occasionally, while he was changing a record, the crown prince would slip in some rock music. When this happened, the shah would gesticulate from the floor below while the crown prince pleaded to let the louder, livelier music go on. For the most part, the shah's will prevailed. Once, however, when the crown prince slipped in a particularly cherished record, all the dancing below came to a grinding halt. Up there on the balcony, he and his sister were performing some of the more intricate disco steps of the current generation. Finally the shah subsided, and with good humor relaxed and joined the rest of us in giving the young couple a resounding round of applause.

The next morning, New Year's Day, President and Mrs. Carter were up for an early departure and were seen off at the airport, not only by the shah and members of the embassy staff, but also by a fairly large group of American business people who had come by special invitation to participate in the occasion. Like any accomplished politician, the president worked the crowd, shaking hands as he went down the line and speaking briefly before he boarded his plane.

After we had seen them off, I asked the shah if he wished to meet the Americans who were still lined up behind their restraining ropes waiting for the departure of the dignitaries from the scene. He seemed particularly pleased by this invitation and moved into the line just as he had seen President Carter do ahead of him. At first he was somewhat reserved and perhaps even a bit concerned about what comments he might get from this group of strange Americans. However, by the time he reached the end of the line, he had entered into the spirit of the occasion and was pumping hands like any American political candidate, posing for pictures, exchanging pleasantries, and obviously enjoying himself.

When he came to the end of the line and moved toward the limousines, he turned to me with a glow on his face and a slight mist in his eyes and burst out, "You Americans are really very nice people."

13

Political Rumblings

Security had been extreme in Iran during the president's visit. The police and military were posted everywhere along the route of his travel, and the population was held back from his path so that he had little contact with the Iranian public. These actions were taken because of the Iranian concern that unrest, which had recently been manifesting itself on the campuses, might erupt into altercations that would mar the president's brief stop. The precautions were warmly endorsed by our Secret Service, which was constantly concerned about protecting the president and his entourage from assassination attempts.

However, the social and political tensions which underlay these precautions did not really become evident in the country until the first part of 1978, after the president had come and gone. The first most active incident occurred in the holy city of Qum.

Qum is located at the edge of the desert, almost immediately south of Tehran. It is a city that over the years has developed as the spiritual center of Shi'a Islam. In its cobbled streets and alleyways twisting among the modern brick buildings are a group of madrasseh—schools where young men are trained to be mullahs and to join the ulema of Shi'a Islam. There were in Qum three or four of these schools in 1978, headed by distinguished learned men who preserved the traditions of the Koran. These scholars attempted to mold young men into the pattern of those mullahs who lived by the teachings of Shi'a Islam, with its constant concern for the martyred imams who had led the religion over the centuries.

This concentration of Islamic culture had, of course, also become a concentration of opposition to the shah's secular moves, and of the attitudes of opposition that had informed most of the Shi'a clergy after the sharp conflict that the shah had had with Ayatollah Khomeini in 1962. The young men who came there were mostly from a conservative Islamic background, but in the course of their training they learned many of the more fiery epithets that the Shi'a opposition had forged for use against the shah.

Moreover, among many of the more sophisticated opposition leaders, particularly in Tehran, the language of Shi'a Islam and quotations from the Koran had come to serve a political purpose. Where it was forbidden to speak in bald political terms of opposition to the shah, it became a favorite pastime to devise sayings from the Koran to express political dissidence. This practice, too, had eventually reached Qum and had become popular among some of the younger students of the madrasseh. Coupled with all this potential political activity was the fact that in recent years some young Islamic scholars had found a way to reinterpret the writings of the Prophet in order to provide theological support for social and political programs. Foremost among these had been Ali Shariati, who had written a series of works suggesting that Shi'a Islam could find a modern manifestation in a form of theocratic socialism which would be closer to the communal systems that had prevailed during the Prophet's life, and which would produce a blend of religious and political orthodoxy that could challenge the appeal Communism seemed to have for many young people in the Islamic world. As a result of this activity, a new vigor was introduced into the political and intellectual life of the ancient religious city of Qum.

A lot of ferment simmered in Qum just below the surface of the religious practices that permeated that city. In February of 1978 it boiled over into demonstrations that attracted the attention of the police, who reacted in typical heavy-handed fashion, attempting to break up demonstrations, suppress the religious students, and restore tranquility in the ancient alleyways. The confrontations turned violent, people were killed, and a whole series of events was set in motion. One of these events was the recurrent forty-day period of mourning for martyrs, which built upon itself and had a self-fulfilling periodic explosion. Each period of mourning became an event that produced new confrontations with the police and resulted in new martyrs, thereby creating a continuing cycle of martyrdom, increasing tension, and violence.

Meanwhile, in the industrial city of Tabriz in the north, another type of unrest was beginning to surface. Here a large concentration of young males had come in from the agricultural countryside to join the industrial work force. They were attracted by the high salaries in the cities and by the fact that work on the farms was becoming less and less productive as the inadequacies of the Iranian government's attention to the agricultural sector began to have their effect. These young industrial workers came from a conservative Islamic background. Most of them were from small villages where the village mullah was still held in higher esteem than the administrators from the government in Tehran. These young men, therefore, found themselves completely at a loss as they faced the westernized civilization in Tabriz.

They were confused not only by the automobile traffic and the bustle of the bazaar but also by the prevailing westernized customs. A fairly large group of Italians was engaged in building a refinery for the National Iranian Oil Company, and their wives and daughters, dressed in tight-fitting jeans or short shorts during the summer weather, set the pattern for female styles that was inevitably copied by the younger, more western-ized members of Iranian society. Moreover, the Italian and French movies that were imported into the city, and the gen-eral trappings of western civilization coming across the Turkish border on the international truck route to the west, were not only confusing but anathema to these conservative young men.

Their economic conditions were disturbing to them as well. They were earning far more money than ever before, but were unable to spend it satisfactorily. They looked at the luxury condominiums intended for the elite but standing empty, a stark contrast to their overcrowded dwellings in the slums. They found the cost of food, clothing, and other necessities of life far beyond anything they had experienced in the country-side. Their tangible wealth did not seem to match the relatively high income that their wages brought them.

The only place where they really felt at home was the mosque to which they went on Friday evenings and where they found themselves in the traditional atmosphere of Shi'a Islam, which they understood and in which they had grown up. They recited their prayers and listened to the sermons. At this time, the sermons on Friday evening in mosques throughout the country all began to resemble each other. They were, in fact, the same sermons. Most of them were tape recordings of ser-mons preached by Ayatollah Khomeini from his desert retreat in Najaf. There, in the bleak and inhospitable country of Iraq, the ayatollah had discovered the Sony tape recorder. He began to record his sermons on cassettes and have them smuggled across the border into Iran by pilgrims who came to the holy places in Iraq. In Iran the cassettes were replicated and dis-seminated by the thousands to the Shi'a mosques throughout the country.

Given the ayatollah's deeply held and long-nourished hatred

for the Pahlavis, the content of his sermons was predictable. He railed against the secularism, the westernism, the modernism of the Pahlavi dynasty, and attributed all of Iran's ills to the actions of the shah. His message was a simple one. Whatever your problems may be today, they are all the fault of the shah, and if you wish to solve your problems, get rid of the shah, get rid of the Pahlavis.

This message fell on religious students in Qum and on industrial workers in Tabriz as a spark falls on dry tinder. In both Tabriz and Qum, the net result was protest meetings, marches in the streets, and eventual violence. When protests first broke out in Tabriz, the police again proved inept in their manner of handling them. Their first action was to announce that the mosques would be closed and to barricade them against entry by the young industrial workers. Predictably, this resulted in the workers going on a rampage throughout the city, destroying motion-picture theaters, liquor stores, and other manifestations of Western civilization that they found offensive.

By March this same pattern had spread to other cities, particularly Isfahan and Shiraz. There, too, the preachings of the ayatollah had been a centerpiece of the Friday religious ceremonies in the mosques, and there, too, the pattern of discontent among industrial laborers and religious youth had taken root. By late spring the same sort of dissonance and dissidence had spread throughout the country. The confrontation that the shah's regime had long attempted to avert began to emerge as a major problem.

At first there was little political content to the turmoil. The old political leaders, whether from the former aristocracy, the Social Democrats, or the more radical Communist group, were kept under such close surveillance by SAVAK that they were really unable to exploit the opportunities that might be available in these initial disturbances. Moreover, most of them had been so seriously cowed by jail terms, physical abuse, or the constant use of police power that they were not eager to step out into the streets and become leaders of dissent.

Therefore, to most observers the events of the early spring of 1978, particularly as they tapered off in the later spring, seemed a part of the growing pains of a society that was attempting to move too rapidly from the traditional, conservative Islamic culture based largely on agriculture to a modern, westernized society that would be based heavily on industry. Corruption, social dislocations, and religious resistance were seen as key factors in the disturbances racking the country. Few observers, either domestic or foreign, suggested that the regime of the shah was in deep trouble.

The one exception was a young intelligence officer in the French embassy who made known his view that he expected the shah to be overthrown within a year. This observation soon made its way through the closely knit diplomatic community in Tehran and was discussed in some detail within embassies and by diplomats with each other. In general, the conclusion that was reached was the one we reached in our embassy. We felt that the shah was in trouble, we thought that his economic plan and his forced industrialization were wrenching his society in ways that could cause political difficulties, but we did not see the beginnings of a revolution. Our political section spent a good portion of the month of May putting together a lengthy assessment of the events that were troubling the country; it came to the conclusion that the shah faced a long, rough road ahead and that he had not yet shown evidence that he had developed the political and economic instruments to deal with the dissidence facing him. The embassy declined to make a prediction concerning the ultimate outcome of the struggle, but did make the assessment that it would be a deep and abiding struggle and that there were no easy, quick solutions to the problems confronting the Pahlavi dynasty.

Largely because of this conclusion, and also because we had not had home leave for three years, I decided it would be prudent for me to take leave during the summer of 1978, on the assumption that events beyond that time might preclude my being able to leave the country again. The British ambassador had come to the same conclusion, and after consultation with each other, we decided that we would both go on leave in the summer of 1978 and return after the month of Ramadan, which that year fell in August of the Christian calendar.

In the latter part of the spring, as we were preparing to go on leave, new and significant developments arose in the area of political dissidence. They came from the older political factions, which had been stirred into motion by the events in the streets. Most of them were remnants of the Social Democratic party, which had had a brief flowering under the regime of Mohammed Mossadeq. In general they were Western-educated people who had considered themselves liberals in the Western sense of the term. They were decidedly not Communists, and although the shah treated them all with scorn as tools and puppets of the Communists, many of them had distinguished political credentials from their earlier years.

By 1978, most of these men were in their late sixties or their seventies and had been subjected to a long period of surveillance by the police. Several of them had been arrested and imprisoned. Some of them had been tortured. As a group, they no longer met with each other, although they did maintain a loose affiliation known as the National Front. They were not allowed to operate as a political party, and they did not always see eye to eye in their approach to various issues. But as events of 1978 indicated a political stirring, many of them began to surface and to speak out publicly.

At first their efforts were anonymous, consisting of unsigned letters and manifestos that were circulated privately. Then some of them began to meet with each other and to sign letters publicly or to address them privately to the shah. One or two of them made themselves known to me and indicated that they wished to have contact with the American embassy.

On one occasion, while I was attending a dinner at the home of a former agricultural minister who was sympathetic with the National Front, I was approached by one of the former Mossadeq ministers who identified himself and said he would like to talk with me. Immediately he and I withdrew to a corner. He had hardly gotten more than a few words out of his mouth when one of the other guests, a staunch supporter of the shah, intruded and began to take part in the conversation. It was clear that this sort of interference was beyond the National Front politician's capabilities to handle. He broke off the conversation and stayed clear of me for the rest of the evening.

Because of this experience, I decided it would be better for my embassy to maintain contact with some of these dissident politicians through officers of our political section rather than by my own direct contact. Therefore, I steered those who had indicated a desire to see me toward two of my political officers, and they, in turn, developed a practice of meeting these political figures in discreet locations, usually not at their own homes or at those of the political figures. Thus in the late spring of 1978 the embassy began to extend its antenna into the network of political dissidence that had been outside our purview for some time.

There has been much discussion about the fact that the embassy did not have contact with political dissidents in the period before 1978. By and large, this observation is true, and, having arrived there myself only in 1977, I cannot say how long that absence of contact had endured. Nor can I speak directly to the circumstances that led to the rupture in such contact. However, I can indicate my own experience with the problem of associations between the embassy and the political dissidents.

Having come to Iran from the Philippines, where the embassy's contact with political dissidents was a regular feature of our life, I was aware of its absence as soon as I arrived in Tehran. When I sought to rectify this omission, it became clear to me that the political dissidents wanted nothing to do with the American embassy. In the first place, most of them distrusted the embassy, since they considered us to be in close association with SAVAK and with the government to which they were opposed. Second, they were under such close surveillance that they believed an association with the embassy would be detected immediately and would cause retribution against them. Third, they had more or less given up any hope of changing the system through political action and were consequently not willing to demonstrate by contacts with an embassy how thoroughly impotent they really were.

When this situation changed in the spring of 1978, the embassy reacted rapidly in establishing contact, and the political officers were able to restore a degree of confidence and confidentiality to the relations that we had with the political dissidents. I am told by some political officers who came back later to assist the embassy in expanding the scope of that contact that they had earlier been discouraged from such activity. It was never clear to me whether that was at the initiative of the ambassador serving in Iran at that time, or at the insistence of the shah. In any event, I never received pressure from any Iranian quarter suggesting that the embassy should not conduct itself in the normal fashion of having contacts as widely and broadly as we wished in the Iranian political spectrum.

In the late spring of 1978, this activity by the old leaders of the National Front did not go undetected by the shah's regime, nor did it go unpunished. On several occasions meetings were broken up by thugs who appeared with clubs and staves and who never identified themselves as members of SAVAK. Members of the National Front were accosted and beaten on the very streets of Tehran, apparently by robbers and muggers. There were searches of houses and occasionally looting, all intended to look like the work of outsiders rather than of the constituted authorities. There were even some arrests, but usually they resulted in short periods of incarceration and subsequent release.

During all this time, the embassy continued to expand its network of contacts among the dissidents and to gain their confidence. Many of them were genuinely surprised to discover that we were intellectually sympathetic with them even though we did not in any way encourage their roles of opposition to the shah. I recall one rather emotional evening when I was taken to the home of an old professor by one of my younger officers who had regularly been meeting with him. On that occasion, the professor had assembled a number of people from the academic and literary world, most of whom had at one time or another been arrested by SAVAK and had served time in jail. I am not sure what they expected from us, or what they felt the American embassy had done about them in the past. But I do recall the almost pathetic toast that the host made to me and to the embassy at the end of our excellent Persian meal. He was keenly aware of President Carter's human-rights program and extolled it at great length.

Other embassies in Tehran began to have similar experiences, sometimes with surprising results. The Goethe Society, which was sponsored by the German embassy, had a poetry-reading evening in which they brought together some of the leading Iranian poets whose Farsi had been influenced by the writings of Goethe. The German hosts had anticipated that a maximum of two hundred people would come to their rather esoteric gathering. Instead, several thousand came, spilling over into the gardens, trampling the trees, and creating an incident that, of course, came to the attention of SAVAK and the civil police.

Similarly, the French embassy, which had always maintained a certain amount of contact with the National Front through the *Cercle Français* and which took some pride in being the intellectual home of most of these Social Democrats, found that their officers were deluged with political projects by erstwhile politicians seeking French endorsement.

The endemic Iranian xenophobia began to turn into an eager search for foreign sympathy and support.

14

Home Leave

Home leave in the summer of 1978 provided me with an opportunity to visit Washington twice, first on my way in from Iran and then on my way back. Both of these occasions were for brief periods of one week each, but they did make it possible for me to discuss some of the important aspects of our bilateral relations with Iran with those government officials directly concerned.

Perhaps the most prolonged discussions concerned the political turmoil in the country. The question was not so much where this turmoil was leading and what the consequences would be if the dissidents should succeed in overthrowing the shah's government, but rather what actions the United States should take in response to requests from the Iranian government for assistance in meeting the problem. The issue ran headlong into the human-rights policy in which the Carter administration took such great pride. In the Department of State the chief proponent of the cause of human rights was Ms. Patt Derian, who had been appointed at the assistant-secretary level to supervise our concern for human rights on a global basis. Ms. Derian and some of her assistants were totally unsympathetic to the shah and aligned themselves with the opponents of his regime, regardless of what cause those opponents might serve. They were consequently against giving any assistance to the shah in suppressing his opponents.

The assistance that the shah's government was seeking from the United States boiled down largely to tear gas. Previous requests for tear gas had been granted only after much discussion and the personal intercession of the secretary of state. During my visit I attempted to set some sort of standard policy on this item so that we would not have to undergo a major bureaucratic struggle each time a request came to us.

Because tear gas is not a lethal weapon, its export was not subject to the same rules that apply to other military equipment. However, it was regarded as police equipment and the Congress had enacted strict regulations concerning the foreign sale of police equipment. A licensing requirement was therefore attached to its export. Consequently, even though the gas might be purchased commercially, it had to undergo government scrutiny in each instance.

In the Department of State, I took the position that tear gas was by far the lesser of evils as far as human rights were concerned. I pointed out that the shah and his government would react against the riots and demonstrations in any case and that it would be better for his forces to use tear gas than the more lethal equipment available to them. Although this argument was generally granted, there was nevertheless a reluctance to accept the fact that tear gas could be generally considered an exportable item not subject to the discretion of the human-rights division in the Department of State. Eventually, Secretary of State Vance stepped into this argument and agreed that tear gas would be regularly licensed for export to Iran unless some new facts intervened that made this decision inappropriate.

Another major but related issue had to do with the purchase of military equipment by the Iranian armed forces. The Iranians had an outstanding list of sophisticated weapons that they wished to buy from the United States. These included the new F-16 fighter-interceptor, additional F-14 aircraft, a specially equipped F-4 aircraft that would serve as a platform for electronic countermeasures, and a number of modifications to existing aircraft in their inventory to bring them up to the current state of the art. In addition to this shopping list, they had a significant request for naval equipment, embracing not only four Spruance-class flotilla leaders but also submarines and missiles to be launched from surface vessels.

This rather extravagant military-sales program sharply divided the Washington bureaucracy. Some in the U.S. military services were eager to provide the Iranians with all the equipment they were seeking. This position derived partly from their desire for a strong military presence in the Persian Gulf and Indian Ocean, and partly from their recognition that the acquisition of significant numbers of American weapons by the Iranians would make it cheaper for the United States services to purchase the same equipment, because of economies realized from increased production. On the other hand there were those in the Pentagon who expressed concern over the ability of the Iranians to digest and maintain this new equipment. They appreciated the limitations that the Iranians suffered in regard to skilled manpower, and they were afraid that the United States, through its military missions and military contractors, would have an insurmountable task in trying to train raw Iranian recruits to use and maintain effectively the equipment that the shah wished to purchase.

The Department of State was also divided. Essentially, those in the geographic-area bureaus were not averse to permitting the shah to acquire the military equipment he sought. This was in some measure a residue of the Nixon doctrine that considered the Iranians surrogates for Western military power in the Persian Gulf and Southwest Asia. These advocates deemed the shah a safe and reliable ally whose strength was a material asset to the United States.

In the human-rights bureau, some opposed the shah's having weapons of any sort, primarily because they opposed the shah. They accepted intellectually the fact that these weapons had little to do with the police repression practiced by SAVAK, but they also felt that any enhancement of the shah's strength would make that repression more effective. They were joined in their opposition by members of the policy-planning staff who considered that the additional acquisition of weapons would strain the military premise of the shah's government in such measure as to impede economic and social advancement. These latter arguments were not well founded from an economic point of view, but they did have a certain validity insofar as the armed forces preempted scarce skilled manpower that might otherwise have gone into schemes for economic and social development.

In the bureaucratic course of events, the political-military bureau of the Department of State assumed basic responsibility for chairing the various discussion groups that concerned themselves with the military-equipment program. Leslie Gelb, who was head of that bureau with the rank of assistant secretary of state, comprehended the arguments on all sides of the issue and sought to steer some sort of rational course among them. He and I eventually worked out an understanding that we thought would satisfy the legitimate concerns of those who felt the military-sales program sought by the shah was extravagant, and that would nevertheless meet the legitimate national-security interests of both Iran and the United States. This program called for me to undertake a review, on my return to Iran, which would force the Iranians to look critically, not only at the equipment they wished to acquire, but also at the resources they would need in terms of money and manpower if that equipment were to be effectively maintained in the future. The burden of this review would be placed on our military-advisory group in Iran, which would discuss the matter with their counterparts in the Iranian military. Since we knew that the Iranian

Meeting with President Carter prior to leaving for Iran, May 1977.

Demonstrators in front of the White House protesting the visit of the shah to the United States, November 1977. UNITED PRESS INTERNATIONAL

The Carters and the Pahlevis as tear gas wafts over the south lawn of the White House, November 1977.

President Carter toasts the shah at a White House dinner, November 1977.

The shah and the Sullivans waiting for the arrival of the Carters in Teheran, December 1977.

Meeting in Teheran between U. S. and Iranian officials, December 1977. *From left*: Ambassador Zahedi and the shah; *from right*: Zbigniew Brzezinski, President Carter, Secretary of State Vance, Ambassador Sullivan, and Assistant Secretary of State Atherton.

En route to present his credentials to the shah, Ambassador Sullivan with U. S. and Iranian officials.

Mrs. Sullivan and daughter
Peggy, dressed in chadors, at
the tomb of Imam Reza,
Mashad.

A view of the U. S. Embassy residence in Teheran.

January 1979. Shortly after the shah's departure from the country, a statue of his father is pulled down by demonstrators in Teheran. UNITED PRESS INTERNATIONAL

Street demonstrations in Teheran, February 1979. OLIVIER REBBOT

American Embassy employees and U. S. Marines are held captive after the fall of the embassy, February 14, 1979. UNITED PRESS INTERNATIONAL

Ambassador Sullivan surrounded by Iranian militants. OLIVIER REBBOT

military had never really costed the maintenance and man-power schedule involved in this acquisition program, and since we also knew that several of them—especially the air force commander—had grave doubts about their ability to assimilate all the shah wished to purchase, we thought it best to put this matter on a technical level rather than to make it a policy issue. If we were to make it a policy issue, I was convinced, the shah would rebel at our efforts to cut back his programs and would merely acquire the equipment elsewhere. On the other hand, if we put it on technical grounds, he would find a face-saving way to reduce his demands, essentially at his own initiative.

The third item that I pursued during these Washington consultations concerned my old bugaboo, the Iranian econ-omy. Once again I tried to encourage the Department of State and CIA to continue and elaborate the examination of the Iranian economy that they had halfheartedly begun a year earlier. Once again this bogged down in the miasma of Wash-ington bureaucracy. I could not seem to get a group that was willing to invest the time necessary to undertake a serious examination of the issue. On the other hand, I found some who were all too eager to turn such a review into a broader examina-tion of the entire Iranian political system, introducing subjec-tive factors that would have made the basic economic review meaningless. This was essentially the last effort I ever made to try to generate a careful look at the direction in which the Iranian economic-development program was tending. After having been defeated on this occasion, I gave up my struggles with the bureaucracy on the issue.

In between these forays into Washington, we spent home leave visiting relatives and friends and making a trip to Mexico for one very important piece of unfinished business that we had planned some time before. It had long been our intention to build our retirement home in Cuernavaca, south of Mexico City. During this home leave we found and purchased a piece of property overlooking the Cuernavaca valley. I recall with a sense of irony that, after my return to Tehran, I was discussing this acquisition with the shah one day. He said he knew Mexico City and Acapulco but was not acquainted with Cuernavaca, and asked me to describe it. I characterized the area as having roughly the same altitude as Tehran and a benign climate and lovely scenery. Some months later, when the shah himself was in Cuernavaca as an exile, he was asked by the Mexican television service why he had chosen that city as a place to sojourn. I recall hearing him say that "it was about the same altitude as Tehran, had a benign climate, and beautiful scenery."

While we were on home leave, little news of Iran was reaching the United States. In Washington, I therefore avidly reviewed the cables that had come in describing the political events, particularly during the month of Ramadan. In general, while the underlying turbulence that characterized the spring of 1978 remained, there did not seem to be any acceleration in the pace of political activity or any accentuation in the campaign of dissidence and disorder. The same opposition groups seemed to be functioning in roughly the same way, and the only ominous notes were reports that several elements of the outlawed Communist Tudeh party were beginning to move back into the country from their exile in East Germany.

When we had left Washington the second time and were visiting relatives in the Adirondacks before flying back to Iran, we heard a radio broadcast one morning reporting that a theater had burned in Abadan and that nearly three hundred persons had been killed. Shortly afterward we heard news reports that opposition groups were attributing the disaster to SAVAK and claiming that the fire had been deliberately lit to entrap dissidents within the theater building and eliminate them. I remember thinking at the time what a complication this would be for the Iranian government, because the forty-day mourning period for those lost in the theater fire would constitute another occasion for rioting and discord. I found it hard to believe that SAVAK would have resorted to such flagrant brutality and considered that, whatever the cause of the fire, it had been seized upon by dissidents as a major propaganda opportunity.

Subsequent events were never to clarify the issues surrounding the Abadan fire. People were arrested as perpetrators of the crime, but the facts remain murky and, in my mind, it has never been properly established where the blame lay for this enormous tragedy. Whatever the cause, it became a symbol in the oratory and rhetoric of the revolution that was gathering momentum in the country.

When we returned to Iran in late August, we discovered that despite the absence of any major events while we were away —other than the Abadan fire—the mood had turned angry beyond what had been discernible when we went to the United States in June. The irritability that always accompanied the fasting and other restrictions of Ramadan had been compounded by the sense of political frustration that now seemed manifest, even in the streets of Tehran.

15

Martial Law and Massacre

My first order of business was to obtain a thorough briefing from the senior officers who had been in charge of the mission in my absence. From them I obtained a bleak picture of the general situation in the country. Although disturbances had not significantly multiplied, a widespread bitterness toward the regime was seeping through in many conversations. Our young consul in Tabriz, Mike Metrinko, had submitted a series of reports from conversations he had held with young intellectuals and others in that northern city who had been traditionally well disposed toward the shah. From these encounters, Mike got the impression that opposition to the regime was growing and spreading among the middle class as well as among the industrial workers. Similarly, our consuls in Shiraz and Isfahan began to notice that opposition was far more widespread than it had been a few months earlier. They were receiving evidence of increasingly outspoken resentment at corruption, political repression, and the ineptness of the Iranian government. Even in the armed forces there were signs of discontent, for example, among the homofars in the air force. These were a special grade of technicians who had been recruited with the promise of significant salary benefits but who served as quasi-military members of the air force. When their term of duty had been extended to eleven years, they considered this contrary to the conditions under which they had been originally recruited. We had reports from several of our military-advisory elements indicating that the disgruntlement among this particular military cadre was widespread.

Considerable grumbling was also reported among the merchant class and those who had previously benefited from inflationary speculation. The Amouzegar government had tightened credit policies, had enforced a number of laws that had earlier been benignly neglected, and had in general made the realization of spectacular profits somewhat less tangible. This had brought a rumbling of discontent with Amouzegar and his government out into the open, along with a number of critical comments concerning the general policies of the shah and his regime. On August 26, Amouzegar, resigned and was replaced by Ja'afar Sharif-Emami, the former president of the senate.

Rumors were also circulating about the shah himself. He had spent most of the summer out of the public eye, reportedly at one of his summer residences on the Caspian. However, the rumors had it that he was absent because of illness, and all sorts of speculative stories were abroad in Tehran concerning his state of health. Officially, we knew that the shah had medical problems, but I did not know their exact nature. In fact, I doubt that anyone in the United States government was fully informed of his lymphoma as it had been diagnosed by French physicians. I was aware that he took constant medication but had no precise knowledge of his actual malady. The question of the shah's health was something that was of interest not only to the gossips in Tehran but also to officials in Washington.

Consequently, when I asked for an audience with the shah shortly after my return, and when it was promptly granted, I approached the occasion with more than casual interest. He received me in his usual office at Niavaran and appeared to be tanned, healthy, and relaxed. We engaged in several minutes of pleasant conversation concerning the way in which we had spent the summer months, and there was no indication of tension on his part until we started to discuss the state of political matters in Iran.

At this point he suddenly became grim and less than communicative. He did not seem to wish to discuss much about the situation and instead lapsed into a moody silence. After several attempts to encourage him to more constructive conversation, I finally stopped, looked at him, and said, "What's the matter with you?" in a more accusatory tone than was normal in these conversations.

Suddenly it all tumbled out. For nearly ten minutes the shah related incident after incident that had taken place throughout the country, each one constituting an assault on his government's authority and on the forces of law and order. He traced them not only to students but also to industrial workers, to members of the various religious factions, to the Shi'a ulema itself, and to the merchants of the bazaar. He said the pattern was widespread and that it was like an outbreak of a sudden rash in the country. He said it gave evidence of sophisticated planning and was not the work of spontaneous oppositionists. He then turned to me and in an almost supplicant tone said he had thought this over at great length and had concluded that the actions that he had just outlined represented the work of foreign intrigue. What bothered him, he said, was that this intrigue went beyond the capabilities of the Soviet KGB and must therefore also involve the British and the American CIA. He said he could understand the British intrigue to some extent, because there were those in the United Kingdom who had never forgiven him for nationalizing the oil industry. He pointed out that negotiations with the oil consortium were currently under way and that this gave the British antagonists all the excuse they needed to attempt a resumption of their ancient subversion in Iran. In listening to the BBC broadcasts that were critical of his government, he was, he said, confirmed in this analysis.

What bothered him most, he continued, was the role of the CIA. Why was the CIA suddenly turning against him? What had he done to deserve this sort of action from the United States? He spoke of his visit with President Carter in Washington and of Carter's return trip to Iran. He said that he thought he had a solid understanding with the United States as a result of those two visits and that our government was sympathetic to him and to his policies for gradual political reform in Iran. Why, he wanted to know, was that understanding being undermined? Had he done something? Or had we and the Soviets reached some grand design in which we had decided to divide up Iran between ourselves as part of an overall division of power throughout the entire world?

I was staggered by this outburst. It was not delivered in peremptory tones, but rather in the manner of a man who had felt himself unjustly betrayed. The shah was clearly distraught, his whole manner pleading—almost pathetic. I was frankly astounded by what I had just heard.

I set out as rationally as I could to try to reassure him of United States support and of continuing understanding on the part of the president and all other senior U.S. officials for the problems he was facing. After doing that, I set about giving him the information I had received from my embassy staff concerning the dissident incidents he had enumerated. I traced each local situation on which I had information to the particular circumstance that had generated it, and attempted to dissuade him from the conclusion that these incidents grew out of foreign intrigue. He listened carefully and seemed surprised that we should have been so well informed about these matters, which had not been publicized in Iran or in the international press.

The shah finally seemed to accept much of my explanation but asked where the dissidents got the money. He felt, in particular, that the clergy did not have access to the kinds of funds that were now at their disposal. When I said that I did not know in detail but that my information was that most of the money was coming from the bazaars, he reacted with incredulity. He said the bazaars had always done well under the Pahlavis; they were his staunch supporters. He refused to believe money was pouring from the bazaars into campaigns against him. He recounted in some detail the events of 1953 in which the street crowds pouring out of the bazaars had been a critical element in his return to power. I suggested he take a closer look at the current attitude of the bazaars, and particularly at their reaction to his recent economic policies.

This rather tense conversation seemed to be cathartic to the shah. Although he appeared somewhat drawn, I felt he was at least more at ease when I rose to take my leave. This meeting established a pattern of frank discussion of political events in Iran that would be followed on a regular basis from that day until the shah eventually left the country. It was clear that he had no one, with the possible exception of the empress, with whom he could talk as he had just talked to me.

As we were leaving, he walked across the room to the door with me, and I noticed that he was limping slightly. When I asked him whether he had had an accident, he was suddenly flustered but then recovered rapidly to say that he had twisted his knee water-skiing. At the time, I accepted the explanation, but I have since wondered whether his limp did not betray a more serious illness of the kind that later consumed him.

On my return to the embassy, I recounted this strange audience in some detail in a cable to Washington and recommended that a letter from the president to the shah, reaffirming policy support for him, was in order. I felt it would be inappropriate for the president in any way to take cognizance of the wild accusations about CIA support for the shah's opponents, but I suggested that the message be so written as to give the lie to any such speculation. I recommended that the message be sent immediately, since the shah's psyche obviously needed some tender care.

This cable arrived in Washington when the Camp David activity concerning the Arab-Israel dispute was at its height. I was informed by the State Department that a message had been prepared for the president's signature and that I could expect to have it in hand in the near future. Because of the president's preoccupation with Camp David and his presence there, I was advised that, although the urgency of the situation was apparent, there might be some delay before I received the actual message. Within a matter of days this delay was overtaken by events.

The end of Ramadan came on September 6, and on that occasion the traditional processions to the mosques took on new significance. We began picking up reports that they would, in effect, become marches and that the marches would have political overtones. Shortly before the event, we received confirmation of these rumors from official Iranian intelligence sources who spoke of a procession that would move down from the northern part of the city, split in two just north of our embassy compound, and then proceed to the center of Tehran. No numbers were given, but we received the impression that it would not be a very large group, composed primarily of mullahs and other acolytes of the Shi'a ulema. In view of the religious nature of the event, the Iranian authorities, according to our information, had decided not to place any restrictions in the way of the procession but rather to let it proceed without incident. Since even this was unusual, we had a number of embassy observers stationed along the projected route of the procession, in order to get a better assessment of just what this phenomenon might turn out to be.

As a demonstration it was unique in the experience of modern Iran. At least a hundred thousand Iranians participated in the march—well organized and marshaled in their parade with almost military efficiency. The marshals themselves were young men, often moving on Honda motorcycles ahead of the route of march, organizing traffic, blocking cross streets, and preparing the right of way. There were walkie-talkie radios, first-aid groups, water and refreshment units, as well as cheerleaders. Groups in the march were drawn largely from the congregations of various mosques. All in all, it was an awesome display of political power on behalf of the Islamic opposition.

As the observers who had been posted by the embassy called in their reports and eventually assembled back at the embassy compound, one of them, knowing the shah's penchant for attributing disorders to foreign sources, observed that the Japanese would be "in for a rough time this evening." When I asked why, he explained that all the outriders were on Honda motorcycles and all the walkie-talkies seemed to be made by Sony. Given the logic of Iranian rationalization, he concluded that the Japanese could well be given blame for this demonstration by some of the more paranoid elements of the shah's entourage.

I could only marvel at the organization and the preparation that must have gone into the demonstration. I realized that the embassy had had only the sketchiest notion of what might happen in this parade and that our sources of information among the Shi'a hierarchy and in the bazaars were obviously wanting. As soon as we had filed our reports to Washington on this event, I set in motion an effort to try to improve our sources of information both in the Shi'a ulema and among the leaders of the bazaar.

In the weeks that followed I constantly harassed our political and intelligence officers in an effort to improve their information from these two significant areas of the Iranian body politic. Interestingly enough, no matter how hard they tried, they seemed unable to develop any satisfactory and reliable sources in either area. It was apparent that neither the leaders of the Shi'a clergy nor the leaders of the bazaar wished to have much contact with the American embassy. Eventually, a few weeks later, I did persuade an American business consultant who had long-standing associations with both communities to put our political officers in touch with a leader from the bazaar who was also well connected with the clergy. In due course these same political officers developed good working relationships with one branch of the political opposition that had a close connection with the clergy. Through these associations we eventually reached quiet contact with Dr. Mehdi Bazargan, the head of the liberation movement, a pious and devout Shi'a Muslim, and the man who was eventually Ayatollah Khomeini's choice to become prime minister of Iran after the revolution.

In the aftermath of this demonstration, I nearly forgot about the pending letter from the president to the shah. Since events had taken a sudden change, I questioned whether the letter as originally drafted would serve its original purpose and recommended in a cable to Washington that it be revised to take account of the actions that marked the end of Ramadan.

The shah himself was not idle. Jolted by the events of September 7, he summoned his military commanders to the palace that evening and held a long meeting. The city and the country awoke the next morning to announcements that martial law had been declared during the preceding night and was in effect as of September 8.

This declaration posed an immediate challenge to the opposition. A demonstration had been organized and scheduled for September 8 in Jaleh Square, immediately facing the parliament, to mark mourning for some of the opposition group who had been killed in previous rioting in Qum. In short order, therefore, a confrontation shaped up in Jaleh Square between the demonstrators who had gathered there and the troops who were brought in to disperse them.

According to eyewitnesses, the confrontation first took the form of a shouting match across the reaches of Jaleh Square. The military commander, equipped with a bullhorn, informed the demonstrators that martial law had been declared and that gatherings of the type he confronted were illegal. He ordered the demonstrators to disperse. The demonstrators, on the other hand, began shouting at the troops, jeering at them, and yelling antigovernment slogans. As the confrontation wore on, some of the more zealous demonstrators, who appeared to be students, moved across the square toward the troops. At this point the troops began to advance and to begin the tactic of removing the demonstrators from the square.

What happened after that is not entirely clear. Some sources indicated that students tried to grab the rifles from the soldiers and others suggested that stones and staves were thrown at the troops. In any event, a melee soon developed and shoving took place on both sides. After a few minutes of this, the troop commander called his forces back to a firing line and ordered them to fire their weapons. Whether the first volleys were fired into the air or whether the rifles were leveled at the crowd in the first instance is again unclear. What is clear is that the soldiers did fire into the crowd and that, by the time the smoke cleared, over two hundred demonstrators were killed.

There have been exaggerated accounts of the numbers killed in Jaleh Square, even though the figure of two hundred is itself shocking by most standards. Given the size of the square and the number of demonstrators who were involved, it seems unlikely that there could have been anywhere near the thousands of casualties subsequently reported by many sources, both Iranian and foreign, after this black Friday.

The massacre was a shock to both sides. The oppositionists seemed sobered by the force of military action; the government —and particularly the shah—seemed astounded by the number of casualties. There was a brief pause throughout the nation in the actions of the opposition as the military deployed forces to all major cities and as the full effect of martial law was felt in those cities. People were arrested, opposition groups were broken up, and the iron fist of the military seemed to have asserted itself.

In the United States, meanwhile, a Camp David summit meeting on the Middle East was in progress. Reports of the situation in Iran drifted into the mountain retreat, and President Anwar Sadat of Egypt, as a close friend of the shah, decided to telephone his fellow chief of state to express his sympathy and support. Within a short period after that call had been made, President Carter also called the shah. Although I was never informed of the exact content of their conversation, I was later told that it was a substitute for the letter that had earlier been recommended and that had now been overtaken by events.

A group of American businessmen who had been visiting Iran had an audience with the shah the afternoon he received these two telephone calls. When they came to my residence for a reception later that evening, they told me that the shah had been briefly delayed at the outset of their audience by a call from President Carter and that he had seemed considerably buoyed up by the event. In any case, he had obviously at last captured the president's attention, and after that occasion I never again heard complaints from him that the CIA or the United States government was in any way seeking to undermine his authority.

16

Feeding the Crocodiles

Even before martial law had been put into effect, the shah had moved to revise his government. He accepted the collective resignation of the cabinet of Prime Minister Amouzegar and immediately announced that he had appointed the president of the senate, Ja'afar Sharif-Emami, prime minister, and had commissioned him to form a government. It was semiofficially suggested that Sharif-Emami was named to this post partly because he and his family had long enjoyed a close relationship with the Shi'a ulema.

Actually, from the point of view of the opposition in general and the Shi'a ulema in particular, the selection of Sharif-Emami probably could not have been worse. He had been intimately associated with the shah in the work of the Pahlavi Foundation and was regarded as personally corrupt. Although he enjoyed a reputation for Islamic piety, his relationship with the forces behind the Islamic opposition was tenuous at best.

I had met Sharif-Emami when I first arrived in Iran and was making my courtesy calls on senior officials. Martin Herz, then our ambassador to Bulgaria, who had previously served as political counselor in Iran, had given me a particular introduction

to him. Herz had developed a good working relationship with
Sharif-Emami when the latter was a political leader in some
ostensible opposition to the government of that time. He was
a man who enjoyed political discourse and who had taken
particular pleasure in leading the American embassy through
the maze of personal, political, and family relations that had
made up the matrix of Iranian politics in the 1960s. A heavyset
man with a large bald head and a ponderous manner, Sharif-
Emami seemed to me lacking in any great depth of wisdom or
political shrewdness. I thought him an unlikely candidate to
lead the shah's political fortunes through the turbulent conditions that had produced the need for martial law.

Shortly after he assumed office, the prime minister asked the
British ambassador and me to meet with him jointly. Neither
Ambassador Parsons nor I knew that the other had been invited to this session, and therefore we found our joint meeting
with Sharif-Emami somewhat extraordinary. However, since
British and American interests in Iran coincided closely, and
since Parsons and I had developed a close working relationship,
this pattern of joint calls and joint action was later repeated
time and again, not only with Sharif-Emami but eventually also
with the shah.

In our first meeting with the new prime minister, he took
great pains to establish the fact that he was operating independently of the shah. He suggested that all his predecessors had
merely been executive extensions of the shah's will and that he,
by contrast, had a Cabinet that was responsible to him and to
the parliament with only a nominal operational liaison with the
shah. He laid out a plan of action that would involve massive
concessions to the political opposition. He said his purpose was
to give them so many of the things they had been asking for
that they would find themselves surfeited with their new status
and cease their opposition tactics. It was a program that we
later labeled "feeding the crocodiles."

For example, he lifted all censorship of the press, permitted the broadcast of debates from the parliament, and declared that all political activity would now be free of government constraint. He confidently predicted that in these circumstances the various strands of the opposition would talk themselves into internecine political conflict and thereby divert their energies from attacks on the government or the crown.

His next action was doomed to be an even greater miscalculation than were his political measures. He had decided that the most nettlesome burr in the shah's political side was Ayatollah Khomeini, who was in exile in Najaf, deep in the deserts of Iraq. Sharif-Emami, who had been instrumental in the effort to reach a rapprochement with Iraq, knew that the Iraqis were tiring of the agitation emanating from the ayatollah. They were concerned not only with the friction that this agitation was producing with Iran, but also with the difficulties it was causing with their own Shi'a Islam population, which constituted nearly 60 percent of the country's inhabitants. Therefore, Sharif-Emami reasoned, he would prevail upon the Iraqis to expel the ayatollah from Najaf, where he had contact with pilgrims from Iran and from where he was able to smuggle his tape-recorded sermons back to Iranian territory. Sharif-Emami's thesis was that the ayatollah, expelled from Iraq, would have to head westward, probably toward Europe, and that this would put him out of touch with most of the religious dissidents in Iran. He told Ambassador Parsons and me that once the ayatollah got to Paris he would fade from public view and probably never be heard from again.

In general, measures such as these, which had not been carefully thought through, were the hallmark of Sharif-Emami's administration. They were clearly in sharp contrast with the essence of martial law, which was still nominally in effect. In fact, General Oveissi, commander of the Iranian ground forces and martial-law administrator, found himself in direct conflict with the basic premises of the administration's policies and puzzled as to how he could administer martial law in circumstances of such political leniency. When he and other military officers took the case to the shah, however, they found that he accepted Sharif-Emami's interpretation of his independent mandate and refused to inject himself into the internal governmental dispute.

During this period, largely at the shah's initiative, Ambassador Parsons and I began seeing him almost every other day for long, discursive audiences. The shah would go over with us endlessly the options he saw for his regime. He would point out that he had moved toward becoming a constitutional monarch and did not wish to reverse his course back to one of dictatorship. He made much of the view that a king cannot rule his subjects exclusively by force, but must have them accept the logic and the objectives of his regime. He said that he expected the young Western-educated technocrats to recognize the folly that would result if he were to accede to the requests of Islamic fundamentalists to turn his various reforms back toward a literal restoration of Islamic practices. He felt that if these young people received the political opportunities being afforded them by Sharif-Emami's government, they would step into positions of political responsibility and preempt the political success of the mullahs. He ridiculed the influence and authority of the mullahs and said they were out of touch with modern Iran. He was sure the more sophisticated elements of Iranian society would recognize the mullahs' incompetence to rule and would see that a clerical regime would only produce reactions that could lead to radical Communist opportunities.

He often indicated that he had considered the use of the military option and had rejected it. He felt he could suppress political dissidence by military force and keep it suppressed so long as he was personally on the throne. But then, in the first allusion to his ill health, he said he would probably be turning over authority to his son, the crown prince, in the course of the next few years, and after his departure from the scene the young man would not be able to continue to rule by military force. He felt, therefore, that it was essential for him to move rapidly to establish a democratic political system that would sustain the dynasty after his own departure. He reasoned this through with us on several occasions and always came to the same conclusion.

He did not specifically ask for our guidance, and we had none to give him. Although Parsons and I both reported these conversations in detail to London and Washington, neither of us ever received any overall guidance from our governments to pass on to the shah. From time to time we continued to receive urgings on human-rights matters, which generally dealt with specific cases and events, but as far as the Washington concentration on Iran was concerned, I could detect neither high-level concern nor any comprehensive attitude toward the events that were in progress. The focus of Washington's attention seemed to be on the Camp David process and the continuing effort to reach a resolution of the Arab-Israeli crisis in the Middle East.

However, as the months of September and October unfolded, things in Iran went from bad to worse. The military, after the first shock of Jaleh Square, were given orders to refrain from firing at demonstrators. Instead they made a belated effort to develop riot-control tactics and sought additional equipment and training from the United States and the United Kingdom. Since our Congress had specifically prohibited police training for foreigners, the British were required to pick up the responsibility for much of this work. They did send a small military mission under the direction of an expert in riot control, and he, in turn, made arrangements for the sale to the Iranians of rubber bullets, plastic shields, and other riot-control equipment that the British had developed in the course of their experience in Northern Ireland. We continued to ship tear gas but otherwise to take no direct responsibility for its application.

As the opposition forces began to recognize that they could resume their demonstrations in the streets without fear of mortal consequences, their actions became bolder. They developed tactics of fraternization with the troops, and young female students began placing flowers in the muzzles of their weapons, as had been done during the revolution in Portugal. There was also a great flowering of opposition and criticism as the new freedoms of the Sharif-Emami administration began to be exploited by the public.

Moreover, as these experiences multiplied, so did the number and variety of the oppositionists. In addition to the Islamic fundamentalists who had begun the early marches at the end of Ramadan, student groups started to spill out from the universities, the old Social Democrats were meeting publicly and circulating letters and petitions, tribal leaders came back from exile, Tudeh party activists returned from East Germany, and even some of the old Qajar aristocracy began to take part in the opposition. The babble of dissidence spread from the streets to the press and to the parliament itself. Speakers in the parliament, finding the opportunity to be broadcast first on radio and then on television, vied with each other in demagogic denunciation of the government. Sharif-Emami stood endlessly in the chamber of the Majlis, defending himself against these attacks and announcing additional changes and concessions to the political opponents. Up to this point the criticism had all been directed against the government, without specific reference to the shah.

As October wore on, a new tactic emerged. In the evenings, people throughout the city climbed to the rooftops and shouted slogans into the night air—mostly choruses of *"Allah-u-akbhar"* ("God is great") and similar anodyne phrases. Troops in the street below answered these calls by firing their rifles into the air. The nights in this period thus became a frenzied nightmare of shouting and keening that swept from one end of the city to the other and was accompanied by the staccato barrage of rifle fire, all of which lasted well into the night.

During the daytime hours, gangs of young men swept through the city in assault groups that would charge down a street, tipping over automobiles and setting fire to the rubbish that had begun to accumulate as the city's services broke down. When military units charged to meet them, the groups would break up, melt along streets and alleys, and re-form somewhere else for a similar charge. Each one of these encounters was punctuated by the firing of military rifles into the air and the discharge of tear-gas canisters as the demonstrators broke and ran. The city grew increasingly chaotic, and similar scenes were repeated in Shiraz, Isfahan, Tabriz, and other urban centers throughout the country.

It became apparent that the shah's tactic and Sharif-Emami's administration were failing. Not only were the oppositionists not appeased by the concessions that were made, but they were emboldened by each successive concession to raise the level of their demands and to begin to think in far more revolutionary terms than they had done at the outset. At about this time the shouts and slogans began to include the name of the shah and, in due course, the phrase "death to the shah."

It was clear to me that Sharif-Emami's days were numbered and that the shah had little recourse but to install a military government. In anticipation of this I sent a message to Washington late in October, giving my assessment of the situation and suggesting that a military government was imminent. I felt certain that the shah, before taking this step, would like to have our views on such an action. I wished to anticipate such a request and therefore asked that Washington give me its instructions in advance so that I would know how to answer the question when it was put to me by the shah.

Much to my surprise I received a rapid and clear answer within forty-eight hours. I was told the United States government felt that the political survival of the shah was of the greatest importance to us and that the shah should take whatever measures he felt necessary to preserve his position. If this involved the installation of a military government, then the United States would accept the shah's judgment in this matter and give him its full support. Clearly this instruction was written on the assumption that a military government would apply the full force of martial law and that the political opposition would be crushed by the use of military force.

This instruction represented a sharp departure from the platitudinous messages I had been receiving up to that point, and it also marked a departure from my previous experience of usually receiving no specific answers to policy questions that I put to Washington. It was also of interest because it seemed to finesse an assessment that the embassy had earlier sent to Washington suggesting that even the installation of a military government would probably not be successful in turning around the opposition that had now become so widespread.

Within a short time two other events took place that seemed to give some explanation for this sudden shift in Washington's policies. The first was a telephone call from Brzezinski informing me he had just spoken on the telephone with the shah and conveyed to him the president's strong support for any actions that the shah considered necessary. The second event, following hard upon this, was the arrival in Tehran of Ardeshir Zahedi, who called me shortly after he had bounded into the city.

When I went to see Zahedi at his home, he took me into his study and in his most conspiratorial tone told me that "Brzezinski has taken over Iran policy." He described how he had been summoned to the White House by Brzezinski and been told that the situation in Iran had alarmed the president and that the shah needed to be stiffened in his resolve. According to Zahedi, Brzezinski had then encouraged him to return to Tehran to inspire the shah to take stronger measures to protect his regime. Zahedi said that when he had protested that he could not leave his embassy in Washington, Brzezinski had ushered him in to see the president, who told him that he,

President Carter, would be the Iranian ambassador in Washington and that Zahedi should feel it was his primary duty to return to Tehran and stiffen the shah's spine as he confronted these sharp political challenges.

Shortly after this meeting with Zahedi, the shah summoned me to the palace and repeated to me what Zahedi had already told me. He said that Zahedi had informed him I would receive a message confirming all these statements, and asked me whether I had such a message and whether I could inform him of its contents.

At this stage, all I had received in the way of messages from Washington was the answer to my inquiry concerning the prospect of a military government. I did quote to the shah from that message about Washington's view that he should take whatever measures he considered necessary and that they would be supported. This did not seem to be what the shah expected, and he asked me for more explicit instructions, presumably a message urging him to use military force to suppress the revolution.

When I reported this conversation and asked for explicit instructions, I received a cable that was far more reserved than Zahedi's rhetoric or than the message that the shah seemed to be expecting. I relayed its contents to the shah. He seemed less than satisfied with what I had to say but continued to review the crisis in the same way he had done previously.

Events in the street soon began to overtake the message traffic. As we turned the corner into November, the rioting became more violent and the confrontations between the troops and the demonstrators more frequent.

17

Military Government

Travel in the city, particularly in the central business areas, grew more dangerous. We established a control room in the embassy and an emergency network to the large American business community. This network consisted of telephone and radio communications to selected offices in various parts of the city that could serve as marshals and monitors for the Americans who lived and worked in those neighborhoods. It became a two-way system as these monitors reported in to us when riots and disturbances took place in their vicinity. Thus we were able to alert the American community to which parts of the city they should avoid and when we felt they should evacuate their business areas to move out of the way of an arsonist mob.

A structure of civil-defense committees was developed within the business community that reported to my embassy security officers, and I began to meet more regularly with community representatives to give them our assessment of advancing events. This was a rather tricky enterprise. We were naturally concerned for the welfare of our citizens and wished to keep them as far away from harm as we possibly could by this monitoring and marshal system. At the same time, we wished to avoid the impression of panic that we knew would result if we began to evacuate Americans. Fortunately, the American citizens who were in Iran at that time were a cool, mature, and experienced lot. Because of the nature of their work, many of them had had previous military experience and were prepared to accept the discipline of a civil-defense network of the type we established. Many of them also had experienced similar civil disorders in places like Beirut and Vietnam. They handled themselves with great sophistication in some very trying times.

Despite all our precautions, circumstances arose in which Americans or other foreigners became trapped in the riots. In some instances their automobiles were smashed, their clothing was torn, or they were physically roughed up. However, given the widespread nature of the disturbances and the amount of random firing in the air that the Iranian military was doing, it is something of a miracle that we had no casualties in those times.

On one occasion the British ambassador and I nearly spoiled this record. We had been meeting with the prime minister at the latter's request in his office in downtown Tehran. After the meeting, we decided to compare notes back at the British embassy en route to my compound. Although we had traveled there separately in our two automobiles, I chose to join Ambassador Parsons in his small Rolls-Royce for the return to his chancery. Haikaz, my intrepid driver, followed us in the large armor-plated Chrysler limousine that was my official vehicle. Behind him came the chase car containing four Iranian national police; also monitoring us in this procession was the major in charge of our Iranian security guards, who was driving a small unmarked car of the variety assembled in Iran.

As we left the prime minister's office, the major, who had scouted the route ahead, advised where the riots were occurring then and suggested a circuitous route that would get us around them. Our small procession started off according to this plan, but because a large riot was taking place just to the east of our projected route, much traffic was spilling into the area we sought to traverse. In moving up one of the streets, we soon found ourselves blocked by a long string of automobiles stopped because of problems ahead. While our cars were stalled by the traffic, we soon saw the cause of the blockage. A large demonstration headed by thuggish-looking types with large clubs and pipes came swinging around the corner about two blocks ahead of us and started down our street. As they came upon automobiles standing by the side of the rode, they tipped them over into the drainage ditches and set them on fire.

The British ambassador's driver, seeing what was happening, quickly swung his Rolls out to the left toward the drainage ditch, backed it up, and managed to reverse direction along the route from which we had come. The police major, behind us, did the same thing with his car and ended up ahead of us, leading us out of the way of the advancing mob. Haikaz, in my Chrysler, attempted to do the same thing but discovered that his car was too long to make the turn; he therefore had to fall back into the procession of blocked cars and await the mob's arrival. Fortunately, we had taken the precaution of changing the registration plates on the car from the diplomatic tags that would readily identify it to nondescript tags that had been supplied by the local police precinct.

Led by our major, we swung out across the city and into the basement of a bank building that he had obviously staked out earlier as a potential refuge. In the basement garage the Rolls was quickly stashed in an inconspicuous spot while Ambassador Parsons and I took the elevator up to the office of the managing director. There we were comfortably received and could look out from his panoramic windows over the portion of the city where the burgeoning riot was taking place. In half an hour or so, shock troops had broken up the mob and dispersed them by firing bullets into the air and tear gas into the crowd. At this stage, Ambassador Parsons and I returned to the basement, got into a small unmarked French sedan provided by the bank, and, accompanied by our police major, worked our way back through the dispersing crowds to the British-embassy compound.

In due course Haikaz and the Chrysler arrived there as well. Although the car had suffered a few dents from the clubs and pipes carried by the mob, Haikaz took great delight in chuckling at the rioters' inability to turn it over because of the enormous weight of its armor plate. We then returned to our compound without becoming another statistic on the increasing casualty lists from the rioting in Tehran.

A couple of days later the riots burst out of control. On the morning of November 4, a well-organized group of arson squads swept with lightning rapidity through the city. They stormed into buildings they had obviously targeted in advance and put them to the torch. Most of these buildings were banks, but some were motion-picture theaters or liquor stores. The arson squads' tactic was to pile all the furniture in some large central room or foyer, soak it in gasoline, and set it afire after having evacuated all the inhabitants. The buildings went up in sheets of flame and within two hours the entire city seemed to be burning.

When the burning of Tehran began, Ambassador Parsons was in my office consulting about the prospect that the shah would have to install a military government. Although I had received clear instructions on this matter, he had no precise guidance from London.

As the arsonists spread through the city and it became apparent that buildings in our neighborhood were being targeted, my military attaché succeeded in having the nearest military garrison send Iranian soldiers to block off the streets that gave access to our compound. Cordons of troops drawn up across four intersections leading to the embassy were able to keep the traffic and the mobs away from our immediate vicinity, but on the streets directly adjacent to us, buildings soon began to spout flames and smoke from their windows. One large eleven-story building two streets away became a towering inferno, burning for several hours before it collapsed in a heap of rubble with a resounding swoosh.

In the middle of all this, an emergency call came in from the British embassy reporting that it was under attack from a mob. Ambassador Parsons immediately wanted to return to his own compound, but our network of riot watchers in that section of the city warned us there was no way he could penetrate the mobs and arrive safely. In fact, within a very short time the mobs had torn down his compound gate, scaled the wall, and set fire to his chancery. The British and local employees had been evacuated before the fire was set, so fortunately no one was seriously hurt. The invaders did not go beyond the immediate area of the chancery itself and left the residences in the rear of the compound unscathed.

By late afternoon the city looked like a battleground. Buildings were still in flames, automobiles were burning in the streets, and piles of old tires had been set afire, billowing huge clouds of black, acrid smoke wherever they were strewn. Troops and police milled around without direction, firing constantly into the air. People who had been on the streets had taken refuge in homes and buildings that had been spared the torch. By then the streets had cleared enough for Ambassador Parsons to attempt to make it back to his compound. He never got there, because of continuing disturbances in that immediate vicinity, but he did arrive at the French embassy, only a couple of blocks away from his own.

At about this time, I received a telephone call from the shah's office asking whether I could come and see him. I said I would be there as soon as I could pick my way through the rubble. Half an hour later Haikaz and the police major assured me the route was adequately clear to make a dash for the Niavaran palace, and we set out with the major in advance,

Haikaz driving the armored Chrysler, and a chase car behind us. It was nearly dusk in the city, and the eerie drive to the palace had a surrealistic quality.

We found the entire area near the palace surrounded by Chieftain tanks and elements of the imperial-guard force stationed at all strong points. Machine guns, antiaircraft weapons, and other equipment were in place. We were swept through the main gate without delay and drove up to the front door, which was usually manned by a doorman. No one was there, and the door was unlocked. I pushed it open and walked into the lobby, where an aide-de-camp was usually stationed. I could find no aide or anyone else in the immediate vicinity. I walked through into the main drawing room. There was no one there either. While I was puzzling what to do next, a door from one of the small rooms off the drawing room opened and the shahbanou came in. She was obviously surprised to see me, and I had clearly not expected that she would be the first person I would encounter there.

When I told her I had been asked to come to see the shah, she went back into one of the rooms and shortly rounded up one aide-de-camp, who was then followed by two or three others. They told me the shah was upstairs in his study, and one of them escorted me there without delay.

I found the shah strangely calm. He told me that he had just returned from a helicopter trip over the city shortly before dusk and that it looked like a wasteland. He said that hundreds of buildings were burning and that destruction seemed to be everywhere. He said he felt he had no choice but to establish a military government. He asked me whether I could quickly ascertain whether Washington would support him in this move. I told him that I had already anticipated this request and had received Washington's assurance that he would be supported in this action by the president and the United States government. He seemed enormously relieved and ordered a whiskey for me. He then told me he had also asked the British ambassador to attend, suggesting that we await his arrival.

He seemed surprised when I told him that the British chancery had been burned and that the British ambassador was at the French compound. He said this would explain why Ambassador Parsons had asked for an armored personnel carrier to pick him up at the French embassy and bring him to the palace. He then began a rambling discourse about the activities of the British Broadcasting Company and the reports they had broadcast concerning Iran. He felt, he said, that any attack on the British compound had probably been inspired by those broadcasts, which he considered sympathetic to his opponents and overly critical of his regime.

All day long I had heard rumors that the burnings were an action by professional arson squads of SAVAK, who were using this means to provoke the shah into a drastic reaction that would install a military government. I told the shah I had heard these rumors and asked him whether he felt they were true. He looked at me tiredly, shrugged his shoulders, and said, "Who knows? These days I am prepared to believe anything."

It was nearly another hour before the British ambassador arrived, and during that period the shah rehearsed once again his familiar arguments about the options open to him. In the middle of this he received a telephone call from the shahbanou. Although my understanding of Farsi was less than adequate, I could make out that he was telling her of his intention to install a military government and answering some of the reservations she was expressing about such a decision. It was a gentle, patient sort of conversation with nothing peremptory in its tone. He informed her at the end that the United States government had agreed with the wisdom of this course of action. Once this conversation was concluded, he picked up the phone and called General Azhari, the chief of staff, asking him to come to the palace as soon as he could get there.

After the arrival of the British ambassador, the shah offered elaborate apologies for the destruction of the British chancery and asked him to assure his government that it would be rebuilt at Iranian expense. He then proceeded to lay out his decision to install a military government and asked whether the British government had expressed any views on this subject. Ambassador Parsons indicated he had no instructions and probably would be unable to seek them immediately, because his communications equipment had been destroyed in the chancery fire. The shah did not press the matter further except to say he would install the government that evening and announce it in the morning.

On the way out of the palace, we met Azhari in the waiting room below. We confirmed his assumption as to why he had been summoned and wished him sincere good luck as he assumed his new duties. Azhari, who was anything but a power-hungry general, looked dejected as he climbed the stairs to see the shah and receive his new assignment.

18

Political Manuevers

With the installation of the military government, five separate courses of action began to take shape in Iran. The first, an effort to restore law and order, was directed by General Azhari and his government. It concentrated not only on the resolution of strikes that had spread throughout the industrial sector of the country, but also on preparations for an election and for the installation of a democratically controlled government.

At the same time, and with no mutual consultation, a movement began to attempt a negotiated political settlement between the shah and the oppositionists. This effort was directed by the shah himself and involved all sorts of intermediaries, most of them drawn from political leaders of a generation past. The personalities involved were not necessarily directly associated with the leaders of the political actions against the shah's regime; they were people the shah felt to be capable of influencing those oppositionists.

A third strand was a line of activity that was directed primarily by Ardeshir Zahedi but that tied into the United States government through the person of Zbigniew Brzezinski. This was an effort by Zahedi to rally forces loyal to the shah in order to preclude a compromise political solution and to achieve enough strength among those forces to dissuade the oppositionists from staging a successful revolution.

The fourth line of action and the one that received the most public attention was the activity of the oppositionists themselves. This was led largely by Ayatollah Khomeini from his exile in Paris, where he was surrounded by a group of political activists such as Ibrahim Yazdi, who had moved there from the United States. In Iran, the actions of this group were headed by two ayatollahs, Beheshti and Taleghani, and by a group of civilians led by Mehdi Bazargan, Amir Entezam, and Nasser Minatchi.

Finally, in counterpoint to all these actions were preparations I was making in an effort to preserve United States national interests as the turmoil enveloped Iran. My assumption was a contingency in which the shah would lose power, and my purpose, in that contingency, was to try to preserve a working relationship for the United States that would preempt Soviet opportunities flowing from a successful revolution.

Our embassy was plugged in to all these various lines of action and attempted to keep a watch on them as they developed. Their development, over the course of November and December, confirmed my worst fears that a preservation of the shah and his authority would be impossible and that the contingency of his departure was one for which we should seriously prepare.

In all these various lines of activity, the work of Prime Minister Azhari and his military government was doubtless the most straightforward. As a career military man, Azhari had learned to tackle problems in a direct manner. He saw his task as one in which he could use the authority of his office and the force of the military to bring the citizens of Iran to an appreciation of their national responsibilities. He considered the widespread strikes, particularly those in the oil fields, detrimental to the national interests and welfare of the country. He believed that, by persuasion and by his own personality, he could bring people to divorce this sort of action from the political measures that were in progress. Indeed, he considered the political process to be outside the effective functioning of the national economy and hoped he could confine his own efforts to the restoration of an orderly process in the everyday life of the country.

He began his work by appointing a cabinet made up exclusively of military officers. Since the task of government had been given to him late one evening and since he had to assume his responsibilities immediately, he had little opportunity to solicit support from a broader civilian spectrum of competence. Accordingly, he merely assigned senior military officers to various portfolios and instructed them to move into their cabinet positions and try to restore the working spirit of the country. Within a few days, however, he released most of these officers from their functions and permitted them to return to their primary responsibilities in the armed forces. In their stead he recruited competent administrators from various elements of Iranian public life and eventually created a cabinet in which only two portfolios in addition to his own were held by members of the military. It therefore became something of an anomaly, after the first few days, to refer to his government as a "military" government.

Among the senior military officials who did retain cabinet portfolios was General Abbas Gharabaghi, the commander of the gendarmerie. A senior army officer with impressive credentials, Gharabaghi had been one of those chosen by Reza Shah to be educated along with Mohammed Reza Pahlavi as a leader of the country. He had attended the Iranian military academy as a classmate of the shah and had been a close associate of the imperial family ever since.

His basic education, outside of Iran, had been received in France, where he had attended a number of senior military courses and where he had learned to speak impeccable French.

He was married to an attractive woman of good Iranian family, whose relatives were closely associated with the Shi'a ulema. Her immediate family was known for being devoutly Moslem, and her influence had extended to making the general, despite his military profession and military bearing, well known as a devout supporter of Shi'a Islamic issues.

My wife and I had come to know the Gharabaghis quite well in the course of our term of office in Iran, and we often had them as guests in our home. Because Gharabaghi could not speak English very well, and because he was head of the gendarmerie with which our military mission was not directly associated, he had had only limited contact with our military representatives in Iran. We found him to be well disposed toward the United States, an admirer of our political system, and a man greatly concerned about Soviet intentions with respect to his country.

Shortly after he had assumed his cabinet responsibilities, I went to call on Gharabaghi in his new office at the ministry of interior. He laid out in some detail his perceptions of the immediate situation and his responsibilities for handling the functions of the interior ministry. He regarded as his foremost task the organization of elections to a national parliament. With considerable French logic, he described to me the manner in which he expected to proceed down this course and seemed to be turning most of his energies toward it. As far as the gendarmerie was concerned, he felt that under martial law its command had effectively passed to the military headquarters and seemed relieved not to have a continuing responsibility in that area.

Azhari himself, whom I saw regularly in his office, felt that his prime effort should be directed toward achieving a more cooperative relationship between the governing authorities and the population at large. Accordingly, he made several television appeals to the nation and spoke in hortatory terms about the responsibilities of civilians to the nation, without invoking any particular reference, other than the rhetorical one, to the government of the shah.

Moreover, he appeared in public debate in the parliament as he presented his new cabinet for confirmation. This debate was broadcast on national television and provided an opportunity for him to lay out some of the tasks he saw facing the nation. The debate also provided an opportunity for many of the oppositionists within the parliament to express their criticism of the shah and of the current constitutional system. It was a spectacle that most living Iranians had never witnessed, and it involved the closest thing to a free political debate that had taken place in the country over the past thirty years.

Privately, in his office, Azhari confided to me his concern for the situation in the oil fields. He felt that the strikes being conducted there and in other key sectors of the economy were run from behind the scenes by the Tudeh party and organized for the benefit of the Soviet Union. He seemed to have no specific evidence to back up this concern, but the nature and tactics of those who were leading the strikes convinced him that they were not Iranians of Islamic persuasion. The struggle to restore oil production became a sort of barometer that Azhari used to test and record the success of his prime-ministerial mission. He did succeed in the first few weeks in office in bringing back daily production to respectable levels; these fell short of the 1977 average but indicated that some sort of progress was being made in the struggle for law and order in Iranian industry.

Nevertheless, shortages of fuel, stoppages in electrical production, and hoarding of food continued apace. In the month of November the economy of the country was in a parlous state, and many foreign observers reached the conclusion that economic problems would soon force the government and the shah to their knees.

The situation in the streets was only temporarily improved. For the first few days of the Azhari government, the presence of the military in office and of large numbers of tanks, armored vehicles, and troops within the city, had produced a calming effect on those who had previously been demonstrating with such violence. Moreover, the shock that had been caused by the arsonist rampage on November 4 had some aftereffects. Some Iranians recognized that the violence had gone much further than people had anticipated, and preferred to have a period of calm rather than a continuation of the disorders that had beset the city in October. Cleaning up the rubble from the burned-out buildings and establishing a semblance of tidiness in the city became paramount preoccupations of the army and the police. By the end of November, the city and the country had achieved a better balance than had prevailed at the beginning of the month.

The shah, in the meantime, was engaged in quite different activities. He seemed detached from the day-to-day work of the Azhari cabinet, and both he and Azhari made something of the fact that the latter was operating independently. This was, of course, a significant departure from past practice, in which the shah concerned himself with almost every little detail of governmental administration. Now the shah was preoccupied with an effort to reshape the basic constitutional structure of his regime.

In this effort he began to meet with a whole series of political figures from the past. The first and most prominent of these was Ali Amini, a former prime minister who had been regarded in his time as a special favorite of the Americans. Amini, a wealthy landowner, had served as ambassador to the United States and had introduced various political, economic, and social reforms during his brief tenure as prime minister in 1961–62. The conventional wisdom at that time was that he had been installed in office at the urging of President John Kennedy and that his reforms reflected American attitudes toward the Iranian situation of the time.

Amini was consulted by the shah in an effort to make political adjustments that would, in effect, cut the ground out from under the more radical changes being sought by Ayatollah Khomeini. The discussions that the shah had with Amini centered on a reduction of the shah's overall power, a restoration of certain constitutional authorities to the parliament, and a series of reforms that would introduce the symbols of democracy to political practice in Iran.

In holding these talks with Amini, the shah hoped he could persuade a number of other political figures—principally from the old Social Democrat and Mossadeq tendencies—to join with him and to accept governmental responsibilities. He was, for example, prepared to hold genuinely free parliamentary elections and to let the parliament nominate the prime minister. He was also prepared to have the prime minister function in a Western European manner, without daily interference from the palace. He was also prepared to let the parliament handle such matters as the budget and the development of national petroleum policy. This would include the subordination of the National Iranian Oil Company to the decisions of the cabinet government.

On the other hand, the shah was not prepared to give up his position as commander in chief of the armed forces or even to permit the parliament and the cabinet to determine the military budget. He stated that the armed forces were the "instrument of the king" and that they were needed for national-defense responsibilities that could be vested only in a sovereign who had the objective interests of the country in mind. Although Amini did not agree with him on this point, he nevertheless undertook to go to Paris to discuss this sort of political action with members of Ayatollah Khomeini's entourage and to see whether a compromise might be reached that would defuse the developing revolution.

During the course of these negotiations and discussions, I met about every other day with the shah for lengthy conversations concerning his activities and the thoughts that underlay them. Time and again he described to me his reluctance to use military force to suppress the growing rebellion, and time and again he suggested that he was prepared to take political actions that, in his own judgment, were more progressive than he felt the Iranian society was prepared to absorb. His constant theme was that a revolution led "by the mullahs" would only be a stepping stone to a revolution dominated by the Communists under the direction of the Soviet Union. He therefore felt it was necessary to take actions that he would normally consider politically imprudent in order to save the country from the two-step deterioration he saw in a "black and red" revolution. In this phrase of his the black referred to the turbans of the ayatollahs, the red to the banners of the Communists.

At the same time, I was meeting, regularly but in a curious fashion, with Amini in order to hear his version of the negotiations. Since Amini did not wish to exaggerate the accusations that he was an American agent, he declined to come to our embassy and was reluctant to have me meet with him in his home. We therefore met—in what he considered a clandestine mode—at the home of an employee of the United States Information Service. Due to the strikes and the shortage of fuel and electricity, we usually held these meetings huddled in our overcoats in a cold and lightless living room, sipping tea and munching on small Iranian cookies. Because of the quaint "clandestine" manner of our meeting and because I was always accompanied by my bodyguards from the Iranian national police, I am sure the suspicious authorities of SAVAK and the shah concluded that Amini was indeed an American agent. They would have been less likely to reach this conclusion if we had met openly at the American embassy.

These discussions made it clear that Amini remained pessimistic about the shah's political program. He told me his own advice to the shah was that he would have to surrender not only the political power that he claimed he was prepared to transfer to the parliament, but also control over the armed forces and the military budget. Amini reminded me that in his previous function as prime minister the issue on which he and the shah had parted was control of the military budget. He therefore felt strongly about this point.

Moreover, Amini said he had told the shah that no political figure would believe the promises he was offering unless he and his family took extended leave from Iran and stayed abroad while the political process was being worked out. In his conversations with me, the shah had not mentioned this aspect of Amini's reaction.

After Amini's visit to Paris and his consultation with the ayatollah's retinue, he returned to tell the shah that he did not believe the compromise offer would be adequate or that it would forestall the political activities of the ayatollah. Privately he told me that he felt the ayatollah and his people were unwilling to accept any compromise and that they would hold out bitterly until the shah had actually abdicated. In his conversation with the shah, however, he said he had left the issue unresolved on the basis of the shah's reluctance to accept a military-budget responsibility for the parliament and of his unwillingness to take an extended vacation.

After the Amini interlude, the shah began to meet with other political figures, most of them of the same vintage. These were men in their seventies who had had previous political experience and who were generally held in high public regard. As these conversations took place over the next few weeks, the shah's position gradually changed. In due course he accepted the fact that a military budget would have to be the responsibility of the parliament and the cabinet. He even accepted the idea of an extended absence from the country. This acceptance took place in a curious set of stages.

On one day he would talk to me in terms of going to Bandar 'Abbas, down on the Persian Gulf, and living in a navy compound where he would be out of public communication but where he would not physically be absent from the country. A few days later he amended this to a willingness to go to the island of Kish in the Persian Gulf, where he had a winter home. Subsequently, he talked in terms of going out on the imperial yacht and staying within the Persian Gulf. Finally, he was prepared to have the yacht moved out into international waters and be literally absent from Iranian territory. It was only in the last part of December, when his desperation became acute, that he was willing to talk in terms of leaving the country for an extended period and naming a regency council to rule in his absence.

In short, all the steps the shah was willing to take politically were always too little and too late. In retrospect it is improbable that any action he might have taken would have defused the revolution. In fact, by the time he was brought to contemplate these measures, the revolution had accumulated such momentum that it is unlikely it could have been averted. Indeed, as his opponents saw the concessions he was willing to make, he only whetted their appetite for further concessions and convinced them he was on the run. Nevertheless, for nearly two months the shah engaged in these rather feckless political maneuvers, always seeking to find some formula that would attract political support from a broad enough segment of the population that it would pull a majority of the public away from those who, like Khomeini, were insisting on the dismissal of the Pahlavi regime as the ultimate course of political action.

19

Washington Emissaries

During the weeks when I was meeting regularly with the shah and reporting the results of our conversations to Washington, I received no specific political guidance about the attitude of the government of the United States. The shah had ceased the practice of having the British ambassador accompany me after the British government had failed to endorse the establishment of a military government in the wake of the events of November 4. Moreover, with the burning of the British chancery and the continued Iranian vexation with the BBC, the British embassy had assumed a far lower profile in Iran. In fact, Ambassador Parsons, who had spent more than four years in the country, was informed that he would shortly be leaving Iran for another posting. My conversations with the shah during this critical period were therefore of rather empty measure. In his own autobiography, the shah, in describing these conversations, said, "Whenever I met Sullivan and asked him to confirm these official statements, he promised he would. But a day or two later he would return, gravely shake his head and say that he had received 'no instructions' and therefore could not comment. Sullivan appeared to me always polite, always grave, always concerned. He came to see me several times a week. He seemed to take seriously everything I said to him. But his answer was always the same: 'I have received no instructions.' "*

While the shah was engaged in his political maneuvers, another player in the Iranian scenario was Ardeshir Zahedi. He installed himself in his home, which was perched on a lofty promontory overlooking Tehran, and operated at his usual high velocity. Because of his close friendship with the imperial family, he spent a great deal of time at the palace, dining with the shah and members of his family and pressing his views on them. The rest of the time he spent working with a small staff of old friends, attempting to build political support for the shah. In this effort he worked in two dimensions—the domestic Iranian level and the international level, particularly focusing on the United States. Domestically, he concentrated on those factions of Iranian society that had supported the shah, especially in the 1953 countercoup. On the international level, he concentrated primarily on American journalists and public opinion leaders, whom he invited to his home.

I saw quite a bit of Zahedi at this time, and he invited me to his home at least once a week. There I found a curious group of confederates, including members of the bazaar, clergymen, and military officers. Among the military was General Manuchehr Khowsradad, the commander of the helicopter forces and airborne troops. Khowsradad was a colorful hawk, outspoken in his support of the shah and contemptuous of the revolutionary forces building against him.

Zahedi's hope was to have the members of the clergy who were well disposed toward the shah, supported by those members of the bazaar who saw their economic and financial forces affiliated with the continuation of the Pahlavi regime, back the

---

*Mohammad Reza Pahlavi, *Answer to History* (New York: Stein and Day, 1980), p. 161.

more hawkish members of the military in a coalition like the one that his father had built in 1953. He then attempted to convince the visiting American journalists that this grouping, many of whom he would display to the journalists, constituted a "silent majority" that would eventually come out of their lethargy and preclude a revolution.

The enthusiasm with which Zahedi attacked his task was not shared by the shah. The shah would regularly speak to me about Zahedi's activities and tell me he did not approve of them. He would say that we should not be deceived into thinking that Zahedi's course of action was a fruitful one. He asked me to inform Washington that Zahedi did not understand the domestic situation in Iran and that, although his heart was in the right place, he was out of touch with reality.

Zahedi, on the other hand, was regularly in touch with Washington through Brzezinski. He would tell me that he had been reporting his efforts to Washington through this channel and had been encouraged to continue them. He said that he believed he was serving the expressed wishes of the United States government by attempting to stiffen the shah's spine and that he felt confident he had Washington's official blessing for his work.

Although I reported my conversations both with the shah and with Zahedi to Washington, I never received any clear indications of the official attitude of the United States government in regard to this entire realm of activity. In fact, during this period my communications from Washington grew increasingly confused. One of their extraordinary features was the increasing number of visitors who came from Washington to Iran in official or quasi-official capacities, carrying various messages to the shah. The first of these was an executive of a large American corporation who had formerly been the CIA station chief in Iran. Despite the fact that his company was negotiating with the government of Iran for a multibillion-dollar contract, this corporate official came on a diplomatic mission for Brzezinski. His purpose was to have a private meeting with the shah, assess the shah's state of mind, assure him of steadfast support, and urge him to take more forceful action against the political dissidents. Brzezinski sent me a message informing me of this mission and asking me to give all necessary support, including communications facilities, to the emissary.

Although I did and although the man involved in the mission comported himself as far as I could determine with considerable discretion, I nevertheless sent a message to Brzezinski expressing my reservations about using an official of a private corporation seeking a large contract with the shah as an emissary for the administration. Brzezinski sent back a sharp, tart report suggesting that what the administration chose to do was none of my business. I was aware from the tenor of this reply that my views were no longer held in much regard at the White House.

The next emissary from Washington to arrive was Mike Blumenthal, the secretary of the treasury. He had been in Iran the preceding year, primarily concerned with Iranian attitudes toward the price of oil. That same concern prompted him to make a trip to the region in 1978. Although he knew that the shah had led the movement toward price stability in international petroleum sales, and although he knew that the shah was preoccupied with political problems, he asked for an opportunity to meet with him once again to discuss these issues.

Blumenthal's visit was an interesting one. We went straight from the airport to a meeting with the new minister of finance, an old friend of the United States whose wife was American, who had received his education in our country, and who understood our concerns for stability in oil pricing. The meeting between Blumenthal and the minister was pleasant enough but not very productive, because the minister did not have much guidance regarding Iranian attitudes on oil prices.

The circumstances of the session were more instructive to

Blumenthal. As we left the Finance Ministry and were driving through some of the more teeming precincts of the Tehran bazaar, we came upon a demonstration that was in the process of being broken up by the armed forces. There was considerable firing into the air and scrambling by the fleeing demonstrators. A few cans of tear gas were thrown, and there were the usual accoutrements of a street clash. Although this had become an everyday occurrence to us in the embassy and although Haikaz took it all in stride, the event caused much consternation among Blumenthal's Secret Service detail. The upshot of their concern was that the Secret Service driver of the chase car—one of our armored vehicles—crashed into the rear of my Chrysler, in which Blumenthal and I were riding, when Haikaz was forced to make an abrupt stop and change direction as we threaded our way through the turmoil. In an effort to ease the Secret Service tension, I told the head of the detail, who was riding in our car, that I expected full Treasury Department compensation for the damage to our two vehicles. Without the slightest trace of humor, he assured me that the Secret Service would accept the responsibility, and a few weeks later I received a memorandum from Washington asking for a bill to cover the costs of repair to the cars.

Blumenthal's audience with the shah was equally instructive. When we called at the palace, we found him in one of his more depressed moods. His efforts to reach a political compromise were running out, and he seemed aware that few options remained. His interest in the price of oil or any other economic matter was minimal. He sat lethargically through the conversation with Blumenthal, his contribution to the dialogue desultory.

In a luncheon that followed, in which he was joined by the shahbanou, he was scarcely more animated. Blumenthal, who, like other emissaries from Washington, had been charged to stiffen the shah's resolve, was shocked by his attitude and later told me he saw no prospect that a man in such a mood could attain the resolve to take political or other forceful action to preserve his authority.

And yet the emissaries continued to come. The next was Bob Bowie, the number-three man in the CIA, who came as a suddenly added supernumerary in a previously scheduled military-intelligence mission. For some years the United States Defense Intelligence Agency had arranged to give the shah an annual briefing concerning military developments that had a direct bearing on the national security of Iran. This briefing concerned not only the disposition of potential enemy forces but also detailed descriptions of new weapons systems that were introduced into positions that could threaten Iran. General Tighe, the chief of DIA, was scheduled to give this briefing, and when he arrived he was accompanied by Bob Bowie, who sat in on the session but did not take an active part.

Bowie was an old Washington hand who had moved into the political and intelligence community from his academic experience at Harvard. He had at one time served as counselor of the Department of State and was a man of considerable experience and wisdom.

During the briefing, the shah, who had usually been animated and interested in this annual event, was detached, uninspired, almost uninterested. He asked a number of casual questions but took little active part in the proceedings. Like Blumenthal, Bowie went away with the impression that the shah was not a man who was prepared to take vigorous action to defend his position.

The final and perhaps most prestigious Washington emissary was the then Senate majority leader, Robert C. Byrd. Bob Byrd, who is not only an astute politician but also a shrewd judge of personalities, has a son-in-law who was originally of Iranian nationality. He therefore had a certain background in Iran and had for years maintained a lively interest in the country. He arrived in Iran aboard a presidential aircraft in November with a fairly large group of his staff. On the evening of his arrival, he and his staff met with me and several members of my staff at the embassy residence. He asked me to give my view of events and my evaluation of the shah's position. After I had painted a rather gloomy picture of the situation and of the shah's will, Byrd told me that that was not the way the situation seemed to be perceived in Washington. He then described a briefing he had received from Brzezinski that suggested that the shah was fully prepared to take action to defend himself but was being inhibited from that course of action by the confusing signals he was receiving from the Department of State and our embassy. He said he had been asked to convey to the shah the strongest assurances of our support and to encourage him to take the action necessary to defend his throne. I asked Byrd whether this message was intended to entail a United States encouragement for the shah to use force in order to kill the political opposition in the streets. He immediately recoiled from any such thought and said he would never intend to convey that sort of suggestion to the shah. I told him that if he did intend to express the message he had just laid out to me, he should anticipate a question from the shah about whether the United States government wished him to shoot his political opponents. This shocked Byrd, but he immediately recognized the implications that would be involved in delivering the message he had been prompted to bring.

In an effort to resolve the parallax that Byrd seemed to find between the perception he had received in Washington and the one we had given him in Tehran, I suggested he have private breakfast the next morning with his son-in-law's relatives and obtain an assessment from Iranians about the state of events.

Byrd agreed, although he asked that the breakfast include a few other Americans so that it would not be exclusively a family affair.

The breakfast went off about as I had expected. The older

members of the son-in-law's family expressed their support for, but grave concern about, the situation of the shah, while the younger ones voiced their strong opposition to the shah and their feeling that he should abdicate his throne. This discussion proved a sobering experience for the senator, who told me en route to the palace that he found the situation in the country somewhat more depressing and certainly more complicated than he had realized in Washington.

The meeting at the palace confirmed the atmosphere of depression. Although the shah was not quite as lethargic as he had been during the Blumenthal meeting, he was, nevertheless, thoroughly negative in his assessment of the situation and in his response to the senator's expression of support. The luncheon that followed was a disaster. Although the shahbanou attempted to maintain some conversation and to keep the impression of civility going, the shah merely sat in his place and looked at the ceiling throughout the entire ordeal. He hardly touched his food, and his expression was one of hangdog indifference. His face had now become more ashen, his age was beginning to show, and his former physical vigor had clearly waned.

Unfortunately, I could not have an extended discussion with Senator Byrd after the luncheon. I had scheduled some time in advance a meeting with the American business community, in order to give them our assessment of the security problems that the Ashura demonstrations would pose in the next few days, and I wanted to lay out for them a program of staged evacuation that would remove some of the dependents and some of the unnecessary personnel from the country. I thus had to go from the palace directly back to the embassy while the senator went by helicopter from the palace to the airport. It is nevertheless my impression from the few words we were able to exchange privately that he had come to accept our generally gloomy assessment of the shah's situation rather than the more upbeat views he had heard at the White House.

20

Thinking the Unthinkable

Sharif-Emami's decision to encourage the Iraqis to expel Ayatollah Khomeini boomeranged. The ayatollah went to Paris,
taking advantage of a "no visa" provision that the French had
previously arranged for holders of Iranian passports. There he
established residence colorfully in a small villa on the outskirts
of the city and surrounded himself with advisors and acolytes
from the United States, Iran, and other parts of the world. He
was the cynosure of the world press and had access to television
almost daily. This exotic figure, sitting under a tree in the
garden of a French villa, hurling verbal thunderbolts at the
shah, and apparently controlling an Islamic revolution several
thousand miles away, attracted the attention of the world.

The sophisticated telephone- and radio-communication system that we had built for the Iranians enabled the ayatollah
and his group to have instantaneous contact with their followers in Tehran. Most of their work was done through a network
of ayatollahs and mullahs headed by two clerics, Ayatollah
Beheshti and Ayatollah Taleghani, who were by far the most
interesting among the Iranian ayatollahs. Both of them were
intelligent, educated men who had attended a university and

Mission to Iran

seen something of the outside world. Beheshti, in particular, who had a degree from the University of Tübingen in Germany, appreciated the more secular aspects of the revolution that were beyond the experience of Ayatollah Khomeini. For eight years Beheshti had lived in Hamburg and directed the Shi'a Islamic center there. During that time he acquired not only a Western education but also a deep distrust of the Soviets and the East German Communists who controlled the Communist Tudeh party in Iran.

In addition to these religious figures, a network of the ayatollah's supporters also centered on Mehdi Bazargan, Amir Entezam, and Nasser Minatchi, the leaders of the so-called Liberation Front. They too had direct contact with the ayatollah's entourage, primarily through Ibrahim Yazdi, an Iranian immigrant to the United States who had lived many years in Houston, Texas, and acquired United States nationality.

In Tehran, our political section was actively in touch with the Liberation Front group under the direction of Bazargan and kept well informed of their attitudes toward the revolution. In due course we also established direct contact with Ayatollah Beheshti through one of the Farsi-speaking foreign-service officers who had previously served in Tehran and whom I brought back to the country to assist us in broadening our associations with the revolutionary groups. We found both of these men to be interesting personalities, generally well disposed toward the United States despite our government's ties with the shah and his regime, which they were pledged to overthrow. They seemed to recognize that the prime threat to the future of Iran came from the Soviet Union and that the United States, despite its close association with the shah, had long been a force for social, economic, and political improvement for the people of Iran. We were never quite certain, however, whether the attitudes they represented to us were reflected in their followers, particularly in those young radical groups that had led so much of the opposition activities in the streets of major Iranian cities.

Faced with all these conflicting tendencies, I tried to make an objective assessment of the situation and determine the proper course of action that the United States government should pursue in order to protect our national interests in Iran. Shortly after General Azhari had taken office as prime minister, I reached the conclusion that this military government, in effect, represented the shah's last chance for survival. If it failed to restore law and order and if it did not succeed in resuming the industrial production in the country, the success of the revolution, I felt, was inevitable and we should face the consequences of that fact. On November 9, 1978, I wrote a cable setting forth some of these fundamental considerations and making recommendations for our future policy.

In that cable, which I entitled "Thinking the Unthinkable," I restated some fundamental clichés about Iran and examined how they were changing. For example, I pointed out the conventional wisdom that stability in Iran rested on two pillars— the monarchy and the Shi'a religion. I noted that, for the preceding fifteen years, the religious pillar had been largely subordinate to the monarchic. The changes in the vitality of the religious side were manifest, but it was necessary to examine what was happening on the monarchic side.

There, it was clear that the shah's public support had shrunk dramatically. His only real strength came from the military. This change had been so widely noted that it had become commonplace among most observers to refer to the monarchic pillar as the shah—supported by the military.

However, I went on, even that relationship had changed with the installation of a military government. It had been converted into a situation that reflected the strength of the military—"which currently supports the shah." I felt that these altered circumstances required us to examine the relationship, both actual and potential, between the military and the religious.

In this examination, I argued that the relationship would be determined by the success that the Azhari government would have in breaking the religious grip over the economy that was manifested by the strikes and civil-disobedience campaigns they were directing. I felt that, even if the military succeeded, the results would be a continuation of tension and an increase in terrorism.

If, on the other hand, the military failed to dominate the religious, then we should, I thought, examine the consequences for United States interests that might result from an accommodation between the two institutions. My conclusion was that such an accommodation might be "essentially satisfactory" for us, particularly if it worked out peacefully along the lines I then laid out for Washington's consideration.

In these lines, I posited a situation in which not only the shah but most of the senior Iranian military officers would leave the country. Understandings about the nature of a successor regime would be reached between the religious leadership and the new, younger military leadership. In such understandings, Ayatollah Khomeini would have to choose a government headed by moderate figures like Bazargan and Minatchi, and eschew the "Nasser-Qadhafi" types, which I assumed he would prefer. Arrangements would have to be made for an orderly series of elections to produce a constituent assembly, a new constitution, and eventually a parliament.

My assumption was that the religious leadership, including Khomeini, might accept such an arrangement because it would give them their essential objective, the elimination of the shah, avoid a bloodbath, and endow them with armed forces willing to maintain law and order on behalf of the new regime.

From our point of view, it would be satisfactory because it would avoid chaos, ensure the continued integrity of the country, preclude a radical leadership, and effectively block Soviet domination of the Persian Gulf. In these circumstances, the major losses, as I saw them would be a reduction in the intimacy of our military and security relations, a shift on Iran's part from a pro-Israeli to an anti-Zionist position, and a certain aloofness in our overall dealings.

While this situation would certainly be less appealing than the arrangements we had enjoyed under the shah, it would obviously be better than one in which an inchoate revolution would succeed and the integrity of the armed forces be destroyed. I therefore suggested we begin to "think the unthinkable" and prepare for this contingency.

It is my understanding, from subsequent reports, that this cable caused some consternation in Washington. That result, however, followed not from any detailed debate over my analysis and recommendation but rather from the president's reaction when he read it. According to these reports, it was the first time he became aware that the shah might not survive. If this is so, it meant either that he was so preoccupied with the Camp David process that he had neglected to notice our cables or else that his national-security briefers had chosen not to trouble him with the problems in Iran.

In any event, it is said that after reading this cable, he wrote notes in longhand to Vance, Brzezinski, Brown, and CIA Director Stansfield Turner asking why he had not been informed of the situation in Iran. For some mysterious reason, which had to do with the White House perception of political leadership, the existence of these handwritten notes was then forthwith leaked to the press.

Given the peculiar nature of Washington symbiotics, this leakage seems to have produced a strange and unpredictable reaction to my cable. Instead of making a reasoned, responsible study of the suggestions I had posed, the bureaucracy apparently began to focus instead on the implications of the president's notes. Each element tried its best to deflect and deny responsibility for the president's alleged ignorance of the true situation in Iran. Brzezinski, in particular, seemed to have been especially sensitive to the implications and reportedly appeared to have chosen to react by attempting to demonstrate that the dire nature of my prognosis was untrue. Some published reports suggest that, in order to disprove my thesis that the shah might not survive, he was spurred to take every sort of action to assure that the shah would survive and thereby exculpate himself from any failure to have kept the president informed of an impending crisis.

Whatever the situation in Washington, and whatever the motivations of the individuals involved, I did not seem able to get any serious "thinking the unthinkable" by those responsible for policy formulation. My normal experience with cables of this sort led me to expect that a significant review of our policy would take place in Washington and that I would receive some guidance concerning the attitudes of our administration toward my recommendations. I waited in vain for any such response. In fact, the cable was never answered by Washington.

We drifted through the remainder of November and into December with no guidance from the Department of State or from Washington in general. The Department of State spokesman and the president himself publicly reasserted the administration's support for the shah. These pronouncements were made with such regularity that they became something of a joke among the American news media. In fact, the shah himself in due course told me that he was somewhat embarrassed by the constant reiteration of our public support, saying that it made him look like a puppet of the United States in such a manner as to undermine the credibility of his independence.

The journalists who were flocking to Iran at this time were people who, in general, had little experience in the Persian Gulf area and who did not choose to stay in Iran for any length of time. Before the onset of the revolution, most American press services had closed their offices in Iran, largely because it had become enormously expensive to maintain journalists in the country and because the atmosphere for their operations was not congenial. Moreover, the costs of transmitting their copy, either by satellite for television or by cable for printed news, had become prohibitive in the judgment of their American headquarters.

As a result, with the exception of one or two young stringers, there were no permanent press representatives in Iran. One of the few journalists with some continuity in the area and therefore some understanding of the local scene was Joe Alex Morris of the *Los Angeles Times*. Morris, whose father had before him been a journalist in the Middle East, made his home in Athens but undertook frequent visits to Iran and other surrounding countries. He was well informed, understood the history and culture of the country, and had excellent contacts among the Iranians. But he was definitely an exception to the rule.

Most of the journalists who came to cover events during the turbulent days of November and early December were veterans of Indo-Chinese journalism, chosen to come to Iran largely because of their experience in living in and reporting stressful situations where flying bullets were a daily fact of life. With the end of the American involvement in Vietnam, these journalists had been scattered to various quarters of the country and the world. They therefore came to Tehran on short notice from other journalistic beats and usually spent only a few weeks at a time in the country. They were then relieved by other journalists of similar background who made similarly short stays in the country. As a consequence of this pattern of press coverage, much of the reporting that the American public saw and read was impressionistic, written by journalists who were stumbling onto a story for the first time.

Inevitably, many of these journalists sought some sort of embassy guidance and information in order to pick up the thread of events when they first arrived in the country. Since most of them wished to see the American ambassador shortly after they arrived, I made a practice of receiving them in groups about once a week and answering their questions on a background basis. I deliberately sought to stay off the record in these conversations and succeeded in doing so except in one instance when a reporter chose to violate the understanding on which we had conversed.

These background briefings presented something of a problem for me. I wished to be as candid and honest with the press as I could, yet I was under constant prodding from Washington to avoid giving an impression of pessimism in our assessment of the shah's situation. When press stories appeared in the United States giving a gloomy picture of the situation in Iran, and when their content clearly indicated that they reflected official briefings from the embassy, I regularly received messages from Washington reminding me that the United States government's policy was to support the shah and that I should avoid undermining that policy in my relations with the press.

The journalists, of course, did not need instruction from me to be gloomy about the situation. After a few hours in the country, they were able to establish contact with dissident groups and at the same time make objective assessments of the situation on the ground. This generally resulted in press coverage that was in sharp contrast to the expressions of support and confidence emanating from Washington spokesmen. It was an awkward situation that none of us in the embassy particularly enjoyed.

In December of 1978, a delegation of Americans who were not associated with the press came to see me. This small group was headed by Ramsey Clark and included a professor from Princeton University. They described themselves as concerned citizens and asked for my candid view of the situation. Since Clark gave me assurances that I could speak with candor and that nothing I said would be repeated publicly, I gave them a pessimistic assessment of conditions and expressed the view that the revolution was probably going to succeed. This, of course, coincided with their own conclusions; their interests and sympathies obviously lay far more with the revolutionaries than with the shah. Unfortunately, when the group was in Paris in an effort to see the ayatollah, the Princeton professor could not resist making my assessment public. This publication brought a sharp cable from Washington reminding me of the United States government's policy of support for the shah and asking whether I had been directly quoted. I replied that the substance of what I had said appeared to be correctly reported, but that the people to whom I said it had agreed not to make it public. This incident created further tension between the embassy and the White House.

At about this time I also discovered that messages we had sent from our embassy in Tehran with the highest security classification began to appear, almost verbatim, in the *New York Times*. It seemed clear that sharp policy differences existed between various groups in Washington and that the leaking of cables was being used as an instrument to further particular viewpoints in this internal bureaucratic battle. Accordingly, I informed Washington that in the future I would refrain from sending sensitive messages through the normal cable traffic and would conduct the bulk of my sensitive business on the secure scramble telephone linking the embassy with selected senior officers of the Department of State. While this had the effect of stopping much of the leakage, it also introduced an additional problem. Because Iran is nine hours out of phase with Washington, it usually meant that I had to walk across the compound in the middle of the night to conduct my conversations from the secure-radio shack in the chancery whenever either Washington had something important to say to me or I had something I wished to convey to the secretary of state.

While all this rather confusing activity was taking place on the political side, a great deal of our energies in the embassy during November and early December were occupied with the protection of the American community in the face of increasing violence. At the beginning of 1978, approximately thirty-five thousand Americans lived in Iran. As the year wore on and violence continued, there were some limited reductions in this number, primarily families leaving because the civil disorders had disrupted the business in which they were engaged. After a number of business offices were burned on November 4, that quiet trickle of departures became more pronounced. Nevertheless, by the beginning of December an informal census indicated that we still had nearly twenty thousand Americans in the country. As troubles multiplied and as we met regularly with the American community, the embassy began to recommend selective departures for those who had no urgent need to stay in the country and for those families whose presence could be spared.

As we approached the Shi'a holy month of Moharram, the American community's uneasiness increased. Moharram is a period of mourning climaxed by two days of Ashura, when the Shi'a faithful usually display their piety by acts of public flagellation and processions honoring the martyrs of Shi'a history. In the past these events had often given rise to violence as the mourners confronted police authorities.

In the light of this past experience, and in anticipation of a major Shi'a emphasis on the ashura observance in 1978, the American community, largely at its own initiative, began to make preparations for extended Christmas holidays. Since the days of Ashura fell on December 10 and 11 in 1978, and since arrangements were made to close the American school before those dates, it became convenient for American families to think in terms of long Christmas holidays.

Seeing these preparations going forward in the private business community, members of the official American community also made inquiries about their prospects for similar temporary departures from Iran. In due course the Department of State granted authorization for the dependents of U.S. government officials in the country to have the same opportunity to depart as had been arranged by American business concerns for the families of their employees. This meant the activation of a "safe-haven" plan that would permit the families of American officials to go to designated cities in Europe, where they could remain temporarily until events sorted themselves out.

As this authorization arrived at the embassy and families began to sign up for the safe-haven program, I felt that I should, in all candor, advise them that, in my judgment, any families that left would probably not be returning to Iran, since I expected the situation to get worse rather than better. Some of the families to whom this advice was conveyed misinterpreted it as an effort on my part to prevent them from leaving the country because of the consequences their departure would have for the morale of the Iranian government. It took some persuasion for me to convince them and the officials whose dependents they were that I was merely giving them a stark expression of my assessment and suggesting that they condition themselves for a permanent departure from Iran rather than a temporary interlude over the Christmas holidays. For many of these officials and their families, this was the first intimation they had of the pessimism with which I viewed the future of Iran. Because the official Washington position had been so upbeat and because I did not choose to air my differences with Washington for the benefit of all those serving in the Tehran embassy, this revelation of my attitude came as something of a surprise.

At this stage the choice concerning departure was left on a voluntary basis, both in the official and the business community. Our census at the time of Ashura indicated that the American presence had been reduced to approximately twelve thousand people as the result of the voluntary exodus. This still left us a considerable problem to cope with in the protection of American citizens, but it made our mission somewhat more manageable as the days of Ashura drew near.

In the event, Ashura itself turned out to be peaceful. Arrangements were negotiated between the Azhari government and the representatives of the various revolutionary groups, so that no confrontations took place on those two days. The outpouring of people into the streets, however, was formidable. Estimates ranged from four hundred thousand on the part of Ardeshir Zahedi, who overflew the route of march in a helicopter, to two million on the part of the BBC correspondent. As best the embassy could determine, participants in the events that took place on those two days numbered at least one million on each day. In general, despite the somber occasion of mourning, the spirit of the marchers and demonstrators was relatively calm. Once again the organizational capability of the marshals who organized the processions was impressive. What was more significant, however, was the fact that the military and police abided by their understandings and stayed carefully away from the prescribed routes of march. The occasion of violence and the opportunity for a political confrontation that might have settled the fate of the shah's regime was thus averted by a Persian capacity for compromise. Everybody in Iran breathed a collective sigh of relief when Ashura was behind us.

Yet the old difficulties remained. Strikers in the oil fields, on the Iranian airline service, at electrical power plants, and in other key sectors of the nation's industry resumed their activities. Acute shortages of heating fuel, gasoline, and other vital commodities developed. It became commonplace to see people standing in long queues for cooking and heating oil, and long lines of motorists waiting a turn at the few gasoline stations that had fuel. Rioting broke out again, particularly around Tehran University. Other incidents involving shooting deaths took place daily. The nights once again erupted with sounds of staccato automatic-weapons fire and shouts of *"Allah-u-akbhar"* from the rooftops. The prospects for the restoration of law and order by the Azhari government seemed to be growing dim.

I was at home on the evening of December 20 when I

received a telephone call from Prime Minister Azhari. He asked in his gentle voice whether I could come to see him at my convenience. I said if it was urgent I would come immediately, but he assured me that the next day would be timely. Accordingly, I fixed a time for the early afternoon of December 21. Nothing in his voice or in the mild request for a meeting gave me any clue about the nature of the business he wished to transact.

I arrived at the prime minister's office at three o'clock the following afternoon and was taken up the familiar staircase toward the familiar reception room. Much to my surprise, however, the young military aide who was guiding me steered me past the doors to the large reception room and toward a small closed door on the left. He knocked gently, then opened the door into an unlit room. As I stepped in, I saw a light go on in the corner and there, to my astonishment, lay Prime Minister Azhari on a small army cot covered by an army blanket and clad in striped pajamas. My first irreverent reaction was to think of former Prime Minister Mossadeq, who had regularly received government officials, the press, and his public lying in bed wearing pajamas.

These thoughts were immediately banished, however, when I noticed a large oxygen bottle standing alongside the bed and observed the ashen, rather pained expression on Azhari's face. He motioned me toward his cot. My first words were to ask whether his doctors approved of my coming there and disturbing him at this time. He said that the doctors were just outside the door, that they knew I was coming, and that he thought this interview was more important than anything else they could prescribe at this moment.

The aide pulled up a chair alongside the cot while the general rested back on his pillow and began to talk in low, somber tones. He told me first that his illness was not severe, that he had suffered a mild cardiac problem, but that his doctors assured him he would be able to resume work in the near future.

He then said, however, that he was not quite sure what kind of work he could resume. He described to me the problems he had faced in attempting to install law and order, and the repeated instructions he had received from the shah concerning the way in which he should administer martial law. He said that the troops had now been in the streets for nearly four months and that they were becoming badly demoralized. The effect of their orders, which permitted them only to fire in the air, no matter how badly they were abused or how heavily they were pressed, left them in a state of shock.

After reciting all this, he propped himself up on one elbow and, looking at me, said, "You must know this and you must tell it to your government. This country is lost because the king cannot make up his mind." With that he settled back on the pillow. We shook hands and I left.

Given the rather dramatic nature of this interview, I reported it to Washington in much the same terms as I have used here. At the end of my report, I said it was clear to me that the contingency I had foreseen in my cable of November 9 had come to pass. The military government had failed in its mission to restore law and order. The downfall of the shah was inevitable. Therefore, I intended to take the action I had prescribed in my November 9 cable and would begin talks with the opposition and the armed forces, designed to help them reach an accommodation that would prevent the disintegration of the military forces. I received no instructions as a result of this cable that would stop me from my proposed course of action. Nevertheless, I was astounded two days later to hear the familiar refrain from Washington that the United States continued to support the shah and expected his government to survive the current turmoil.

When I saw the shah the next day and discussed with him the matter of Azhari's health, I refrained from repeating what Azhari had told me about the country's being lost. Nevertheless, in view of the comportment of the shah, I could only agree with the general's assessment. The shah talked largely about the need to find a replacement for Azhari because the general's health would not permit his continuation in office. By this time he had agreed to a number of concessions in his discussions with various members of the opposition but had yet to find one political leader who would be willing to assume the burden of the prime ministry. He spoke to me, however, of one or two politicians who he thought might be willing to face the task.

One of these was Shahpour Bakhtiar, a former minister in the Mossadeq government, a leading member of the Bakhtiari tribe, and a leader of a faction among the National Front movement of the Social Democrats. Bakhtiar, who had been educated in France, was an habitué of the French Club in Tehran and a man with whom we had occasional contact. Although he was a charming and articulate individual, our assessment was that he had no popular following and that his ability to act like an effective political leader was almost nil. Ironically enough, despite his indication that he might offer him the prime ministry, the shah's assessment of Bakhtiar seemed to be about the same. He outlined all his weaknesses and then told me he was "one of those worms" that always crawls out of the woodwork in times of trouble. I was therefore somewhat bemused when, a few days later, the shah told me Bakhtiar had agreed to accept the task of forming a government and that he, the shah, was prepared to install him as prime minister.

21

The Eliot Mission

Since I had received no instructions from Washington precluding the effort I had proposed of speaking with the leaders of the opposition and the military in an effort to avoid conflict between the revolution and the armed forces, I set in motion a number of actions by the embassy in pursuit of this objective. In my telephone conversations with Washington, I recommended that a similar set of actions be undertaken in Paris with the entourage of Ayatollah Khomeini.

I knew these actions would be observed by the Iranian intelligence services, and took the precaution of telling one of the shah's confidants, Hushang Ansari, the head of the National Iranian Oil Company, that we were making these various soundings and that the Iranian authorities should regard them as a normal effort to protect American national interests. Ansari seemed alarmed when I passed this information on to him and was clearly concerned that such a hot potato had been dropped in his lap. He telephoned me late the following morning in some agitation. He said that he had informed the shah what I had told him and that the shah seemed to understand. On the other hand the shah had asked him to pass on to me the warning that we should not become engaged, as the British had in 1906, as the protectors of the clergy and the advocates of the constitutional insurrections of that year. I told Ansari I understood the message, and I let the matter stand at that point. In all my subsequent discussions with the shah, he never indicated any concern about our actions and even, toward the very end of his regime, used to ask me with some curiosity what we were hearing from "your friends the mullahs."

Our initial soundings in Iran suggested that both the military leadership and the leadership of the liberation movement, as well as the senior clergy, believed it was important for some understandings to be reached between them. The military officers recognized that the morale of their troops had deteriorated to such a point that many of them were undependable in any confrontation. They also knew what we had observed: many of the demonstrators in the streets confronting the troops were the sons and brothers of the men who held the rifles. Although military units were regularly being rotated from one city to another, in order to avoid the problems inherent in such confrontations, the troop commanders' estimates and the opinions of our military advisors stationed with the Iranian forces suggested that the situation was very spongy indeed.

In response to our suggestions about contacts in Paris, the Department of State instructed our embassy in Paris to designate an officer who could meet with Ibrahim Yazdi. The officer chosen was Warren Zimmerman, head of the embassy political section. Zimmerman was a career professional who followed his instructions explicitly and who met on two or three occasions with Yazdi in a small restaurant near the ayatollah's suburban residence. Since his instructions were limited and since Zimmerman was not familiar with the internal situation in Iran, these contacts were not particularly productive. However, their general nature reflected the same points of view we were obtaining in Tehran. The members of the ayatollah's entourage were deeply concerned about the prospect of a clash with the military and wished to avoid it. Since they did not have weapons and did not particularly desire to have them as an adjunct of their revolution, they felt the prime necessity was to reach some understanding with the armed forces before the ayatollah's return to Iran.

That return had now become a matter of near certainty. It had been publicly stated that the shah was prepared to swear in Shahpour Bakhtiar as the new prime minister, to establish a council of regency, and then to depart Iran on a long vacation. To most Iranian observers this course of action was a fig leaf designed to permit the graceful departure of the shah and obscure the victory of the ayatollah and his revolution. Preparations were therefore seriously under way for the return of the ayatollah and his entourage to Tehran shortly after the start of the new year.

In the meantime, another small crisis struck the embassy. Ever since the assault on the British embassy, we had been protected by Iranian troops stationed at the gates of our compound and patrolling our perimeter. These troops came from different units and on any given day varied in number. If the circumstances looked calm, we would have as few as one platoon, but if Iranian military intelligence suggested that large, unruly crowds would be in the streets near the compound, we could have as many as one whole company deployed for our protection. On Christmas Eve we had one platoon of troops, which had never before been assigned to protect the compound, stationed at the gate of the driveway leading to our residence.

Early that afternoon, demonstrations began to erupt near the National Iranian Oil Company and the municipal buildings only two or three blocks away. They seemed to be composed of employees agitating for more pay or other work-related issues. The Iranian authorities assured us it would be a peaceful demonstration, which would soon disperse.

Their estimates were correct up to a point. The demonstrators began to disperse and move in various directions away from the areas where they had assembled. A fairly large number of them came down Takht-e Jamshid, the broad avenue in front of our embassy compound. In accordance with the security practices we had established, the radio dispatcher for our embassy automobiles warned all drivers to stay away from the compound until this group had passed our perimeter. Unfortunately, one driver who was close enough to be able to observe the street in front of the embassy, felt he could make a dash for it and get in the gate before the crowd arrived at the compound. He therefore drove his automobile to the gate leading into the parking area and asked to be permitted to enter. The marines and local guards, however, had already received instructions to chain the gate shut, and they refused to permit him to come into the compound.

There then ensued a typical stubborn Iranian argument in which the driver got out of his car and gesticulated to the guards at the gate, demanding that they unlock the chains. In the meantime the advance elements of the demonstrators coming down the street saw what was going on and ran toward the car. In a flash one of them threw a Molotov cocktail into the back seat, and the whole thing went up in flames. This spectacle, particularly when the gasoline tank exploded, brought a significantly larger surge of demonstrators and idle passersby to the compound perimeter. The young army captain who was in charge of the platoon stationed at the residence gate half a block away froze in panic. When he saw the flames shooting out of the car and the crowds arriving, he radioed to his headquarters for reinforcements. Under the best of conditions, given the traffic in Tehran streets and the demonstrations in the neighborhood, it would take at least half an hour for reinforcements to arrive.

When I was told what was happening, I dashed out of my office, down the stairs, and to the security officer's position near the marine guard station at the reception desk. By this time our marines had been alerted from their quarters, were donning combat gear, and being issued shotguns and tear-gas cannisters. I sent them out to the motor-pool area and told them to take cover positions but to be prepared to throw their tear-gas grenades on order. At the same time I sent the security officer and our police major to the other gate to propel the young army captain into sending some of his troops down the sidewalk to fire into the air and disperse the crowd.

Within minutes the now excited crowd began to assault the front gate, throwing stones, pieces of brick, and other debris over the embassy wall toward the positions being held by the marines. I gave the order to launch tear-gas grenades, but at the same time gave explicit instructions that no marine was to fire a weapon except under direct orders from my radio command. We had television monitors that were remote controlled from the reception desk, and I could watch skirmishes developing on the screen as I manned the central radio-communications post. The struggle at the gate swayed back and forth for nearly ten minutes. The tear-gas grenades were effective in dispersing most of the mob, but a few hardy souls continued to wrench at the gate in an effort to tear it down, and others succeeded in climbing to the tops of the walls.

At long last the young captain gathered up his courage and sent a jeep load of four soldiers down the sidewalk to the gate. As they drew within fifty feet of the gate, they began firing their automatic weapons rapidly into the air. This had the desired effect, and the crowd dispersed without further incident. Fifteen minutes later, military reinforcements arrived and established a checkpoint farther down the street, blocking off the area and erecting a useful cordon around all potential entrances to the compound. By dusk the situation had returned to normal, the gate had been opened, the charred body of the sedan had been hauled inside, and the marines had been authorized to stand down from their alert.

For most of these young marines, this was their first taste of a combat situation and they were exhilarated by it. As they came back to the command center, stacked their weapons, and stored their combat gear, it reminded me of the atmosphere that used to prevail on our destroyer during World War II after we had successfully come through a combat engagement. While I was pleased with the morale and discipline demonstrated by the marine security guard, I wondered whether they really understood what might be in store for them if an armed attack were to develop on our compound and if the Iranian army behaved in as hesitant a manner as the platoon had done on that Christmas Eve.

The next day, Christmas, we were well protected by deployments of Iranian army troops. Nevertheless, mindful of the attack that had taken place at the British embassy while the ambassador was away, I decided not to attend the Christmas dinner that had been arranged by our consul general in his home four or five blocks from the embassy. It seemed to me prudent to remain on the scene in the event a sudden attack developed.

The young marines, discovering this, and still feeling the aftereffects of the preceding day's activities, came over to the residence at dusk and serenaded my wife and daughter and me with Christmas carols. We invited them in for beer and snacks and sat around the piano singing. They were all in high spirits, eager for another go at the street mobs. I quietly took aside the gunnery sergeant, who was some ten years older than the rest and who had had significant combat experience in Vietnam, and expressed my concern about this ebullience. I pointed out that the preceding day's engagement had been an almost accidental one, that the attackers had not been armed, and that the skirmish had been of minor proportions. I suggested he have a gentle talk with his young troops when they returned to their quarters to point out that a planned armed attack would be of significantly different dimensions and that they should recognize the need in such a circumstance to obey orders explicitly and avoid exuberant independent acts of heroism. The gunny, who understood the import of what I was saying, assured me he would get the point across before the evening was over.

As the year drew to an end, the situation in Iran began to drift. The shah made up his mind to name Bakhtiar prime minister, to appoint a regency council, and to leave the country. However, he insisted on taking all these steps exactly in accordance with custom and the constitution; he would not be hurried by events. The state of the armed forces was becoming tense. Our military advisors assigned to Iranian units reported confusion and despair, particularly among the younger officers. In Iran, the armed forces took an oath to the shah, the country, and God, in that order. The imminence of the shah's departure gave cause for concern about the loyalty of the armed forces and the actions they might take unless they received both assurances and guidance.

The reports we were receiving from Washington were equally disturbing. The president announced that former Deputy Secretary of State George Ball had been brought in as a consultant to the government on the question of Iran. George had a long background in Iranian matters, both as a lawyer and as a government official. He had recently visited Tehran in his capacity as a member of the Lehman Brothers investment firm and had talked with me at some length about his perceptions of the problems in the country. I found his views sound and welcomed the announcement that he would play a consultative role in Washington. I hoped this would serve to consolidate what appeared to be an increasingly shattered administration effort to find some common policy.

At the time Ball was brought into play, events in Iran had passed the point of coherence. The shah was experimenting with all sorts of formulas that might permit him to stay in a position of power, or at least to preserve the Pahlavi dynasty.

While Ball was sympathetic to the shah, he was also pragmatically aware that the dynasty was probably doomed and that it was necessary to establish some sort of transition mechanism that would permit moderate political elements to preempt the revolution.

In Tehran, I was only generally aware of what Ball's thinking was, because he had the Department of State address a number of cabled inquiries to the embassy concerning some political personalities who might assist in the transition that he conjectured. We answered these questions as best we could but gave no comfort to the notion that the individuals concerned might act as effective catalysts at this late stage in the political confusion.

In the final analysis it all did not matter, because the White House rejected Ball's report. A copy of it was never sent to the embassy. I am aware now of what was in Ball's suggestions only because he has described them to me in private conversations after my retirement from the foreign service.

As all these events drew together, our discussions with the leaders of the opposition in Tehran became increasingly more explicit. The members of the liberation movement made clear that they wished to preserve the armed forces and maintain their integrity and strength. At the same time, they advised us that a large number of senior military officers were anathema to them. In the course of these discussions, and in parallel conversations with senior officers of the armed forces, it became apparent that a significant number of senior officers in various strategic positions within the military-command structure were not only sympathetic with the aims of the liberation movement but also closely in touch with its leaders on a regular basis. From this circumstance, it developed that the liberation movement knew quite explicitly the attitudes and operations of the various military officials.

On exploring this information further, we were eventually

given a list of over a hundred senior military officers who would be expected to resign their positions and leave the country when the shah left. We were told there would be no arrests or other acts of revenge. It was even suggested that these military officials could take their wealth and possessions with them, provided they left quietly and without resistance. Although we were never told who would be expected to replace them in the military hierarchy, we got the clear impression that a list of officers for such positions was in the hands of the liberation-movement leaders.

While I found this encouraging in the light of my general recommendation that our interests lay in preserving the integrity of the armed forces, I was still not sure that the views we were receiving from the liberation movement coincided with the views held by the ayatollah and his immediate group in Paris. I was concerned that the ayatollah, on his return, would turn his powerful rhetoric against the proposals that we were hearing from the liberation movement, and that this rhetoric in turn would incite the street mobs to undo the efforts being made to preserve the military.

Accordingly, I recommended that the United States government send a senior emissary to Paris to discuss this matter directly with the ayatollah. I ruled myself out for such an undertaking because of my accreditation to the shah and because it seemed an unwise time to leave Tehran. I talked on the secure telephone with Secretary of State Vance about this proposal and subsequently with Under Secretary David Newsom. In due course they informed me by way of a teletype system called Telecom that my proposal had been accepted, and they suggested that I frame the terms of reference for the proposed mission. I then laid out a talking paper much along the lines of the discussions we had been having in Tehran, indicating that our primary concern was for the preservation of the territorial integrity of the country and that we thought it important in that perspective for the armed forces to be as strong and as effective as possible. I suggested we inform the ayatollah that we would be prepared to continue the military-assistance and sales programs currently in effect and that we thought a conflict between the Islamic forces and the Iranian military would benefit only the Soviet Union and their agents inside Iran.

After some further exchanges on the Telecom, this rather explicit statement became considerably more anodyne but nevertheless left open the general concept underlying my proposals. I was much less concerned about the explicit content of the talking paper when I learned of Secretary Vance's choice of representative to conduct the mission to the ayatollah.

The man he named was the Honorable Theodore L. Eliot, the inspector general of the foreign service, who had only recently returned from four years as ambassador to Afghanistan. A career foreign-service officer, Ted Eliot had earlier served as the economic counselor in Tehran and spoke fluent Farsi. He was a tall, imposing man with a quick mind and a direct demeanor. He was an excellent choice for this mission, and I felt comforted that he would be able to deal on positive terms with the ayatollah.

With these aspects of the mission established, I received a further instruction telling me to explain the entire undertaking to the shah. While there was no suggestion that he would have a veto over our intentions, the opportunity was certainly afforded to him to register objections if he so chose. When I saw the shah and laid out the action we were taking, he listened gravely and without enthusiasm. However, he voiced no opposition whatsoever, asking merely that he be kept informed of the results of the mission. I cabled this information to Washington and was informed that Eliot would leave for Paris on January 6.

After months of imprecision in our dealings with Washington, and given the absence of any answer to my basic cable of November 9, the new, crisp attitude that seemed to emerge from these arrangements was refreshing. I was aware that Secretary Vance had been traveling most of November and December on missions associated with the Camp David process and had been out of touch with events affecting Iran. I therefore credited this new precision to his return to Washington. Some members of my staff who had been privy to this exchange suggested that the new realism resulted from the allied summit meeting in Guadeloupe that had just ended. There, President Carter had met with French President Giscard d'Estaing, German Chancellor Schmidt, and Japanese Prime Minister Ohira. One of my officers concluded that these leaders had convinced President Carter that the shah was doomed and that it would be the better part of valor to seek some accommodations to protect our national interests in this vital part of the world. The president himself, who had completed the business portion of the summit meeting, was staying on in the Caribbean for some deep-sea fishing, accompanied by Zbigniew Brzezinski. I assumed he had turned over the detailed direction of Iranian policy to Secretary of State Vance.

My surprise and anguish could not have been more complete when, in the early hours of January 5, I was awakened by the duty officer, who handed me a cable. The Eliot mission had been canceled. The shah was to be advised that we no longer intended to have any discussions with Ayatollah Khomeini. No explanation was given for this complete turnaround, and no opportunity for rebuttal was presented. I was told that the decision had been taken by the president and that my views were not invited.

At this point the frustrations that had beset me for so many months spilled over. I sent a short, sharp message to Secretary Vance saying that I thought the president had made a gross mistake and that a cancellation of the Eliot mission would be an irretrievable error. I urged that the decision be rescinded and the mission be restored. I then returned to bed for the rest of a sleepless night.

In the morning, I received a terse reply. It informed me that not only the president but the vice-president, the secretary of state, the secretary of defense, the secretary of the treasury, the head of CIA, and the national-security advisor had all agreed with the president on his decision to cancel the mission. I was therefore instructed to proceed as previously directed. Accordingly, I called the palace and asked for an audience with the shah. It was granted immediately, and I set off up the hill with grave thoughts racing through my mind.

As far as I could see, the United States government was facing the situation in Iran with no policy whatsoever. The shah's collapse, in my judgment, was inevitable, and unless some understandings were reached for an accommodation between the armed forces and the Islamic forces, I felt that an explosion would occur. Up to this point I had moved rather slowly in suggesting to the American business community that additional evacuations should take place. I had hoped that in a peaceful transition the continued presence of Americans in Iran would be tolerable and that casualties would be avoided. I had felt that the absence of any traumatic decisions about evacuation would enhance the possibilities for a more normal situation and make a peaceful transition more likely. I now foresaw all that going by the boards. Approximately ten thousand Americans were still in the country, and we had very few days in which to move if we were going to get them out of the path of revolutionary violence. Although one section of my mind was rehearsing what I should say to the shah to explain the sudden reversal in our plans, the other section was concerned with the enormous logistics operation that would be necessary to evacuate these American citizens.

I was not quite sure what to expect from my meeting with the shah. He was, on that morning, more drawn and tense than usual. It appeared that he had not slept very much and that events were crowding in on him. He was nevertheless his usual urbane self as he received me and as we sat down to drink our ritual small cup of tea.

When I told him of the instructions I had received from Washington, he became agitated. He asked why the mission had been canceled. I said I had received no information on that score. He then asked how we expected to influence these people if we would not even talk with them. He threw up his hands in despair and asked what we intended to do now. I had no answer.

It is clear from reading the shah's autobiography that, until this point, he felt we had some grand national design that was intended to save his country and perhaps, somehow or other, his dynasty. In the light of that assumption, he was prepared to make personal sacrifices for the larger goal. It now suddenly became clear to him, as it had to me, that we had no design whatsoever and that our government's actions were being guided by some inexplicable whim. It was a bad day for both of us.

I returned down the hill to the embassy, wrote a cable describing the meeting with the shah, and then summoned the embassy officers who were responsible for the protection of our American citizens and the evacuation plans. We spent most of the rest of the day going over the task facing us, lining up the arrangements for transportation, and preparing to move our evacuation program ahead at a fast pace.

22

The Huyser Mission

During the days immediately preceding these events, I had received information from Washington suggesting that Secretary of Energy Schlesinger might make a visit to Iran, presumably to discuss the petroleum situation. While it struck me that the Iranian government was in no position to discuss such matters coherently, I nevertheless welcomed the idea of seeing Schlesinger, who was an old friend and whose judgment I respected. I felt he might take back to Washington a more realistic view of the conditions we were facing. In due course, however, I had been informed that he would not make the trip, and the matter passed from my mind.

I was surprised, therefore, on the evening of January 2, to receive a call on the secure telephone from the supreme commander of the allied forces in Europe, General Alexander Haig. Haig told me he had received informal information from Washington that his deputy, Dutch Huyser, was being asked to undertake a mission to Tehran to help stabilize the Iranian armed forces. As Haig understood it, the reports that we had been sending in regarding the unrest in the armed forces and their concern about the departure of the shah had caused

Washington to propose that Huyser come to Tehran to help the military make the transition in loyalty from the shah, in a situation in which they would presumably be responsible to the government of Prime Minister Designate Shahpour Bakhtiar.

Haig told me he was vigorously opposed to this idea and did not think it was appropriate for Huyser to undertake such a mission. He said he was informing Washington that he did not approve and hoped I would do the same. He even went on to say that if Washington insisted on this step, he would make a major issue of it and would announce his retirement.

I told Haig that I had not been informed of any proposal to send Huyser but that I shared Washington's concern over the situation in the armed forces. I was not sure Huyser could do any good by coming to Iran, but I did feel he had the confidence of most of the senior officers and might be able to assess their attitudes in the current situation better than could the more junior two-star officer who was the MAAG chief. Consequently, while I doubted the propriety of sending an officer out of the NATO command structure to Iran at this particular juncture, I was not as vehemently opposed to it as Haig was. I thought it better to wait until I received some official information about the nature of the proposed mission before I protested. I asked Haig to keep me informed of any further developments, and he undertook to do so. The next day he telephoned me again to say that the mission had been approved and that Huyser was being instructed to come to Iran. He also said that within the next hour he intended to announce his resignation from his NATO command.

Later that day I was informally advised by Under Secretary Newsom of the Huyser mission. He told me the secretary of state had concurred in it, and suggested in a friendly manner that I would only complicate the secretary's life if I were to object. He was aware of the contretemps with Haig and indicated that there was quite a bit of tension at the White House about all this. I told Newsom that while it was not quite clear to me what Huyser was expected to accomplish, I had great respect for him as a person and would not register any objections to his coming to Tehran at this juncture. I also said I considered it highly important that the mission be undertaken with discretion and that Huyser arrive incognito. Newsom agreed and said he would stress this point in Washington.

The next day Huyser arrived in Tehran, clad in civilian clothes, having flown in the cockpit of a 747 cargo plane transporting supplies to our military mission. He arrived at our residence in somewhat of a fluster. His prime preoccupation seemed to be Haig's resignation and the consternation this would introduce into the European military picture. He told me in some confidence that the circumstances leading to Haig's resignation had been building for some time and were only indirectly related to this Tehran mission. He described it as the straw that broke the camel's back and said that the inconsistencies of the Carter administration with respect to NATO policies had been more than Haig could tolerate.

Huyser then showed me the brief instructions he had received concerning his mission, which he said he had read several times en route. Although they were vaguely worded, they indicated that his task was to meet with the senior officers of the Iranian military command in order to assure them of the continuity of American logistical support and to urge them to maintain the integrity of their forces in the difficult period that would accompany the departure of the shah and the investiture of the Bakhtiar government. It was further indicated that one of his tasks would be to assist the military in the difficult psychological task of abandoning their traditional oath to the shah and transferring their loyalties to the civilian authority of the prime minister, to whom they would be subordinate.

Despite his misgivings, Huyser set out gamely to try to carry out his instructions.

He moved in with my wife and me, and we established a curious modus vivendi. Huyser would spend his days with the

Iranian general staff at their military headquarters or else with the MAAG chief and his staff at their offices. I would spend mine in the embassy, at the palace, on my various appointed rounds throughout the city, and then we would return in the evening to compare notes over dinner. After dinner we would stroll across the compound to the chancery and take up our positions at the two secure-telephone circuits to Washington. On one line I would speak to Under Secretary of State Newsom or Assistant Secretary Saunders. On the other, Huyser would speak with the chairman of the Joint Chiefs of Staff, David Jones, or with Secretary of Defense Harold Brown. We would then compare notes after our conversations to try to sort out what Washington was attempting to convey to us. There were times when we felt we must have been talking to two different cities.

In the meantime political change was moving apace in Tehran. The shah had finally organized the actions that were necessary for a constitutional investiture of Bakhtiar. The cursory parliamentary debates in both houses had taken place, a regency council had been appointed, and all was in preparation for the governmental transition.

About this time I received a message asking me to see the shah and inform him that the United States government felt it was in his best interests and in Iran's for him to leave the country. This is not the sort of casual message that an ambassador usually carries to a chief of state, but the relationship that had developed over the past few months had become so extraordinary that somehow or other the task of delivering this suggestion did not seem surrealistic. The shah listened to me state it as simply and gently as I could and then turned to me, almost beseeching, throwing out his hands and saying, "Yes, but where will I go?"

The cable of instruction had said nothing about this point. Accordingly, when the shah asked this question I told him I had no guidance, but said, "What about your home in Switzerland?" The shah immediately dismissed this suggestion, saying that Swiss security was no good. Then, apparently anticipating another suggestion, he said that "we also have a home in England, but the weather is so bad." With that he sat there in silence, looking at me with soulful eyes.

I then asked, "Would you like me to seek an invitation for you to go to the United States?"

He leaned forward, almost like a small boy, and said, "Oh, would you?"

When I reported this conversation to Washington and asked whether such an invitation would be extended, I was surprised by the alacrity of the reply. Within twenty-four hours I received a lengthy cable informing me that the shah would be welcome temporarily at the estate of former Ambassador Walter Annenberg in the desert near Palm Springs, California. I was assured that security there would be excellent and that transportation could be arranged by military helicopter without extraordinary problems. The instructions authorized me to convey the invitation to the shah in the name of the president of the United States. I was asked to obtain the shah's travel plans, itinerary, and the anticipated number of persons who would be in his official party.

About the time that this exchange was taking place, Ayatollah Khomeini and his entourage in Paris began to anticipate the shah's departure. Their tactics, at this time, were to encourage his safe and orderly withdrawal from Iran to a place of refuge abroad. In order to make this more palatable to all concerned, the ayatollah issued a statement from Paris to the effect that the leaders of the revolution would welcome the actions taken by any state to provide the shah a safe haven and would not take any measures against the interests of any state that provided it. Consequently, at this particular juncture, there seemed no risk to U.S. interests in offering the shah asylum in the United States. On the contrary, it appeared we might even gain some credit with the ayatollah for making the shah's orderly departure feasible.

I asked to see the shah the next day and also inquired whether I could bring General Huyser with me. Both requests were immediately granted, and we had a lengthy audience on the morning of January 12. The shah described this briefly in his autobiography, suggesting that the only things we seemed concerned about were his departure plans.

In actual fact he seemed relieved to receive the invitation and was eager to work out departure plans with us. We, on the other hand, were more interested in discussing our concern for the integrity of the armed forces and the way in which he saw the transition of authority from him as commander in chief to Prime Minister Bakhtiar. Although he addressed this question casually, his mind was clearly focused on something else, and he did not seem to regard this as a subject worthy of much attention. Once again, poor Huyser was left to wing it on his own.

Instead, we discussed the shah's impending trip to the United States. He suggested that he might like to fly by way of Andrews Air Force Base as he entered the country, the implication being that he would meet with senior U.S. officials en route to California. From conversations that both Huyser and I had had with Washington, we knew such a plan would be neither feasible nor welcome. Massive demonstrations against the shah could be anticipated in any such undertaking. We therefore advised him that his plane should come through one of the more obscure United States air force bases, probably in Maine, on an itinerary that would call for the transit during the hours of darkness. He would then go to Travis Air Force Base in California and be helicoptered to the Annenberg estate. The shah seemed to accept this with equanimity and suggested that Huyser work out the details with General Rabii, the commander in chief of the air force. He said that Rabii could also give us details about the size of the accompanying party and the exact time scheduled for departure.

That same evening, I made one final, rather impassioned effort to convince Washington to throw its weight behind a reconciliation between the military and the religious forces in Iran. I sent off a cable saying that "our national interests demand that we attempt to structure a modus vivendi between the military and the religious, in order to preempt the Tudeh."

In effect, I addressed my plea directly to President Carter, by pointing out that it was possible he would be meeting with the shah when the latter reached his asylum. I said that the public consequences of such a meeting would be of enormous importance to our future relations with Iran. "It would be disastrous if the image that should emerge would convey the idea that we continue to 'support' the shah and that we expect to assist him somehow to return to power in Iran."

I went on to suggest that the president discuss with him frankly and candidly our feeling that the integrity of Iran and its preservation from the Communists demanded a rapid reconciliation between the military and the religious, who shared a common antipathy toward communism. I pointed out that the U.S. government and the president personally had more than adequately discharged their obligations of loyalty to the shah. "We cannot, by continued avowal of that loyalty, do for the shah what he has been unable or unwilling to do for himself. . . . We must put the shah behind us and look to our own national interests as foremost in Iran."

As usual, I received no answer to this cable and no indication that the White House comprehended the nature of the situation developing in Iran. Instead, Huyser continued to get his telephone instructions designed to brace the military for a confrontation with the revolution.

Two days before the shah was scheduled to leave, I received a cable from Ambassador Hermann Eilts in Cairo transmitting an invitation from President Sadat of Egypt for him to pass through Aswan and to rest there en route to the United States. When I first relayed this invitation to him, the shah was less than enthusiastic. He asked me to send back a gracious message to Sadat but stated that he would have to consider the invitation.

The next day the chief of the imperial staff telephoned to say that the shah wished to accept the Sadat invitation and would fly from Tehran directly to Aswan. He said that his stay there would be of only twenty-four hours duration and that we should therefore set back all the arrival plans for the United States by one day. I immediately sent this message off to Cairo and was assured by Eilts that the Egyptians were prepared to receive the shah and his party. Eilts also told me that, by coincidence, former President Gerald Ford and a small group accompanying him were in Aswan at the same time.

As all these plans were in motion, the shah and his party quietly left Iran after a brief private ceremony in the imperial pavilion at Mehrabad Airport. This ceremony was televised a short time later by the national television station and a pandemonium of delirium broke out in the city of Tehran. Automobiles roared through the streets with demonstrators hanging out the windows. Truckloads of young people passed up and down Takht-e Jamshid. Horns blew everywhere, and the shouting and celebrating lasted for three or four hours.

The reins of government were now in the hands of Shahpour Bakhtiar.

23

Confusion Compounded

The day after Bakhtiar was installed in office, I made my first call on him. During that interview and in my subsequent meetings with him, I constantly had to pinch myself to remind me that I was talking with an Iranian. Bakhtiar was one of the most complete francophiles I have ever encountered. He spoke exclusively in French, he dressed in French-tailored clothes, he had French mannerisms, and he even looked like a French country gentleman.

Although I knew from my conversations with the shah that Bakhtiar was intended to be nothing more than a fig leaf that would permit the shah to leave the country in good constitutional form, I was somewhat surprised to discover that the new prime minister considered himself something else. He spoke with ebullience about his plans for his government and about his intention to "steal the revolution away" from the ayatollah. He seemed to feel that, with the departure of the shah, he could now capture the leadership of the Iranian people, whose attitudes he felt had been distorted by the posture of the ayatollah and the mullahs who surrounded him. He talked to me of going to Paris to meet with the ayatollah and making

arrangements for the latter to have an honorific religious position outside the realm of government, while he, Bakhtiar,
organized the political functions of the state.

I listened to this discourse with considerable disbelief and
then returned to my embassy to report the substance of the
conversation to Washington and to add my own observations
that Bakhtiar was a "quixotic" character who did not seem to
realize that he and his government would be swept aside by the
tide of the revolution once the ayatollah and his followers had
returned to the country. I was later told by a secure-telephone
call from a senior State Department official telling me that this
cable was not well received at the White House, because it was
the U.S. government's official position to support Bakhtiar. I
began to wonder just how unrealistic the White House had
become.

As I pondered our situation and reviewed the various instructions I had received from Washington, I became aware once
again that I had never been told there was any Washington
objection to my continuing the embassy's efforts to arrange
some sort of accommodation between the armed forces and the
leaders of the impending revolution. Accordingly, I decided to
take a personal hand in this effort.

I instructed one of my political officers that I would accept
a long-standing invitation from Mehdi Bazargan, the leader of
the liberation movement, to meet with him at his convenience.
Bazargan accepted immediately and designated an evening
rendezvous in the home of one of his followers in the northern
part of the city. I went there accompanied by a political officer
and my usual retinue of five Iranian-national-police bodyguards. Since the house was unfamiliar to them, they and my
driver were naturally curious about this activity.

On entering the house, we were greeted by Bazargan and
Ayatollah Moussavi, who, with his black turban and gray beard,
bore a striking resemblance to Ayatollah Khomeini. The four
of us sat in a small living room facing a window that, in turn,

opened onto the front courtyard. The conversation was a curious one. Bazargan and I spoke in French, and then he deferentially translated the gist of the conversation into Farsi for the benefit of the ayatollah, who said very little throughout. Bazargan repeated to me what his associates had been telling embassy officers for some time. They wanted the armed forces to remain intact and to work with the new government. They had a list of designated military officers who would be required to leave the country but who could take their possessions with them and escape any retribution. They wanted a continuation of the military associations and other security arrangements with the United States. Bazargan said that he spoke for the Liberation Front and that the ayatollah spoke for the religious elements of the revolution. Unfortunately, although the ayatollah was attentive, benign, and constructive throughout the conversation, he never did ratify the statements of Bazargan in quite the explicit terms I would have preferred. It was, nevertheless, a satisfactory beginning to the policy that I had hoped to put into action.

After we had been in the house for over two hours and had completed the essence of our conversation, the front gate of the compound opened, and I could see the figure of Amir Entezam coming across the courtyard toward the kitchen part of the house. Shortly thereafter another figure, not familiar to me, entered the same way. I assumed that the shadow cabinet of Bazargan was beginning to gather for discussions that would analyze the substance of our conversation. The gate opened once again, and in slipped one of my police bodyguards, whose curiosity about the place had obviously gotten the better of him. We watched as he closed the gate quietly behind him and then faced toward the window of our room. Because he obviously did not recognize the man, the ayatollah stood up and leaned forward. Just then the policeman glanced up and saw this menacing bearded figure glowering down at him. The resemblance to Ayatollah Khomeini was striking. The policeman, obviously startled by what he saw, turned and fled out the gate as the whole room broke up in laughter.

I reported this conversation to Washington, said that I was encouraged by its implications, and indicated that my next action would be to try to persuade the new chief of staff of the armed forces to enter into discussions with Bazargan and his people. The new chief of staff was the former head of the gendarmerie, General Gharabaghi. He had replaced General Oveissi, who had preferred to retire and leave the country when the shah departed. During our conversation, Bazargan had indicated that he and Gharabaghi were friendly and that he would undertake directly to initiate conversations with him.

Once again, although the report of my action and of my intentions was explicit, Washington did not comment and did not interpose any suggestions concerning the future of this undertaking.

At the same time, however, the signals Huyser was getting through his Defense Department contacts were at variance with these plans. He was being asked to prepare the Iranian armed forces to be able, if necessary, to face and suppress massive civil disorders. He was being pressed particularly to be certain that the armed forces could control the oil fields and, in an emergency, operate the machinery of the oil industry themselves.

In his meetings with the general staff, Huyser felt that a positive attitude was developing toward Bakhtiar. The prime minister had come to staff headquarters and had met extensively with the military high command. They seemed to have gotten along well, and Bakhtiar promised the officers considerable autonomy in the performance of their military duties. Huyser interpreted this as a step in the right direction and said the officers appeared to be willing to transfer their loyalties from the figurehead of the shah to a civilian government headed by Bakhtiar. At the same time, he reported a curious reluctance on the part of the staff to entertain suggestions for serious contingency planning or to make appropriate logistical provisions for the tasks they might face. He was particularly shocked to learn that they had no reserves of diesel oil and gasoline or other middle distillates for their armed forces and that their plans seemed to assume that the oil fields and refineries would always function just as in normal peacetime conditions.

As a result of this discovery, a tanker chartered by the U.S. Navy picked up the middle distillates at Bahrain and proceeded to the Iranian port of Bandar 'Abbas in order to make them available to the Iranian armed forces. However, the Iranian navy kept the tanker offshore and never permitted the cargo of fuel to be discharged. Huyser shook his head over these patterns of behavior but felt that the military still retained the will to act in an emergency.

By contrast, I felt that the military had convincingly lost its will. Many of the dissidents in the streets who might face the armed forces in an emergency were the sons, brothers, and other close relatives of the men behind the rifles and machine guns. In our evening conversations, I suggested to Huyser that the armed forces were not a dependable instrument with which to face the revolution. He heard me out and respected my judgment, but his own conclusions were to the contrary. It is to his great credit, nevertheless, that whenever he reported his views to Washington he always included the caveat that I disagreed with his assessment and that I felt the armed forces would, in a crunch, collapse because they would be unable to face the sort of opposition they would meet in the streets.

My judgment was not entirely based on present conditions in Iran. I had been in Paris in 1968 when the students rioted on the Left Bank and the government brought in fifty thousand police in an effort to quell the disturbances. I was living in the Crillon Hotel, on the side where the police were staged and ready to attack, and was crossing the river daily to deal with the French officials in the Quai d'Orsay. Many of these officials were the fathers of the students mounting the barricades in the

Latin Quarter and the approaches to the Sorbonne. I observed with great interest the way they and their colleagues in the senior elements of the bureaucracy reacted to the problem of using force against the youngsters who were challenging the government. The net result was that the fifty thousand police who awaited orders on the Right Bank were never really called into action, because most of these officials recognized they would be jeopardizing the lives of their own children on the barricades.

It seemed to me that the same situation now obtained in Tehran as far as the armed forces were concerned. I seriously doubted that they would make a successful effort to counter the youngsters in the streets if they were called on to suppress the disturbances with live bullets. I concluded, therefore, that in a confrontation between the armed forces and the revolution, the armed forces would collapse. Huyser faithfully reported these observations to Washington, and I made them myself in my conversations with State Department officials on the secure telephone. Nevertheless, both Bakhtiar and Brzezinski continued to make preparations to produce a confrontation between the military and the revolution.

I was meeting regularly with Bakhtiar in those days and listened with some astonishment as he talked about his intentions to confront the revolution and to disperse its challenge by the minimal use of military force. He remained jocularly confident about his own prospects for success. So, apparently, did Brzezinski and the people who were representing his views in their conversations with Huyser; they reminded Tehran unendingly that there were the Iranian armed forces of four hundred thousand that certainly could manage to overwhelm an unarmed street crowd led by nothing but rhetorical exhortations from the mullahs.

In Egypt, the shah seemed to be convinced of the same considerations, possibly by Ardeshir Zahedi. Contrary to his original plans, he did not stay one day at Aswan and then move in accordance with his previous schedules toward the Annenberg retreat in Palm Springs. Instead, he chose to stay as a guest of the Egyptian government for an indefinite period of time. We learned from our observers in Egypt that he felt there would soon be a military confrontation with the revolution and that the armed forces would prevail. He seemed convinced that, in such an event, he would be recalled to Tehran as he had been in 1953 and would be able to resume the throne as in that earlier experience. This seemed to me to be the most unrealistic sort of thinking on the part of all concerned. Therefore, in due course I sent a message to Washington suggesting that these wishful thoughts were pure moonshine and that we should instead be preparing ourselves for the fact that the revolution was going to succeed and that we needed to accommodate ourselves to it in the most effective way in order to protect United States national interests.

In response to this message, I received a most unpleasant and abrasive cable from Washington, which, in my judgment, contained an unacceptable aspersion upon my loyalty.

In the whole cascade of frustration that had swept over me during the past few months, this proved to be too much for my tolerance. I was, after all, the senior United States foreign-service officer on active duty, and I felt that my reports and assessments deserved some fair consideration at the highest policy levels in Washington. When I was told by telephone from the State Department that the insulting message had originated at the White House, I thought that I no longer had a useful function to perform on behalf of the president in Tehran. I therefore made up my mind to resign and to leave this totally unsatisfactory situation behind.

In discussing this impasse with my wife, however, I realized that my departure from Iran at such a critical moment would be unconscionable as far as the eight thousand remaining Americans in the country were concerned. I foresaw, as the result of the policy the United States government seemed to be pursuing, an all-out clash between the military and the forces of revolution in which chaos would ensue. In such circumstances, I felt, there would be a complete breakdown of law and order and the lives of the eight thousand Americans would be in serious jeopardy. I therefore swallowed my anger and resolved to stay on in my post until the crisis had passed. Nevertheless, I did persuade my wife that it was time for her to leave, and arranged for her transportation back to the United States by way of a military aircraft flying to Athens. From then on my relations with the administration were adversarial. I admit that my communications in the period that followed were not couched in the usual respectful phrases that an ambassador normally employs in writing to his superiors. I frankly felt that since I had apparently lost the confidence of the president and his immediate associates, and since I no longer held them in appropriate respect, there was no need for me to disguise my attitudes throught he use of tactful language. My communications became not only abrupt but occasionally acerbic.

As an apparent prophylaxis against my seditious views, Washington made clear in direct communications to Prime Minister Bakhtiar that he enjoyed the full support and confidence of the United States government and that I was under instructions to render such support to him in all circumstances. In view of my ambassadorial oath to support the Constitution and consequently the authority of the president to make and direct foreign policy, I accepted that situation and assured Bakhtiar that I would act in the light of those instructions. In his own writings, he has suggested that I was always "cool" in my dealings with him, but I think it is fair to say that I never deviated from the letter and spirit of support for him that were inherent in the positions of the president of the United States.

The most severe test of this anomalous situation came in a confrontation that developed between Bakhtiar and the commander in chief of the Iranian armed forces. As the chief of staff, General Gharabaghi began to appreciate the nature of the confrontation that was forming as the result of the policies of the prime minister and the attitudes of the United States government. He decided to resign his function and his commission, informing his colleagues of his decision in a dramatic meeting at the armed-forces headquarters. General Huyser, who was told shortly thereafter, attempted to persuade Gharabaghi to change his mind. When Gharabaghi declined and indicated he was going ahead with his resignation that same evening, Huyser returned to my residence in a considerably distraught state. He told me he feared this action on the part of Gharabaghi would precipitate the collapse of morale in the senior echelons of the military, which, in turn, would be rapidly communicated to the troops in the field.

Within minutes after Huyser had told me of this situation, the prime minister called, asking me to join him in his office at six o'clock that evening. I arrived about six and was ushered immediately into Bakhtiar's office. He waved me to a seat, saying with a cryptic gesture, *"Nous serons trois"*—"We will be three"—and smiled enigmatically. After we had discussed political matters for about twenty minutes, General Gharabaghi was ushered into the office. He was obviously astounded to see me already there and saluted in the French manner to both the prime minister and me.

The prime minister ushered him to a seat between the two of us and began talking gently with him in French. Gharabaghi attempted to shift the conversation into Farsi but Bakhtiar continually forced him back into the French language.

It became apparent that Gharabaghi had a written resignation in his pocket that he kept fingering and trying to deliver to the prime minister. The prime minister, on the other hand, kept dissuading him from making his resignation and argued about the difficulties that such an action would produce. He kept turning to me for support of his arguments. Although I personally agreed with Gharabaghi's position, I was under instructions to maintain the military loyalty to Bakhtiar; therefore, with all the force at my command, I argued with him against the action he was contemplating. The discussion went on for more than half an hour, and in the end Gharabaghi tucked his resignation back into his pocket, saluted, clicked his heels, and withdrew. After the general's departure Bakhtiar thanked me profusely for my assistance in precluding the general's resignation and then went on to tell me with some elaboration about his anticipation that, on the return of Ayatollah Khomeini, the confrontation would develop in a manner favorable to the Bakhtiar government.

At this point, the telephone rang, and Bakhtiar began an animated conversation with his caller. When he hung up, he told me with great relish that the caller was Mehdi Bazargan, and that the two of them had arranged to meet the following day in the home of a former speaker of the parliament, whose house happened to be within two blocks of my residence and immediately next door to my CIA station chief. The house was also close to a stadium where Bakhtiar had arranged a large rally of his forces in an effort to demonstrate that he had popular support against the revolution.

I knew, too, that conversations were taking place between the armed forces and the leaders of the revolutionary forces. Several talks had ensued between General Moghaddam, the chief of SAVAK, and representatives of Mehdi Bazargan. In addition, Bazargan himself had met with Gharabaghi and Moghaddam. Bakhtiar apparently knew about these developments, but it was unclear to me how he viewed them relative to the confrontation he anticipated between the armed forces and the revolutionary forces that would be led by Ayatollah Khomeini. In short, there seemed to be little logical consistency between what Bakhtiar was doing throughout this period and what he was planning to do when the ayatollah returned.

The prime minister had publicly made clear that he wished to go to Paris to talk with the ayatollah and that, indeed, he felt he had some understandings that would permit such an event. He therefore publicly announced that there would be a meeting and that he and the ayatollah would be able to reach a compromise. Shortly before this intended meeting was to take place, however, the ayatollah made public his conditions. These included a prior announcement by Bakhtiar that he was resigning as prime minister of Iran. This total confusion preceded by only a few days the planned triumphant return of the ayatollah and his retinue to Tehran.

At this point I could only fear and prepare for the worst. I encouraged a more rapid exodus of American citizens from the country and began to cut drastically the size of our official representation. We organized a military airlift with a regular series of aircraft flying between Tehran and Athens. (Although by this time the civil air controllers at Mehrabad Airport were on strike, the Iranian air force manned the tower and kept the airlanes open.) Huyser, in the meantime, was growing increasingly restive about his role and sought authorization to leave the country on the grounds that he had done all he could possibly do in the confusing circumstances. I endorsed his position, but given the mood at the White House, that probably only contributed to the extension of his tenure in Tehran.

I was also becoming increasingly concerned about the status of our military-sales program in Iran. We had nearly six billion dollars worth of contracts to deliver military equipment to the Iranian armed forces that were negotiated on a government-to-government basis but that involved production by independent, private military contractors in the United States. If, as I suspected, the incoming revolutionary government was to cancel all those contracts, the United States government would be stuck with the obligation to pay the private American corporations for the contractual obligations. I therefore urgently suggested to Washington that the matter should be negotiated with the Iranian government in order to work out a program for the orderly liquidation of these obligations in a manner that would absolve the United States government from further liability. To my astonishment, I could not persuade the administration officially to take such an action. Apparently Washington considered that such a negotiation would suggest a lack of confidence in the Bakhtiar government and in future relations between the Iranian armed forces and the United States.

Nevertheless, through long-standing personal association with the Pentagon officials who dealt with military sales programs, I was able to arrange for Eric von Marbod, one of those bureaucratic geniuses who had been able to persevere through several administrations in Washington, to come to Tehran to examine the situation. On his arrival, von Marbod immediately sensed the urgency of the situation and set about attempting to work out a memorandum of understanding with the Iranian authorities that would resolve the inherent difficulties. He also moved in with me and he and Huyser, and I led a strange existence in those last few days before the collapse of law and order in the country. Eric would venture out every morning with a small Derringer strapped into a holster on his leg and would seek to find someone in authority on the Iranian side who would be prepared not only to negotiate but also to sign an understanding that would provide for an orderly resolution of this enormously expensive problem.

Eventually, shortly before the country collapsed in disorder, he worked out an agreement that was acceptable to the Iranians, and we cabled the text back to Washington. At this stage we should not have been as astonished as we were when the State Department and Pentagon lawyers sent us back a whole series of amendments they felt were necessary, which would have taken weeks to work out. In total exasperation I told von Marbod to sign the document himself as it existed; I would take responsibility for any bureaucratic repercussions. He did so, and the agreement now appears as an official document in the series of executive actions signed by the United States government. It probably saved U.S. taxpayers about four billion dollars, but we never received a single word of appreciation from the administration, or any real indication that the White House understood what had been involved in the whole transaction.

24

Attack on the Embassy

Events muddled on for the next few days, and eventually Huyser and von Marbod were given permission to leave the country. They quietly departed on separate aircraft and flew off in different directions. On February 1, Ayatollah Khomeini, with an extensive entourage, returned to Tehran aboard an Air France 747. Ecstatic mobs met them at the airport and escorted them through the streets of Tehran to the cemetery south of the city where many of those who had fought in the revolution were buried. With an exquisite sense of public relations, the ayatollah moved to a small religious school in the south of Tehran. His every action was carried on national television.

Even though the Bakhtiar government had, by this time, become irrelevant and several of its ministers had quietly left the country, Bakhtiar continued to make a number of pronouncements that were promptly swept aside in the overwhelming attention being paid to the ayatollah. Among the first pronouncements made by the ayatollah himself after his arrival was that he would set up a government and that the government would be headed by Mehdi Bazargan.

During these hectic days, the embassy kept in touch with both Bakhtiar and Bazargan, but most of our efforts were concentrated on the continuing evacuation of the American community from the country. Washington had ceased to send us instructions of any import.

The tension in the city grew increasingly electric. Clashes between military units and the ayatollah's followers were endemic and the nightly fusillade of stray automatic-weapons fire become a regularly accepted phenomenon. Then, on February 9, the situation came to a head. A unit of air force cadets joined by technicians at Doshen Toppeh Air Force Base rebelled and took up arms against the air force command located there. An armored unit of the imperial guard was brought in to crush the rebellion, and fighting broke out in the middle of the base. Many of our air force advisory personnel were stationed at Doshen Toppeh and were thus caught in the military activity; however, General Rabii, the air force commander, called in helicopters to evacuate those most endangered, and the rest left in buses, using a circuitous route. By nightfall, while the fighting within the perimeter of the air force base had stalemated, the situation came to a head. A mob of civilians descended on the perimeter and set up barricades along all approaching streets, throwing automobiles, buses, furniture, and any other handy objects into their construction. As this motley force of civilians began to man the barricades, it was noted that for the first time in the course of the revolution automatic weapons appeared in their hands. Many of these weapons were AK-47s of Soviet manufacture.

The fighting around Doshen Toppeh became increasingly chaotic during the day of February 10. Even though the civilians were pouring weapons fire into the base, the imperial-guard unit seemed reluctant to use its heavy tank weapons, and great confusion reigned. Since we had evacuated all our official American personnel from the installation, it was difficult to get an accurate fix on exactly what was happening. However, a number of intrepid American newsmen attempted to cover the fighting from buildings in the immediate vicinity. One of them, perhaps the most knowledgeable correspondent in the country, Joe Alex Morris, was killed by a bullet that struck him in the heart.

By the end of the day, not only did Doshen Toppeh seem to be in the hands of the rebellious airmen, but a number of the imperial guard tanks exited from the base and joined the revolutionary forces. I never knew whether the crews had mutinied or whether the tanks had been taken over by rebels. However, since it seemed unlikely that the rebels could handle anything as complicated as a Chieftain tank, I always assumed the imperial guard had mutinied.

These tanks, followed by a large armed mob that had picked up a great many weapons from the garrison at Doshen Toppeh, then began to surge up the avenues toward the northern part of the city where the headquarters of the Iranian military command was located. At the corner of Takht-e Jamshid Boulevard, just a couple of blocks from our embassy compound, they met resistance from the military-police headquarters, and a vicious battle ensued. Stray rounds from the fighting fell into our compound all afternoon and evening. As darkness came, I watched some of the action from the rooftop of my residence, but the increasing number of spent bullets ricocheting off the walls of the house made it an unsafe vantage point.

In the days since the return of the ayatollah to the country, the Iranian armed-forces units that were guarding our compound had begun the practice of stationing themselves inside the gates as a reaction force. Their commanders felt that this was wiser from several points of view. First, they would be less conspicuous and attract less attention to the embassy compound. Second, they would be spared the prospect of being proselytized by young revolutionaries who regularly approached the soldiers and attempted to place flowers in the barrels of their weapons. Third, it was a far more comfortable location for them in the cool February nights. The army attaché, who by this time had taken up the practice of sleeping in his office at the chancery and acting as liaison with these Iranian army troops, reported to me that evening that there was considerable agitation among them as they listened over their radio to the course of the military action occurring only a few blocks away. They were able to follow some of the flow of the battle, but, more particularly, they were aware of the defections and mutinies taking place among elite units of their armed forces.

The battle at the military-police headquarters ended early on the morning of February 11, and for a time quiet settled throughout our sector of the city. Picking up their routine duties again, the senior members of our military-assistance group reported as usual that morning for duty at the Iranian armed-forces headquarters. The hiatus, however, was not to last long. In the early afternoon, the MAAG chief telephoned me to report that a large crowd was forming outside the headquarters building and that he was proposing to remove his personnel. I concurred and suggested that he personally move into the embassy compound and spend the night in my residence. Half an hour later he called again to say that the mob outside had begun firing at the guards around the headquarters building and that their fire was being returned from within. In those circumstances, he considered it unsafe to try to leave and decided to stay in the headquarters offices for the time being. A short while later, his deputy called to tell me that tanks had now been drawn up outside and that 105-mm howitzer fire from the tank cannons was being directed at the building. The twenty-six members of the military-advisory group were therefore evacuating their office space and heading for the bunker below the building, where the Iranian general staff had already taken up positions. I asked that the MAAG chief call me as soon as they had safely reached the bunker and give me a telephone number where I could reach him.

By now I was furiously trying to find senior leaders of the revolutionary forces who could act to extricate our personnel from the increasingly dangerous situation at the armed-forces headquarters. Embassy political officers, military attachés, and members of the military-advisory group who were not trapped in the bunker were all pressed into action. They were to keep me continuously informed of any contacts they developed and any prospects they felt they could exploit for the safe removal of our personnel. My telephone was soon ringing constantly, as these officers reported on the progress they were making to achieve the task I had imposed on them.

In the middle of all this activity, a telephone call came in from Washington. Under Secretary of State Newsom first came on the line and told me he was calling from the situation room in the White House, where a meeting to consider the situation in Tehran was in progress, chaired by Brzezinski. When he asked for my assessment, I gave it to him in a few short phrases, emphasizing my current preoccupation with trying to get my twenty-six military personnel out of the bunker. Newsom seemed to understand the overriding operational concern I had with this project and did not press me significantly further.

Fifteen minutes later the Washington phone rang again; this time it was manned by both Newsom and Deputy Secretary of State Christopher, who said they were again calling from the situation room and wished further exploration of the possibilities in the current situation. This particular call interrupted and overrode a report I was receiving from one of my officers who hoped he had achieved some success in getting Ibrahim Yazdi to undertake responsibility for rescuing our personnel from the bunker. Because this report was cut off by the Washington call, I was not particularly amused to have to answer esoteric questions about courses of action being considered in the situation room while so many American lives were in danger. I was therefore fairly abrupt with my two interlocutors.

I was particularly abrupt when I was told that Brzezinski wanted my views on the possibility of a coup d'etat by the Iranian armed forces to take over authority from what was clearly seen as a faltering Bakhtiar government. The total absurdity of such an inquiry in the circumstances then existing in Tehran provoked me to a scurrilous suggestion for Brzezinski that seemed to shock mild-mannered Under Secretary Newsom. When he told me that it was not a particularly helpful comment, I asked whether he wished me to translate it into Polish and hung up the receiver.

A few minutes later, as I was desperately trying to reestablish contact with the officer who had made arrangements for Yazdi to intercede at the military headquarters, my circuit was again overridden by a call from Washington and Newsom was once again on the line. He said that he had been instructed to ask whether I was in touch with my military-advisory group commander and whether I could obtain from him and relay to Washington his assessment of the possibilities of a military coup d'etat. Almost incredulously I asked Newsom whether he realized that the general was trapped in a bunker and that I was trying to save his life. Newsom said he understood that but that his instructions were to obtain an assessment from the general. Seconds after I hung up, I received a call from the MAAG chief in the bunker. He told me there seemed to be some encouraging activity toward a cease-fire at the headquarters, that several officers had been going from the bunker to the upper levels of the building, and that they seemed to be in conversation with some leaders of the besieging force. With some diffidence, I then told him of the conversations I had with Washington and of the explicit request from the White House for his assessment of the possibilities of a military coup d'etat. Preoccupied as he was with trying to extract his small military unit from almost certain extinction, he nevertheless, like a good soldier, pulled together an assessment. He fixed the chances of a coup at five percent. I later told someone to relay this assessment to Washington, but I am not sure that, in the confusion that followed, it ever reached its ineffable destination.

In less than an hour we received word that a cease-fire had been arranged at the military headquarters, that not only Ibrahim Yazdi but also Ayatollah Beheshti had arrived on the scene and that they had arranged for the safe extraction of our personnel from the bunker. We were told our people would be returned to our compound in a short time. February 11 was almost over. My deputy, Charlie Naas, whose house was also within the compound, took charge of arrangements to receive the convoy that would return the military-assistance group, and he also worked out plans for bedding them down in various locations within the compound once they arrived.

During the earlier part of the night, the compound had been subjected to harassing attacks by marauders firing automatic weapons from passing automobiles, and the marines were particularly vigilant about approaching vehicles. Charlie therefore took great pains to be sure that the convoy bringing our personnel was properly identified, and arranged to have it enter a rear gate rather than the more conspicuous front gates, where a breach in our perimeter defenses might be exploited by armed revolutionaries in the alleys across Takht-e Jamshid Boulevard. However, it was not until nearly five o'clock the following morning that the convoy finally drove up and was admitted through the rear gates. It was headed by Ayatollah Beheshti himself and by Yazdi. The vehicles were official Iranian army vehicles driven by senior Iranian military officers and containing the twenty-six bedraggled members of the military-advisory group who had spent most of the preceding day and night in the bunker. Charlie expressed our profound thanks to Beheshti and Yazdi, who, in turn, made apologies for the inconvenience that had been inflicted on our personnel.

Later that day, February 12, the Iranian military unit that had been protecting our compound received orders to return to its barracks. The young captain in charge drew up his troops in the best possible military formation and made an emotional farewell to our army attaché. After he had mounted his men in their vehicles, he kissed the attaché on both cheeks and, with tears streaming down his face, carried out his orders to return to the barracks and a most uncertain fate. We learned from our various outposts in the city that all other military units stationed throughout Tehran were receiving the same orders. The armed forces were being withdrawn from all the points they had been protecting, and the authority that had previously been exercised by the Bakhtiar government had now evaporated. Bakhtiar himself disappeared and was not heard of again until he turned up in France some weeks later. Mehdi Bazargan and his cabinet moved into the executive offices of the government, and the revolution had been consummated.

With our Iranian military protection gone, I called a meeting in my office that morning of all those immediately concerned with our security situation. These included Charlie Naas, the administrative officer, the army attaché, the CIA station chief, and the gunnery sergeant of the marine guards. I told them that, with the departure of the Iranian army unit that had protected our premises, I anticipated an attack on the embassy compound. I could not say how it would develop, but I assumed it would be in the form of a street mob that would replicate the activity we had experienced on Christmas Eve. I expected that the mob would have weapons among them and that we would face a serious emergency.

We had already, over the preceding two weeks, taken measures to pack up and ship home most of the classified documents in the embassy files. The only items remaining were those that were operationally necessary for the daily functioning of the embassy. However, we had reduced the files to such proportions that they were all kept within the code-room vault, and we had calculated their volume so that they could be destroyed either by burning or shredding in two hours.

I now said that I wanted maximum security alert established.

I wanted the documents, cryptographic material, and communications equipment prepared for immediate destruction. I also asked the group to consider with me the contingencies we faced in the event of a mob attack on the compound.

We reached a decision, in which all present concurred, that we would withdraw the M-16 rifles from the marine guards, furnish them with shotguns that contained nothing more lethal than bird shot, but leave them their .38-caliber sidearms for personal protection. This was done to make it clear to the marines that they were not going to be asked to fight in defense of the compound even when it became invaded. We strongly felt that any casualties suffered by an attacking mob would merely lash them to a frenzy that would result in their literally tearing limb from limb all the Americans they could get their hands on. Despite the bravado the marines had displayed on Christmas Eve, we were preparing them for the prospect that, in the event of attack, they would be required to surrender and leave our defense to other resources.

The immediate problem became one of finding those other resources. We had established contingency plans to evacuate the embassy, in the event of an attack, to a military compound immediately adjacent to us on the northwest corner of our grounds. While this was essentially a quartermaster post, it was surrounded by high walls and did have a small garrison prepared to protect us. The colonel who commanded it had assured us that he could hold out against mob action and that he had communications with the various mobile units that protected the city.

It was therefore a source of considerable discouragement to us that afternoon to watch that military compound be taken over by a small group of urban guerrillas. They balsted their way in through a side entrance and within two hours had set the place ablaze, totally destroying it. The garrison that had undertaken to be our protectors offered no apparent resistance. After this event we scurried about trying to find other military or police assets on which we could rely. We also took our case to Prime Minister Bazargan, to Deputy Prime Minister Entezam, and to Yazdi, all of whom were in the process of attempting to settle into their new government offices. From various quarters we received assurances that we would be assisted in case of attack, but the details were disturbingly vague and our communications were limited. Both Bazargan and Entezam gave us telephone numbers that they assured us were direct lines we could use in case of emergency.

In this tense situation, I directed that most of the embassy staff should stay home and avoid cluttering the compound with unnecessary bodies. Therefore, on February 14 we had fewer than a hundred Americans in the compound and about an equal number of Iranians. For all our trepidations, the day seemed surprisingly calm.

When I came to the office that morning, I found instructions advising me that the United States government had decided to continue diplomatic relations with Iran despite the change in governments and that I was authorized to send a formal diplomatic note to the new foreign minister advising him of that fact. While I was drafting the note, our political officers were attempting to find out where the foreign minister was so that it could be delivered to him. Since he was not at the ministry and not at his home, this presented something of a problem. I therefore telephoned the deputy foreign minister —a career officer—at his residence. I told him what the situation was, and he agreed to receive the note and pass it on to the foreign minister. At about ten o'clock in the morning, my trusty driver Haikaz took the note and started off in the direction of the deputy foreign minister's home.

Twenty minutes later the deputy foreign minister telephoned. He had located the new foreign minister and proposed to send my driver, with the note, directly to the foreign minister at the residence where he was staying. However, since Haikaz had received instructions from me to deliver the note to the deputy foreign minister, he declined to act on the deputy's recommendations without my explicit instructions. I arranged for the deputy to keep the carbon copy of the note while the original was carried on by Haikaz to the foreign minister himself.

I happened to be in my outer office when this call came, so I took it at my secretary's desk and made these fussy arrangements with my back to the waiting room. After I hung up and turned around I was surprised and annoyed to see two American journalists standing there with Barry Rosen, the press attaché. I summoned Rosen into my office and chewed him out for bringing journalists in to overhear this conversation, since Washington had explicitly advised me that the announcement concerning the continuation of diplomatic relations would be made from the State Department and should not emanate from Tehran. Rosen was chagrined but explained that the two journalists were there to obtain papers that would help them ship the remains of their colleague, Joe Alex Morris, out of the country to his family in Greece. Properly abashed, I asked him to seek the journalists' cooperation in refraining from printing what they had heard because of the impending Washington announcement. It was a tribute to Barry's good relations with the press that both journalists agreed without reservation.

Within two minutes of this conversation, and while I was taking another telephone call at my desk, a murderous barrage of automatic-weapon fire opened up on the embassy from all sides. Fifty- and thirty-caliber machine guns had been surreptitiously mounted on the roofs of all the high-rise buildings surrounding the twenty-three acre compound, and on a given signal at 10:30 A.M. they simultaneously opened fire. Window panes shattered, lead flew everywhere, and we had no recourse but to dive for the deck and slither across the floor to the safest spot we could find. Charlie Naas had been holding a meeting in his office concerning plans for the continuing evacuation of American personnel, and in all there were nearly twenty of us in the immediate vicinity of our three-room executive suite. As we lay on the floor, I directed Charlie and the army attaché to use separate telephones to try to reach the numbers that had been given us only two days before as hot lines for use in the event we needed assistance. Fortunately, I had my small walkie-talkie radio and established contact as rapidly as I could with the marine units that were outside the buildings in the compound and with other members of the security network who were in a position to give me some sense of what was going on.

From their reports, I gathered that under cover of the extensive machine-gun fire, about seventy-five guerrillas, armed with automatic rifles, had come over the gate and the wall fronting the residence and were proceeding through the trees in an attack on the residence itself. For the time being, there did not seem to be any direct attack being mounted against the chancery. I therefore directed the group of marines posted near the residence to fall back toward the cafeteria in the northwest corner of the compound and instructed the other marines who were outside the building to fall back toward the chancery. I gave them all explicit instructions not to fire their weapons and to use their sidearms only if required for personal self-defense. Shortly thereafter, one young sergeant radioed me that he was surrounded and trapped, and asked permission to fire. I instructed him to surrender if he could and to fire only if his surrender was declined. It was a hard order for a marine to carry out, but he did it with good discipline. In a few minutes, he was back on the air telling me he had surrendered and was being taken by his captors in the direction of the cafeteria. For some reason or other, the guerrillas had not taken his radio away from him.

The attack on the residence continued for over an hour, thus affording us additional time to seek a reaction force from the Iranian authorities. During this period the machine-gun fire continued and we were unable to move significantly within the chancery building; however, we did manage to scuttle out into the main corridor, and eventually I sent most of the people on the second floor into the communications vault. In due course we also succeeded in getting everyone on the ground floor up to the second floor and into the vault, with the exception of the marines and the army attaché. Once the assault on the residence had been completed and additional guerrillas had come over the wall, an attack was launched against the chancery itself. The high-powered G-3 rifles that were in the hands of these people proved capable of penetrating the metal doors we had installed for security protection on all entrances to the building. Defense of the ground floor appeared improbable, and I instructed the marines to lay a barrier of tear gas near all entrances, to withdraw up the stairwell to the second floor, and to join the rest of the personnel in the communications vault. By this stage only three of us were left outside the vault —the army attaché, an Iranian interpreter, and myself. We could hear the metal doors on the ground floor being battered down. At the same time we could also hear different and rather confusing sounds—cross fire outside the chancery building. Iranians were shooting at each other. It was clear that a rescue force had arrived. What was not clear was whether the rescue force would reach the second floor of the chancery before the attackers did.

Hoping that it would, and assuming that attempted resistance from the vault would be feckless in any event, I placed the army attaché and the interpreter at the steel doors guarding the second floor and withdrew into the vault myself. There I instructed all personnel to dispose of their weapons in a corner of the vault and be prepared to surrender without any show of arms. This produced a certain amount of grumbling, which was immediately suppressed by the general in charge of the military mission, who supervised the disarming as rapidly as possible. I instructed the army attaché and his interpreter to lie on the floor near the steel doors and to advise whoever approached that we were prepared to surrender peacefully and to ask that no shots be fired. Within a few minutes, the Iranians arrived at the doors, which were opened to permit them—and a whole flood of tear gas—to come into the second-floor corridor.

Although it was not immediately apparent, the Iranians who arrived included members of both the attacking force and the rescue element, which resulted in a certain amount of confusion. As they came into the corridor, I swung open the vault door and stepped out with my hands over my head, followed immediately by the general and all the others who had been herded in there. We were immediately directed into the waiting room of the executive suite and were brusquely frisked to see whether we carried any weapons. I stationed myself at the door with my staff aide, who acted as interpreter, because I wanted to be sure that no one was abused and that everyone was accounted for. At this point a certain amount of tugging and hauling was occurring between the two Iranian factions, and we were soon able to determine who the attackers were and who the rescue force. The head of the rescue force was a young man whose only weapon was a bayonet blade; the man who seemed to be leading the attackers carried an AK-47 rifle.

Shortly after we had all been frisked, and while the discussion was going on between the two Iranian factions, a rifle shot came through one of the windows and plunked into the wall over our heads. Everyone automatically dropped to the floor. The man with the AK rifle irrationally assumed that the shot had been fired from within the room and began swinging his weapon wildly in the direction of his hapless prisoners, who were all a tangle of legs and arms as they sought to find floor space in the crowded quarters. At this juncture I became aware that the two journalists whom I had earlier seen in my waiting room were on the floor behind me. I could not resist teasing them with an expression of hope that they were getting all this down carefully in their notebooks.

In due course it all sorted itself out adequately. The Americans were allowed to leave the room one by one and were taken down into the courtyard below, where once again they were welcomed by Yazdi. I insisted on waiting until all had cleared the room; then I went back into my office to pick up my jacket, which I had left there when the shooting began. Thus attired, I walked down and out of the building, the bayonet man holding one of my arms and the AK rifleman holding the other. The press was there in great numbers and photographed my exist in such a manner that the man with the bayonet, who was actually my savior, appeared to be one of the guerrillas.

The scene in the courtyard was considerably disorganized. The embassy employees had been herded out of the building and were now standing in a group along the wall of the parking lot. In the parking lot itself, and reaching out toward the main gate, a group of Iranians milled about, some armed, some obviously spectators. A line of armed men in various pieces of military uniform had their rifles lowered and were pressing toward another group clustered in front of the gate. That group, which apparently had been the nucleus of the attacking force, was making a slow retreat toward the gate. Many of its members wore the familiar checkered scarf of the Fedayeen, indicating that they had been trained in the PLO camps by George Habash. A white-haired man in a well-tailored Western suit, accompanied by a large bearded ayatollah, seemed to be positioned between the two military forces, attempting to urge the Fedayeen group to leave in quiet good order.

Over to the edge of the parking lot, near the wall where the embassy staff was gathered, Ibrahim Yazdi stood on the hood of a parked automobile carrying a battery-powered megaphone and entreating the spectators also to leave the compound. Since the reek of tear gas was everywhere, it did not take too much persuasion for him to accomplish his objective. The international press was very much on the scene, and a group of photographers and reporters descended on me as soon as they saw me approaching the center of all this activity.

My first action was to break loose from the military escort

and the press in order to go over and shake the hand of the ayatollah. He seemed a bit bewildered but reciprocated heartily and then went on with his effort to exhort the Fedayeen to depart. I next crossed over to Yazdi, who slid off the hood of the car, apologizing effusively for what had happened and assuring me that everything was now under control. He then leaped back up on the hood and continued to chatter into his megaphone. After these two small rituals had been accomplished, I joined the rest of the embassy staff in the area against the wall, and we were immediately closed about by a protecting cordon of armed irregulars.

Once all the activity in the courtyard had ceased and the Fedayeen, as well as the spectators, had left through the front gate, Yazdi joined us and suggested that we would be safer if we left the embassy compound. He summoned a large bus that had apparently transported the rescuing force and brought it over to near where we were standing. He suggested we get aboard and be taken to "a safe place." I demurred, since I did not wish to leave the compound and the eventual restoration of our communications there. I therefore suggested to Yazdi that he and I and the rest of the embassy staff walk over to my residence, where we could talk things over in a somewhat less public atmosphere. He readily assented, so we set out on foot across the compound to the residence, a straggling group of about a hundred, the press and photographers nipping at our heels from all sides and a small band, made up largely of Iranian air force personnel with G-3 rifles, acting as our escort.

Once we had reached the embassy residence, I collected the group on the terrace and asked each section head to try to assemble personnel under his supervision in order to take a nose count and find whether anyone was missing. I also checked with my communications people and discovered, to my relief, that they had managed to destroy all the documents stored in the vault, to smash the cryptographic material, and even to dismantle one controlling element in our satellite-communication station, so that our telecommunications could not be used by anyone interloping in the chancery.

As we attempted to line up on the terrace and get our nose count, a shot suddenly rang out and everyone dove for cover. We naturally assumed that the shot had been fired from one of the sniper positions on the high-rise apartment building across the street from the residence. There was, therefore, a moment of comic relief when a young Iranian air force enlisted man sheepishly attempted to explain with great embarrassment that his rifle had gone off accidentally and that the shot had merely gone winging off through the trees. Although this episode relieved tension somewhat, it pointed up that it was not prudent for all of us to remain in such plain sight out on the residence terrace. I therefore herded everyone inside throught the smashed glass doors of the living room into the main reception area, where windows had been riddled, draperies torn, and furniture overturned by those who had vandalized the house. Once again we attempted a nose count and came to the conclusion that none of those who had been in the chancery was missing but that we could not account for the marines and others who had been outside when the attack began.

At this point Yazdi asked to talk to the group. He made a rather eloquent little statement assuring us that the attack had been carried out by undisciplined elements of the revolution, that the government was deeply apologetic for what had happened, and that we would be afforded full protection in the future. He stressed that the government was not ill disposed toward the United States, but that we would have different relations than we had had under the shah. After this little ceremony, I suggested that all of the staff, with the exception of my deputy, the MAAG chief, the military attaché, and myself, move across the compound to the Caravanserai cafeteria, where some food and beverage could be found even though we had no electricity and no way of retaining our refrigeration.

Those of us who remained began a discussion with Yazdi about the prospects for security in the compound after the events of that day. We were joined by the white-haired gentleman whom I had seen near the parking-lot gate and who turned out to be a retired colonel from the Iranian army. He spoke no English, but his French was impeccable. With him and with Yazdi we worked out an arrangement by which there would be forty Iranian guards stationed outside the walls of the embassy to protect its approaches, and forty more stationed inside the walls. Although it was a departure from normal embassy practice, I decided on this latter arrangement because I wanted to have Iranians present with us in the embassy compound area to preclude our being shot up again like fish in a barrel if there were only Americans under the attacking guns. Yazdi agreed to both of these provisions but also made a considerable point about providing me with a personal bodyguard. He brought forward a young man who spoke good English and who said he had a group who would assume responsibility for my personal safety. They would become part of the group that remained within the compound.

In fact, it appeared from later discussions with this group that it was made up of personnel who were members of a student militant organization and that they had previously had an assignment as my "hit squad" but were now readily reversing roles to protect me rather than to assassinate me. It was not the most comforting sort of arrangement.

The other elements of the compound security force were made up partly of air force enlisted personnel and partly of a group of Mujahadeen led by a colorful, burly butcher from the southern part of Tehran. As later events unfolded, we discovered that not one of these three groups could get along with the other two, and we eventually ended up having to mediate squabbles among them.

Having settled these security arrangements, Yazdi and the colonel departed, and we finally had an opportunity to inspect our damage and ponder our future course of action. The house was a shambles. Every window had been shot out, bullet holes studded every wall and mirror, the furniture had been tipped over and used as fortification, and a certain amount of looting had taken place. I decided, nevertheless, that it was habitable, and determined that those of us who had been residing there would stay there again that evening.

Our more immediate tasks were to get the electricity functioning again by starting the generator and to continue our effort to get a final nose count of our personnel. A navy Seabee, who had been helping us with security construction in the chancery, demonstrated his ingenuity by getting the old generator turning over again, and Charlie Naas was in the last stages of reaching some conclusions about the status of our personnel. A few marines, who had been arrested and taken off by the attacking forces, straggled back to the compound, and before darkness fell we concluded that we were all accounted for except for one young marine sergeant who had suffered superficial wounds by the discharge of his own shotgun and been taken to a hospital. Our efforts to communicate with him at the hospital proved futile, and we had to assume he was missing.

While we were engaging in this activity, I began to receive a stream of visitors. The first to arrive was the Swedish ambassador, whose office was in a building on the next block and who had watched the assault and rescue from the windows of his chancery. He arrived marveling that any of us were still alive and offered us the use of the efficient communications of his embassy, which enabled me to report to Washington that all of our American personnel seemed to be alive and accounted for, with the exception of the one missing marine sergeant. The papal nuncio was next, and over the course of the next two days nearly all my diplomatic colleagues came to call on me and express their condolences and their relief that we had survived without loss of life.

Many of them brought messages from their foreign ministers who were acquaintances of mine, and two of them brought messages from their chiefs of state whom I had known in the past. I was bemused by the fact that despite this generous example from other capitals, I never did receive any message whatsoever from the White House indicating that our predicament had been noticed there.

Among the visitors I received two days after the attack was a gentle ayatollah who came to call, accompanied by two or three young mullahs. He told me he had been sent by Ayatollah Khomeini to express the latter's personal apologies for the attack on the embassy and to express his relief that we had come through it alive. He assured me that this attack was contrary to the policies and wishes of the ayatollah and that he was prepared to leave the young mullahs on the scene to help dissuade Islamic groups from making any further attacks if they should be contemplating them. He also asked whether there was anything he or Ayatollah Khomeini could do for us in these circumstances.

I immediately expressed appreciation for the gesture of Ayatollah Khomeini but said I saw no need for the mullahs, since I had worked out arrangements with Minister Yazdi for protection by the armed forces of the Islamic groups. Nevertheless, he could do something for me by finding out where our marine sergeant was and returning him to us as soon as possible. The gentle ayatollah, whose name I never caught, seemed a bit confused by this request and had to have the whole situation explained to him. When, in due course, he understood what was at stake, he assured me that action would be taken immediately. In fact, the sergeant was released from a prison in which he was being held that very afternoon and returned to my residence that evening.

His case had developed into something of a cause célèbre, since the American press had become aware that he was missing and had given the story considerable attention in United

States media. Consequently, when the press got word that he was in the process of being released, this also became a major public-relations event in the United States. This was the sort of thing that attracted White House attention, and I soon received a telephone call informing me that the president wished to know precisely when the sergeant would be returned to the embassy so that he could announce the fact in Washington. I suggested that, given the tenuous situation in Iran, it might be prudent for any announcement to be withheld until the sergeant had actually left the country on a military aircraft that I was holding at the airport for his departure. I received a return call telling me that decisions on the timing of the announcement would be made in Washington and asking once again that I report as soon as the sergeant was safely in our hands.

A short while later, while we were having dinner, the young sergeant walked in. I invited him to join us and he wolfed down a meal in record time while telling us the rather bizarre story of his capture and brief imprisonment. The Washington line rang again, and I was asked whether the sergeant had arrived. When I confirmed that he had, I was told that the White House operator wished to speak to him. With some reluctance, I called the sergeant into the library and turned the phone over to him. Within a few minutes he returned to the table flabbergasted. He reported that he had talked to the president of the United States and also to his mother, and that the president was announcing those two facts at the White House immediately.

Fortunately, there were no repercussions from the announcement, and the sergeant was able to slip quietly out of the country without further attention from the militants who had held him.

25

Aftermath and Departure

Once we had recovered from the shock of the initial attack on the embassy, we set about the urgent business that remained for us. We had three general goals to pursue. First, we had to evacuate all the remaining Americans in the country; second, we had to get the embassy back in some form of operation; and, third, we had to sort out what our relations would be with the new revolutionary government.

As far as the Americans were concerned, I put out an announcement that the embassy could no longer protect American lives in Iran, and therefore strongly recommended that all Americans leave the country. We set up a processing center in the embassy compound and attempted to coordinate the evacuation from there. For a few days we were able to bring in military aircraft from Germany to constitute the bulk of our evacuation fleet; we had also arranged with Pan Am to provide special aircraft for this purpose. Nearly eight thousand Americans were left in the country in scattered spots when the airlift began.

In retrospect I find it extraordinary that we managed to get everyone out without casualties. The American citizens themselves were remarkably well disciplined. They accepted the priorities we arbitrarily assigned to them, they waited patiently in our compound while we arranged surface transportation to the airport, and they did not grumble when that sometimes meant that they had to remain overnight, sleeping on cots and eating dry sandwiches. We took their automobiles, signed receipts for them, and parked them in the compound pending the possibility of their sale in the future. We took records of where they had stored their household furniture and promised to do what we could to try to get it shipped eventually to their new destination. We worked with a constantly changing, unpredictable, and capricious group of revolutionary *komitehs* in carrying out this exodus, adjusting to shifting and arbitrary decisions made by those who were temporarily in command of any particular facility, such as the customs control points at Mehrabad Airport.

On the second or third day of this operation, I received a telephone call from my Israeli colleague, who had literally gone underground with his staff after his building had been taken over by the Fedayeen and given as a gift to the PLO. Since El Al aircraft could no longer come to Iran, he pleaded with me to take his people on one of our planes as soon as possible. He told me he had thirty-two officials and could get them all to the airport within two hours of the moment I gave him notice that the plane was ready. This posed something of a problem, since it meant bumping thirty-two Americans off the airlift, but, under the circumstances, I judged the Israeli danger to be greater than our own. Accordingly, I arranged space for thirty-two people on one of our flights and through a complicated series of signals got the word to the Israelis. With typical efficient discipline, they rounded up their people and arrived at the airport in good time and in good order for departure. There was only one complication. They had thirty-three rather than thirty-two, but one American citizen readily volunteered to cede his position and let all of them go. They left with considerable relief, and I received a nice message of thanks from Foreign Minister Moshe Dayan.

Evacuations from the southern part of Iran proved somewhat more complex, but the task was shared with the British, whose geodetic-survey vessels picked up some of our people from various ports along the Persian Gulf where they were working. In one of these evacuations, an American family was advised that it could not bring its two dogs aboard the British vessel. The family chose, rather than leave the dogs behind, to forfeit the opportunity to depart on the British vessel, to pile their dogs and the family in their car, and to drive overland across hostile territory to Tehran, where we eventually airlifted them out. Their dogs joined a large animal airlift that we eventually dumped on the poor unsuspecting German airport authorities at Frankfurt.

The problem of resuming embassy operations proved every bit as complicated as the evacuation problem. We managed to restore our communications within two or three days, but, because of the heavy infestation of tear gas, the chancery proved to be virtually uninhabitable. All the drapes, furniture, rugs, and other material to which the tear gas clung were stripped out and taken from the chancery building. Nevertheless, the problem persisted, and it became impossible to work more than several minutes at a time in the atmosphere. Moreover, smashed windows, broken doors, and shattered furniture made operations tenuous at best.

Our consulates in Tabriz, Isfahan, and Shiraz had even worse problems. The one in Tabriz was attacked at least twice and finally set afire, and the young consul was nearly lynched. Indeed, a rope was strung around his neck and his life was seriously threatened. He eventually managed to escape and make his way to Tehran.

In Isfahan, our consul was beaten up when he attempted to save a drunken American from a surly mob. At considerable risk to his life, he did save his appreciative fellow citizen and get him into the airlift from that city. Then he, in turn, closed down the consulate and moved to Tehran. There was less violence in Shiraz, but our consulate was hastily closed and its personnel withdrawn to the Tehran compound.

Up on the border with the Soviet Union where we maintained the two listening stations for the surveillance of Soviet missile programs, a number of other American personnel were in difficulty. Their stations were taken over and they were held hostage briefly by unfriendly groups, most of which seemed to be made up of the Iranian air force personnel who worked with them. In due course we came to the conclusion that the principal motivation of their assailants had to do with the concern that, because of the revolution, they would no longer receive their paychecks.

I persuaded Prime Minister Bazargan that these listening posts continued to be of value to the Iranian authorities, since they provided, as a by-product, intelligence information concerning the movement of Soviet troops and other forces that might menace the safety of Iran. Although I felt that we could no longer man such posts with Americans, I suggested that it was in Iran's interest to maintain their integrity and avoid their sabotage. He agreed, and as a result our air attaché and his assistant were permitted to go in an Iranian plane to these stations, carrying the payroll for the Iranians who worked there. Once the pay was delivered, with assurances that we would continue to pay the Iranian staff, the American hostages were released and evacuated from the country. Payments to the Iranians continued to be made during the rest of the time I remained in the country.

The problem of working out our future relations with the Iranians became even more complex than the problem of evacuating American citizens and organizing the work of our mission. This was not for lack of any good will or intention on the part of the Bazargan government, but rather because of the chaos that prevailed in the country. In the first communication

I sent to Washington after our satellite link had been restored, I described this chaos and the situation of the government in a cable.

There, I referred to the *"komitehs"* that had sprung up everywhere as a "sort of vigilante presence throughout the country." I said that, although in principle they reported to the Islamic Revolutionary Council, in practice they had differing loyalties. Some were primarily Mujahadeen, others were Fedayeen or Tudeh, and still others were composed primarily of young homofars who had deserted from the air force. I thought the Communists had a well-developed set of objectives— namely, to seize the radio and television service and then to try to dominate the press. Since the armed forces were in disarray, there was little prospect for law and order. "Islamic justice" seemed to be the order of the day.

As for the Bazargan government, I described it as being "buried somewhere in the middle of this chaos" and expressed grave doubts about its ability to function.

I said that, in these circumstances, immediate U.S. actions ought to be quite explicit. Our first priority ought to be to get as many Americans as possible out of Iran. I felt they not only could get caught in the cross fire but would become targets themselves. Our overall actions ought to tailor our ambitions to realities. We should adopt a low profile.

"As for policy, I continue to recommend the same policy line I first set forth in November, and which Washington has consistently rejected. That is the effort to convince the Khomeini (Bazargan) group and the armed forces that they share a broad community of interests and should work together to eliminate the communists. In rejecting this policy recommendation, Washington directed a series of tactical actions which succeeded in placing the religious and the military in antagonism to each other. This resulted in the consequence we consistently warned about—the disintegration of the military and the spewing of perhaps one hundred thousand weapons into the hands of the street gangs. This, in turn has meant that the U.S. no longer has an integrated military establishment which is responsive to our influence and interests. It has also meant that those who have gained control of these weapons are filled with resentment for the United States because we were the ones who encouraged military resistance to the revolution rather than collaboration."

I went on to say that I would probably never understand the rationale for pursuing the tactics Washington directed, because they seemed devoid of strategic policy objectives. I recommended, nevertheless, that we act in the future on the assumption that the United States and Iran shared fundamental interests and that Iran would, in the long term, wish to restore friendly relations with us.

In the days following the assault on our embassy, I met several times with Prime Minister Bazargan and members of his government, proceeding from the assumption that our relations would be considerably different from what they had been during the time of the shah. Nevertheless, I took for granted that the Iranians wanted to continue friendly relations with the United States and that they wished to continue cooperating with us in both the economic and military spheres. Bazargan and his ministers confirmed this, and we made several efforts to try to determine just what level of cooperation should remain.

I was particularly concerned to try to establish the logical level for the manning of our military-assistance and advisory group. Because of the disintegration of the Iranian armed forces there was very little structural integrity on the Iranian side with which our people could work. I therefore suggested to Bazargan that there should be a drastic reduction in the numbers of our people assigned to this mission.

He agreed, but pleaded with me not to send all of them home. He wanted to continue to have the sort of cooperation with the United States that would be essential to maintain the military capabilities of the Iranian forces, particularly the air force. After much discussion, we finally reached the figure of twenty-five military personnel who would remain in place, to be headed by an officer considerably junior in rank to the major general who now headed the mission. Bazargan did finally produce an Iranian military officer who could meet with and work with the military mission. He was a retired major general who had been familiar with the military-logistics program and who was apparently given a clean bill by the Islamic revolutionaries as being untainted by corruption and politically acceptable to them. Nevertheless, because of the total confusion in the armed forces, it was not possible for the advisory group to function in a normal way.

Once I had set these several actions in train, I turned to the question of my own status. I informed Washington that I intended to leave. However, since this would mean that my deputy, Charlie Naas, would have to stay on for some time until a new ambassador could be found, I suggested that he be permitted to have one month's leave, during which I would remain on post. I suggested he be permitted to return immediately to the United States, spend the month of March there, and come back to Iran on the first of April. I would leave shortly thereafter. Washington approved this plan with what seemed to be a sigh of relief.

The month of March was a nightmare for Iran. Rival forces contended for power within the context of the revolution, and since all of them were armed, this meant constant firefights breaking out around the city. During the night, armed vigilantes fired regularly into our compound, and our makeshift group of defenders returned the fusillades with gusto.

Radio and television stations had been taken over by leftwing groups. Their programs were stridently revolutionary in tone, featuring continual attacks on the United States as well as on the remnants of the shah's regime.

Kangaroo courts had been set up, and executions were a daily affair. Some of those who had worked most closely with us in the shah's government were executed, their bodies displayed in the most grisly manner. Looting was rampant throughout the city, and most services came to a halt. We were largely cut off from meeting with unofficial Iranians, since any contact with us was likely to contaminate them and cause their arrest with great risk to their lives. The small residue of the diplomatic corps that remained in the city met with each other regularly, exchanged rumors, discussed prospects for the future, and worked out plans for survival. Our prognoses were universally gloomy.

In the meantime, the shah lingered in Egypt. Despite his originally announced intention to stay only one day at Aswan, he stayed much longer and then spent another considerable period of time in Morocco. The indirect contact we had with his entourage suggested that the reason for his delay was an inordinate hope that he might somehow or other be called back to the country. In the face of much evidence to the contrary, some of his advisors seemed to entertain the delusion that the armed forces and the general public might rebel against the excesses of the revolution and turn on the Islamic protagonists. They reportedly had persuaded the shah that it would be imprudent for him to become neutralized in the United States—that it would be better if he waited somewhere in the Islamic world for a call to return to his throne. If this was his motivation, it was ill conceived and impossible to execute.

It also raised new problems concerning the relations between the new Islamic government in Iran and the United States. So long as the shah continued to give evidence that he wished to return to the country, it made our position less tenable. It would make it particularly difficult for us, in those circumstances, to take the shah into the United States, because the general presumption in Iran would be that we were moving to assist him in his ambition to return to his throne. If he had come to our country at the outset with the obvious intention of abdicating, that would have been one set of circumstances. But for him to come with the apparent intention of rallying his forces for a return was a quite different situation.

On February 26, in reaction to a message from our ambassador in Morocco suggesting a renewal of the original presidential invitation to the shah, I sent a rather sharp warning to Washington. While I recognized the continuing obligation implicit in the original invitation, I felt Washington should very carefully consider what the results would be of any renewal of the invitation at this time. I felt it would confirm the worst suspicions of those Iranian revolutionaries who assumed that the U.S. was plotting to restore the shah to power.

I said that if we wished to maintain any credible relations with the new authorities in Iran, we should leave our association with the shah on the aloof basis that had developed during his exile. I ended up by saying that, from the point of view of any hope of establishing cooperative relations with Iran, it would be clearly in our interests for the shah to choose some other location for his exile and that it would be counter to our interests in Iran to offer him warm encouragement to go to the United States.

After sending this message, I began to inform Washington, in more explicit terms, that I felt a move by the shah to the United States would result in the personnel of the American Embassy in Tehran being taken hostage. I particularly asked Charlie Naas, when he checked into the Department of State on his return to Washington, to stress this point in his discussions with senior officials.

Charlie seems to have been quite persuasive, since the Washington position began to reflect this view. On March 7, in a discussion with two American intermediaries representing the shah, Under Secretary David Newsom said that if the shah came to the United States, there was a real danger that armed gangs might seek to take Americans hostage. Shortly thereafter, in two messages sent by President Carter to King

Hassan of Morocco and to the shah himself, there was explicit mention of "the very real threat that hostages might be seized" as the reason that it would not be a propitious time for the shah to come to the United States. The prospect for a renewed convulsion in the relations between the United States and Iran seemed, therefore, to have been avoided.

On this note, and in anticipation of the return of my deputy from his brief vacation, I prepared to leave the country. In order not to make a major issue of my departure, I undertook to leave as if I were going on consultation to Washington. I intended to announce my resignation after I arrived there. I felt there was some prospect that my departure would be interrupted if it were known that I was leaving permanently.

Unfortunately, the White House, for reasons I could only guess, chose to leak to the press that my return from Iran would be definitive and that I would be replaced. Happily, this news, which was picked up by my diplomatic colleagues in Tehran, went largely unnoticed by the Iranians, because of their preoccupation with more immediate affairs. There did not seem to be any indication that measures might be taken to prevent my leaving the country.

Nevertheless, we decided to take no chances, and a rather elaborate departure scheme was arranged. The man in charge of this exercise was Mike Coughlin, who had been my security officer in Manila and who had come to replace a rather badly shaken security man whom I had sent home shortly after the attack on the embassy. Mike had volunteered to come to Tehran out of friendship and because he was most expert in handling challenging situations of this type. He spent a few weeks in the embassy compound working out ad hoc security arrangements that would have baffled less imaginative practitioners. He looked on the arrangements for my departure as a challenge to his ingenuity and as an opportunity to mount an interesting operation.

Charlie Naas returned refreshed from his leave, things had

settled down somewhat in Tehran, the American community had all left safely, the embassy compound had resumed more or less normal operations, and our relations with the government were stabilized. Pan Am had resumed an abbreviated flight schedule, and the airport was functioning in a relatively safe manner, the civilian air controllers having returned to their duties in the control tower. However, the situation in the passenger terminal, in the customs area, and on the loading ramps was erratic. At least three separate *komitehs* were functioning in those precincts, and it was always difficult to know which one had the upper hand at any particular moment. Each of them had discovered that there were a great many lucrative opportunities in granting permission for people to leave the country, for their possessions to clear customs, and for the aircraft to be handled and loaded on the ground.

We had worked out fairly good arrangements with the *komitehs* controlling the passenger terminal and the customs, but the group that controlled the ramp and the runways was made up of Fedayeen, the same element that had attacked our embassy. Consequently, we sometimes were able to clear a whole planeload of household effects through the customs and out onto the ramp and then were denied permission to put it aboard an aircraft. At least two of the planes we had chartered to fly out these household possessions were not permitted to load and flew away empty.

In these circumstances Mike Coughlin was, with some justification, concerned that the Fedayeen might attempt to kidnap me when I tried to leave the country. He felt I was particularly vulnerable because the White House leak to the press had made it clear that I was, in effect, expendable as far as United States relations with Iran were concerned. Consequently, his plans for my "extraction" concentrated efforts more on the loading ramp and the runway than on the passenger terminal and the customs area.

After checking all considerations, we determined that I

should depart on the Pan Am flight that transited Tehran early on the morning of April 6. The plane was scheduled to arrive from New Delhi at about 2:30 A.M., and depart for Europe at about 3:30 A.M. The whole exercise would thus be undertaken under cover of darkness and at a time when the number of personnel at the airport would be minimal.

On the day before my scheduled departure, Mike put into effect a number of security precautions. He decided that the reliability of the personal-bodyguard unit assigned to me by Yazdi was questionable, and he worried about their having some association with the Fedayeen. He therefore decreed that they should go out to the airfield ahead of me to make sure that the runway was secure and that there were no potential saboteurs who might try to block the departure of the aircraft. He was particularly concerned that there might be some SAM-7 hand-held antiaircraft rockets among the Fedayeen who might be deployed at the foot of the aircraft. Mike issued this group walkie-talkie radios that contained the standard embassy-security frequency crystal.

He then concentrated his attention on forming the convoy that would take us across town to the airport during the curfew hours. For this exercise he relied primarily on the Mujahadeen under the direction of our trusty butcher, who had, by now, become quite enamored of Americans and devoted to our protection. The butcher's younger brother had been a member of the Iranian Olympic wrestling team, and through him Mike recruited a group of his wrestling colleagues, to whom he issued Uzi submachine guns. After very limited instruction, he made them into a sort of SWAT squad and assigned them to ride in a closed van at the tail of our convoy. In the convoy itself he arranged a group of armored cars around my heavy black Chrysler limousine, which Haikaz had christened "the tank." However, Mike decreed that I should not ride in that car but rather in a smaller armored Chevrolet immediately behind it. He himself sat in the rear right-hand seat of the Chrysler, where the ambassador would normally sit, and became, thereby, the prime target for any well-articulated assassination attempt.

At about 2 A.M. this convoy swung out of the embassy gates into the quiet of the curfew-controlled night. We moved speedily down to the center of town and turned right on what used to be called Eisenhower Boulevard, in order to strike straight for the airport. This path took us immediately in front of Tehran University, where the most radical elements were holed up.

As we approached the university, we found a checkpoint and a barricade strewn across the street. The heavily armed defenders of this barricade stopped the convoy and demanded the right to search the cars. Our butcher friend in the lead car remonstrated with them, showing them his Mujahadeen papers and all his other credentials as a proper member of the revolution. This did not seem to avail, however, and the barricade defenders insisted on their prerogatives to search.

At this point Mike called up the van full of wrestlers. He had taken the precaution of shifting crystals in the convoy's hand-held radios, so that they were on a different frequency from that of the bodyguard unit at the airport. In the dark the van lumbered out from the rear of the convoy and pulled up to the front, where the altercation with the barricade defenders was going on. The van doors slid open, and the wrestling team with their Uzis tumbled out. The butcher's younger brother took up the dialogue at that point, and while he and his colleagues engaged the barricade folk in gentle discussion, the rest of the convoy slid quietly westward into the night. The van full of wrestlers caught up with us before we reached the airport, having, presumably, quietly settled the dispute in our favor.

At the airport, we moved away from the main passenger terminal to a side gate whose personnel Mike had alerted for our arrival. The gate was opened immediately, and we moved across the service areas, past the VIP lounge, and out onto the ramp, heading for the Pan Am 747 that was loading for takeoff. A jeep with four Fedayeen spotted the convoy as we passed the old imperial pavilion and pulled out to cut us off before we got to the aircraft. The Fedayeen, wearing the familiar checkered scarf around their heads, were armed with AK-47 rifles.

Once again Mike gave the signal to his wrestlers, and while the rest of the convoy slowed down, the van pulled out around us and caught up with the jeep just as it neared the loading ramp. Out tumbled the wrestlers with their Uzis, and for a brief moment there was a sharp confrontation with the Fedayeen. When the latter recognized that they were outnumbered and outgunned, however, they quietly pulled off a hundred yards or so away from the aircraft and watched the rest of the proceedings.

The captain of the Pan Am plane, standing at the head of the ramp, was intrigued by the proceedings. He was not at all happy to see quite so many weapons being waved under the fuel tanks in the 747's wings and belly. I made my brief farewells to those who had come out from the embassy in the convoy, thanked Mike and Haikaz, and mounted the ramp. In the cabin, I discovered the Pan Am regional vice-president, who had kindly come along on the trip, as well as the captain of the plane. In his meticulous way, Mike had arranged with the captain in advance for a "lights off" takeoff in order to minimize the chances of making the plane a target for snipers on the ground.

While the vice-president and the captain and I were discussing this takeoff procedure, a curious commotion arose from the ramp. It seems that the Mujahadeen did not think that they had made appropriate farewells to me and were insisting on coming aboard to do so. The Pan Am security personnel at the foot of the ramp refused to let them carry their weapons aboard; with Mike Coughlin's intercession, the weapons were thus being stacked at the foot of the ramp, permitting this bearded, greasy, ragtag, gallant bunch, including the wrestlers, to come up the ramp one at a time to say good-bye. Each of them grasped me around the shoulders, kissed me on both cheeks with their stubbly beards, and then meekly departed down the ramp. The captain, who by this time had retreated to the circular staircase leading to the flight deck, stood shaking his head, bewildered.

As this little ceremony ended and it looked as though we could arrange for takeoff, another clamor arose from the foot of the ramp. By this time my bodyguard unit, which had been cut off from communications because of the change of crystals in the radio sets, had become aware that the moment of departure was at hand. They too insisted on coming and making their farewells, and they too went through the procedure of checking their rifles, pistols, and grenades at the bottom of the ramp. Although they were a somewhat more clean-shaven and sophisticated group than the Mujahadeen, they went through the same procedure of kissing me on both cheeks and wishing me farewell, most of them speaking fluent English. With these matters taken care of, the ramp was withdrawn, the plane was buttoned up, and the darkened takeoff was accomplished without incident.

I learned later that the evening at the airport ended in a fight between the bodyguards and the Mujahadeen; it was fortunately confined to fisticuffs and never deteriorated into the firing of weapons. Haikaz served as the peacemaker to break up the scrap before it reached the mortal phase, and separated the two units for their respective returns to the embassy compound. They were never again, however, able to work together, and their bitter enmity resulted in serious security problems for Charlie Naas and his successors in the embassy compound.

My trip home, with a stop at Frankfurt, was uneventful. Our consul general in Frankfurt and members of his staff met me there and made sure that our ten-year-old Persian cat, who was traveling in the baggage compartment, was properly fed and cleaned before being transferred for the flight to Washington.

I was met at Dulles Airport by my wife, who was much relieved to see me but who looked a little exhausted from her own exertions over the past two months trying to help the wives and children of the embassy personnel who had been evacuated while their husbands and fathers stayed on in Tehran. She had felt, with some justification, that on my return she could turn that task over to others, and had planned a vacation for us in Palm Beach, Florida.

Postscript

Before going on vacation, I reported in to the Department of State and asked for an early appointment with Secretary Vance. He received me warmly on the first day after my return. Much to my surprise, he told me that the president wanted me to take another embassy. Since my relations with the White House during the last few weeks of my tenure in Tehran had been anything but smooth, I was frankly astonished by this suggestion. When I said so to Cy Vance, he replied that the president wanted to indicate by this suggestion that he recognized that my judgments in the Iranian situation had been correct and that the recommendations he had followed had been wrong. Cy said I should look on this as vindication and urged me to consider the offer seriously.

I continued to express the most profound reservations, particularly since I foresaw a situation in which I would still, in any new embassy, have to deal with the same combination of circumstances that had frustrated me so thoroughly in Tehran. I told Vance that I did not see how I could work in an arrangement in which Brzezinski was still able to make end runs around the State Department and, indeed, around the ambassador. Vance was confident that lessons had been learned from the experiences in Iran and that any new post I might take would not be afflicted by these problems. When I was still doubtful and indicated I intended to retire, he asked me to hold up any such action until I could take a brief vacation, sort out my thoughts, and reach a judgment in more deliberate terms. I told him of my plans to go to Palm Beach and play golf for about ten days, and agreed that I would delay taking any definitive steps until that stretch was over.

He then discussed briefly pressures that were being brought to bear on him to change the current policy of denying asylum to the shah in the United States. He thoroughly shared my concern that the entry of the shah into the United States would result in the embassy personnel's being taken hostage, and he was resisting any changes that might bring about an invitation to the shah. He said that, if pressures got worse, he might ask me to help him make the argument, particularly with some of the protagonists who were well known to me. I agreed that I would be at his disposition if I was ever needed, but, in the event, he never did call on me.

Just before we left for Florida, I was telephoned by some friends who were trustees of the prestigious American Assembly, an organization founded by Dwight Eisenhower in 1950 and affiliated with Columbia University. The assembly is a public-policy institution whose charter describes its purpose as "the illumination of issues of United States policy." It has a bipartisan board of trustees, all of whom are nationally prominent figures and many of whom were well known to me. Since the president of the assembly was reaching the age of sixty-five and would retire in the fall, the nominating committee of the board of trustees urged me to take his place. I thanked them for the flattering suggestion and said I would think over my options for the future during my vacation. They told me I would have to decide one way or another within the next seven days, before the next meeting of the board, when the ultimate decision would be made.

Thus we drove off on a leisurely trip to Florida with these

two options very much in need of resolution. After four or five days in the pleasant sunshine, playing golf without a retinue of bodyguards, moving around on my own schedule with no obligations hemming me in, I rapidly came to the conclusion that my retirement was completely in order. This decision was also helped along by a message I received from the State Department, telling me that the White House wished to nominate a close friend and former assistant of mine as my successor, and asking that my resignation from the post be submitted forthwith. I told them to write a pro forma letter of resignation to the president, forge my signature, and hand carry it immediately to the White House. On the same afternoon, I telephoned New York and advised the American Assembly that I would be pleased to be its new president. Then I sat down and wrote a brief handwritten note to Secretary Vance in which I advised him that I had determined to retire from the foreign service because I did not have confidence in the judgment of the president in times of crisis.

With that action, I ended thirty-five years of service to the government of the United States in some of the most fascinating and troubled lands of our national experience. I had served most of those years in areas of violence and crisis, but I found all the service rewarding. Even the last few, frustrating months in Tehran had proved instructive. It was my hope that, through changes in the way we conducted the foreign policy of the United States, these experiences would not have to be repeated again, and that the formation and execution of our policy would be the better for it.

Unfortunately, this hope was to be dashed in the next few months. The feckless manner in which the Carter administration conducted its affairs continued, the erratic ambitions of Brzezinski were unabated, and the failure to understand events in Iran was compounded. All of this led, in November of 1979, to the taking of the hostages in the American embassy and to a period of national humiliation unmatched in our history. It was not our finest hour.

Index